Theatre Praxis

Teaching Drama Through Practice

Edited by
CHRISTOPHER McCULLOUGH

St. Martin's Press
New York

THEATRE PRAXIS

Copyright © 1998 by Christopher McCullough

St. Martin's Press, Scholarly and Reference Division,
175 Fifth Avenue, New York, N.Y. 10010

First published in the United States of America in 1998

This book is printed on paper suitable for recycling and
made from fully managed and sustained forest sources.

Printed in Hong Kong

ISBN 0–312–21610–6 clothbound
ISBN 0–312–21611–4 paperback

Library of Congress Cataloging-in-Publication Data
Theatre praxis : teaching drama through practice / edited by
Christopher McCullough.
p. cm.
Includes bibliographical references and index.
ISBN 0–312–21610–6 (cloth). — ISBN 0–312–21611–4 (pbk.)
1. Theater—Philosophy. 2. Theater—Production and direction.
3. Drama in education. I. McCullough, Christopher, M.A.
PN2039.T55 1998
792—dc21   98–16916
                                                CIP

To the memory of Joyce and James McCullough
and for Carol, Rebecca and Anna

Contents

General Editor's Preface

In the past ten years, Theatre Studies has experienced remarkable international growth, students seeing in its marriage of the practical and the intellectual a creative and rewarding discipline. Some countries are now opening school and degree programmes in Theatre Studies for the first time; others are having to accommodate to the fact that a popular subject attracting large numbers of highly motivated students has to be given greater attention than hitherto. The professional theatre itself is changing, as graduates of degree and diploma programmes make their way through the 'fringe' into established theatre companies, film and television.

Two changes in attitudes have occurred as a result: first, that the relationship between teachers and practitioners has significantly improved, not least because many more people now have experience of both; secondly, that the widespread academic suspicion about theatre as a subject for study has at least been squarely faced, if not fully discredited. Yet there is still much to be done to translate the practical and educational achievements of the past decade into coherent theory, and this series is intended as a contribution to that task. Its contributors are chosen for their combination of professional and didactic skills, and are drawn from a wide range of countries, languages and styles in order to give some impression of the subject in its international perspective.

This series offers no single programme of ideology; yet all its authors have in common the sense of being in a period of transition and debate out of which the theory and practice of theatre cannot but emerge in new form.

JULIAN HILTON

Notes on Contributors

Stephen Cockett is a Senior Lecturer in the School of Education, University of Exeter. He has taught drama in schools and in initial teacher education courses in the UK and Canada, Hungary and Poland. He has written extensively for secondary schools; this work includes the drama series *Plays Plus* and *Upstagers*, and his most recent work is *The Birds Keep on Singing*, a play set in the Second World War.

Anthony Frost studied at RADA and at the University of Birmingham before helping to found the drama degree course at the University of East Anglia (UEA). A former Chair of UEA's Drama Sector, he is currently Director of the recently opened UEA Studio Theatre, which he largely designed. He has taught at the Freie Universität, Berlin, and lectured in the United States and Canada. He is the co-author (with Ralph Yarrow) of *Improvisation in Drama* in this series and currently is completing books on theatre history and dramatic theory.

Dorinda Hulton is a Lecturer in Drama at the University of Exeter. She has worked extensively as an artistic consultant for new work with different companies including Theatre Alibi and Foursight. She co-edited the series *Theatre Papers* and is currently an editor for the documentation project *Arts Archives*.

Graham Ley has taught Greek drama in the universities of London, Auckland and Exeter; he is now a Lecturer in Drama at Exeter. As well as translating, adapting and directing several Greek tragedies for studio performances, he has published a number of studies on ancient Greek performance, including *A Short Introduction to the Ancient Greek Theater* (1991). He has been an advisor to several contemporary productions of Greek plays, in 1994 to the Royal Shakespeare Company for Euripides' *Ion*, and to the director John Barton.

Christopher McCullough is a Senior Lecturer in Drama at the University of Exeter, also working frequently as a visiting professor and director in the United States. His main research interest lies in the field of the politics of culture and twentieth-century political theatre. He has also published on the contemporary mediation of Elizabethan theatre. His book *Theatre and Europe 1957–1995* was published in 1996.

James MacDonald is an Honorary Fellow in Drama at the University of Exeter. He has written thirty plays on a range of themes, most recently the black market in Russia. For Rose Bruford College he has written a distance-learning module. He is a keen advocate of multi-disciplinary education and multi-cultural discourse.

Lesley Wade Soule is Lecturer in Drama at the University of Exeter. She trained at the Central School of Speech and Drama, London, before completing research degrees at the University of British Columbia and the University of Exeter. She is interested in the relationship between the practical and theoretical elements in the performance of character. She has also published on aspects of Elizabethan and medieval performance and directed plays from both the pre-modern and modern repertoire.

Peter Thomson has been Professor of Drama at the University of Exeter since 1974. His books include *Shakespeare's Theatre* (second edition, 1992) and *Shakespeare's Professional Career* (1992), *Brecht* (1981) and *Brecht's Mother Courage* (1997), as well as work on the English theatre in the eighteenth and nineteenth centuries.

Acknowledgements

The debts incurred in the writing of this book are collective and due, in the main part, to those many drama students whose energy, generosity and intellectual and creative curiosity have made possible the questions raised in this volume. Their praxis has helped us towards our praxis and, in that knowledge of our debt to them, our heartfelt thanks are offered. I am also indebted to Dr Görel Garlick, who composed the index. She not only came to my rescue when I was under pressure from other quarters, but brought an energy and rigorous attention to detail that serves the authors very well indeed.

The editor and publishers wish to thank Macmillan for permission to reproduce 'Dick Lander' by Charles Causley from his *Collected Poems*.

General Introduction

Christopher McCullough

---

the inflexible rule that the proof of the pudding is in the eating.
(Attributed to Engels and Brecht)

We are at a point in the history of drama/theatre/performance studies when the relative merits of theory and practice are under renewed scrutiny. Since the inception of the first British university drama department in the 1940s, a still-unresolved debate has gone on over the nature and purpose of practical drama/theatre work within a university drama department.[1] Indeed, in the early years, the debate focused on the question of the validity of such an activity in the scheme of a university faculty of arts. It is all too easy to say that this debate is well behind us. There are many academics (of many ideological persuasions) who see, at worst, the engagement with practical theatre-making as contrary to the essential verities of scholarship in the humanities: at best an enjoyable addition to the curriculum, but a great consumer of time, when the students should be engaged in the more serious matter of readily quantifiable scholarship.

While the misconception was held that the practice of drama in the universities meant simply the 'putting on of plays' as an adjunct to textual and historical studies in drama and theatre, it was little wonder that practical work was held to be marginal to more serious scholarly pursuits. The traditional antagonisms to 'practical work' have, more recently, been supported by attacks from people who may be described as representing, broadly, the 'literary' left. These academics (and some

1

of them are employed in departments of drama), while ideologically distanced from the familiar conservative critique of drama in the university, now vaunt their negativity on a neo-Leavisite platform. 'Performance' is perceived as a transitory form and lacking the rigour of objective (critical) thought by reason of the ephemeral nature of its 'text'. This argument is not without its inconsistencies. Whereas much work emanating from the literary left observes the essentially ephemeral nature of meaning in a given text, there appears to be a simultaneous (and contradictory) acceptance of a text's material value. It is at this point that an alliance is formed between the writer and the literary critic, with both recognising the validity of the literary text as a cultural yardstick by which a performance may be judged.

Skirmishes in the battle between text and performance are regular features within the walls of the theatre itself. Opposing positions were, for example, well exemplified in *The Playwrights' Manifesto* that arose from the Budapest Playwrights' Conference in December 1980.[2] The degree of distress felt by the playwrights is demonstrated by David Edgar's report in *Théâtre International*:

> I think the argument over the *Playwrights' Manifesto* was particularly significant for the British and American delegations, because it brought home the depths of feeling that exist among European playwrights about how their work is mangled by directors, and, indeed their resentment at the way in which directors have become cinema-style 'superstars' over recent years.[3]

The *Manifesto* opens with this statement by Harold Pinter, referring to Visconti's production of his play *Old Times* at the Teatro di Roma in 1973:

> It is certainly an inventive production. Signor Visconti has invented a play, where significant and quite crucial pieces of action are introduced into a play by the director, without consultation with the author. Let me remind you that a play is not public property. It belongs to its author.[4]

Of course, a reply to this statement may declare that this is so until it is performed, then the performers and members of an audience acquire a stake in the construction of meaning. There is a distinction to be made between the, often understandably, proprietorial attitude adopted by the playwright towards meaning in her/his text and the theories of shifting meaning articulated in much modern theory.

However, a common alliance, founded in a concept of poesie, is established when dealing with the actions of the performer/practitioner. We cannot assume that these critical positions are merely reactionary. That would be to fall into a simplistic way of thinking that claims an intrinsic radicalism for theatre practice on the grounds that 'doing' the activity is radically progressive. This, in its turn, has led to the accusation that practical theatre work, at least in the context of pedagogy, leads only to a subjective *cul de sac* of feeling. The subsequent response of many practitioners usually reveals them at their most authoritarian, claiming the unique insight born of a creative sense that transcends ideology.

While it would be unusual to find a university drama department that did not give a serious place in its curriculum to the practice of theatre, equally, theory has never been so strongly promoted as it is being now in these departments. The problems, addressed by the chapters of this book, are located in how we perceive the two activities and how we perceive the tension that may exist between them. Is there any fruitful currency in a curriculum that, while giving serious time to both theory and practice, sees them as essentially separate activities? This arrangement is based, to a large extent, on the perception that theory is a contemplative activity and that the time needed for practice is potentially disruptive to serious thought. Alternatively, when practice is seen to be concerned exclusively with action, talking about the subject of the activity simply blocks progress (don't spend too much time talking about it; get on your feet and act!). So, are the two activities mutually exclusive? One premise which may said to form the basic *raison d'être* of our book could be extracted from the materialist discourses of Bertolt Brecht and Walter Benjamin and employed by Terry Eagleton:

> The audience must 'think above the action', refuse to accept it uncritically, but this is not to discard *emotional* response: 'One thinks feelings and one feels thoughtfully.'[5]

If we are to move forward, we need to understand the radical and progressive possibilities that may be attained by understanding the potential of a dialectical relationship between theory and practice. This may be extended to a trialectical relationship if we include in the equation the playwright. The potential of what may be learned through a dialectical formation should, I believe, reveal the necessity of attaining a symbiotic, rather than an antagonistic, relationship between the elements of theory and practice. Put more simply, by recognising the different sites of the activities under discussion, we may be better enabled to appreciate both the problems and the way forward in our pedagogic practices.

Resistance to theory from drama/theatre practitioners is often founded in the observation that theatre is made through action, rather than on the page. Moreover, theatre cannot be constrained within purely logocentric structures. It is also physical, visual and visceral, and, even where the starting point is the word on the page, the performer's intonation inevitably adds an immediate and new dimension to the author's written word.

There is a common misconception that theory is a recent development, but of course the idea of theory goes back at least as far as ancient Greece. However, much of what we encounter as theory today emanates, in one sense or another, from literature. By that I mean that the broad range of disciplines – such as philosophy, linguistics, political theory, cultural anthropology – the humanities in general – are the significant contributory factors to the concept of theory and all of them are subject to the hegemony of a logocentric language. If anything is significant, it is the idea that, in one way or another, all theory is ultimately concerned with linguistic philosophy. Even theory in the form of semiotics, which constructs meanings from a pattern of signs, is formulated as a language. Further to the point, much of what we term literary theory is drawn from this hegemony of linguistic philosophy and much of what appears as theory in the realm of drama and theatre is derived from 'literary theory'. Hence, the tension between theory and practice in our discipline may be perceived as a further advance on the past subservience of practice/performance to the cultural yardstick of the literary, or logocentric, form.

The precise division between theory as a contemplative activity and practice as all action seems too crude a model. There is, surely, a form of action in theory in the form of verbal discourse, as there is contemplation and decision-making in practice. Given that we may accept that there are small elements of the 'other' in each of the areas of discourse, the tension may then seem to be more precisely between language-based theory and the non-verbal aspects of theatrical practice, even between thought and gesture.

A further distinction in the assumed natures of theory and practice arises out of the observation that theory, as a contemplative activity, implies a socially isolated individual experience, whereas theatre practice is an interactive social group activity. This perception applies equally to the outcome of both theory and practice as to the process. The outcome of theory is, generally, disseminated in a logocentric printed form to be read (rather as one reads a novel), whereas the practice of theatre assumes that performers and spectators gather together, whatever the precise nature of the particular event. In relation to this polarity, Walter Benjamin wrote concerning the need to relate word and action symbiotically:

> For the dialectical treatment of this problem – and I now come to the heart of the matter – the rigid, isolated object (work, novel, book) is no use whatsoever. It must be inserted into the context of living social relations.... Social relations, as we know, are determined by production relations.[6]

Benjamin's argument states, clearly, the productive possibilities involved in locating thought, language and action in the context of social relationships. Our culture recognises a broad spectrum of possibilities for the expression of these social relationships. Literature forges social relationships through language and literary narratives. Theatre practice carries those narratives back into the realm of concrete social relationships when the performer conducts the simultaneous action of fiction and her/his own social reality. The development of a discourse between a variety of 'languages' and kinds of social relationship suggests an emphasis on a distinct process.

This book records the diverse attempts of a number of university teachers to reconcile the claims of theory and practice in their teaching of drama, recognising the need, to paraphrase Eagleton, to think feelings and feel thoughtfully. The key to our pedagogies may be expressed as an emphasis on process and discourse, rather than on an outcome emphasised as a fixed commodity. There is, in a concept of process, that very Hegelian quest for a synthesis of theory and practice that gave rise to a re-examination of the Greek idea of praxis and to its optimistic incorporation in dialectical materialism. While the term praxis was never precisely defined, we are taking its meaning as that which links theory and practice as parts of a process that encourages theory to lead to action, and, further, action that is directed towards enabling people to change that which they wish to change. This does not mean that practice, as the other side of the equation, tests theory in any scientific sense, producing proof, or lack of proof. Social practice cannot work in that precise way because human beings, in their social personae, are not precise creatures. The pedagogic principle by which we aim to work suggests that human beings are, given the intellectual opportunities, constantly self-changing through their actions. Moreover, the process is not linear, but cyclical, moving through thought to action and back to thought. It is this cyclical process that we describe as praxis.

At the heart of this approach to pedagogy is the idea that education through the arts, and in particular theatre, offers the potential for 'self-changing' through and by the means of critical, thoughtful, praxis. At this point we should return to the questions that address the position of drama as a discipline within the academic community. It is to be hoped that drama is no longer questioned in terms of its intellectual rigour, but, equally, it must not be forgotten that the activity is practical and social. Most teachers of drama would wish to advocate the pursuit as one that demands the involvement of both the teacher and the student as collaborators in the experience of making theatre; such teachers would not, normally, wish to remain exclusively as passive scholarly observers of the process. However, the discourse pursued in this book refutes equally the notion that to practise drama implies, *ipso facto*, that it is a radically progressive activity. Without a thoughtful reading of why we pursue an activity, we deny the purpose of that activity. Drama, surely, exists to draw attention to the activities of human beings through the action of women and men enacting their experiences of the world in which they live. This may take the form of the recovery of history, or it may draw upon contemporary experience. Either way, it relates past events to current experience; how we are and how we are made. History, in this sense, is not removed, nor is it contemporary. It is a sensual relationship between then and now, dependent upon thoughtful action. To deny the ideology intrinsic to action in performance is to deny to that worker (the artist) the means by which s/he may understand her/his own identity. Further, to remove the artist – actor, writer, stage-hand, publisher – from the whole means of production is to disempower him/her. At the centre of the whole complex pattern is surely the clear understanding of the material relations that link stage-hand to writer; actor to critic; theoretician to spectator. To isolate one from another is to alienate that individual, or group, from the whole pattern of elements. By allowing the past to inform the present, by allowing each worker in the whole production process to understand the other workers, we offer ourselves the opportunity to make effective changes in our lives. This, in the final analysis, is our argument for praxis.

The synthesising of the different elements of the discipline into a process emanates from, but is not confined to, the Drama Department of the University of Exeter – and that is appropriate because it was there, between 1968 and 1976, that the attempt was first made to compose a syllabus out of a praxis. The syllabus structure that served this pedagogy was founded in the notion of the project. From its inception, the Drama Department rejected the conventions expected by an academic timetable, dispensing with separate timetabled hours for lectures, seminars, tutorials and practical sessions. Instead, the timetable was based on a series of five-week projects, in teaching blocks of three hours, and while in principle the single-honours students' timetable had no constraints, even the combined-honours timetable, with the constraints of the other subject, offered more contact hours than is normally found in a university department. This concentration of time was essential, both for the intensity of the activity and to allow free movement between spaces and modes of teaching. The cohesive quality of the project, and the claim for praxis, was based in the thematic nature of the project. Rather than following a chronological course in theatre history, or dramatic literature, each project would pursue a theme, and each project theme would form the pedagogic narrative of the year. Thus, first-year projects may be broad-based, offering such areas of discourse as dreams, ritual, or storytelling. Second-year projects would approach specific conventions of theatre. While certain historical periods of theatre may be omitted, what is taught is a process and, with the astute student, this process may be applied to any area of theatrical experience. Rather than covering a broad curriculum, this approach to teaching seeks to enable each student to acquire the skills of both word and action that may be carried into any area of discourse. It is not so much what you learn, as how you learn it.

Every approach to teaching should be subject to periodic self-reassessment; however, we are also subject to the invasive changes in the structure of universities. The new systems of management standardisation, quality assurance and, ultimately, the gradual disenfranchisement of university academics within the system have threatened the integrity of all teaching in Exeter, as elsewhere. The changes that are taking place throughout the university system institute a new form of utilitarianism. The demand is that a university education must be quantifiable in terms of the marketplace: the knowledge acquired must be quantifiable according to approved standards; the methodologies of teaching must be of a commensurate standard throughout the country; and all forms of teaching must prove themselves cost-effective. The result is an ideology that perceives knowledge to be a commodity that may be bought (by the client/student) and employed for its currency value in the career marketplace. Universities are rapidly becoming institutions where knowledge is sold in neat parcels and there can be no room for questions that may disrupt the efficiency of quality assurance. The new call for a standard definition of 'graduateness' is only the latest in a long line of actions determined to disrupt any sense of difference.

The concept of standardisation is a curious one. As I understand it, the demand is that a certain class of degree is the same, not only in every institution, but in every discipline. While there is a justification in asking that the education at X university is as good as in Y university, how may an upper second-class degree be the same across disciplines? What are the commensurate criteria that decide a mark in an arts subject and in an engineering subject? They are different, but both with their own intrinsic value systems. While we, presumably, wish to be assured that all courses and institutions are reputable, how is it possible to systematise assessment across disciplines which are, and should be, very different in nature?

Even within disciplines we cannot hope (nor should we) to impose a standard ideology of teaching. The contributors to this book have all tried to express their commitment to praxis in their pedagogy. This does not imply a precise consistency of ideology. The book is addressed to students and fellow teachers, *not* as definitive, but in the more modest hope of being exemplary.

The book is divided into three parts, each discussing specific aspects of a process-orientated approach to the teaching of drama in a university. Part I discusses the question of empowerment: the empowerment of the performer; performers and spectators; and the teacher. Part II discusses the question of dialogues with texts: play-reading; study, reception and understanding; and adaptation. Part III offers three case studies in researched performance, each of which focuses on a specific project undertaken in a university drama department: improvising tragedy and epic; politics of theatricality; and melodrama.

Given a realistic view of the constraints under which we are all being 'encouraged' to teach, and recognising the irony that may be perceived in the use of empowerment in the first part, the chapters of this book record our determination to continue, and develop, the principles of pedagogy that we hold to be efficacious. The students who now apply to university drama departments have benefited from the developments in drama education in the secondary sector. Their experience of an education through drama does not question the appropriateness of understanding theoretical issues through a practical exploration. It remains true that a drama department that fails to accommodate its students' urge to apply what they learn in meaningful social interactions will disappoint their hopes and aspirations.

Notes

1. I am, quite deliberately, using the terms drama and theatre loosely, and regarding them as interchangeable. I am also well aware of the differing uses and meanings ascribed to 'drama': that is, the literary textual aspect of the performing arts; or a word from the ancient Greek verb meaning to 'do' (theatre relating to the verb to 'see'). As long as we are aware of the interchangeable possibilities of the two terms through common usage, I see no point in labouring precise definitions. Across Britain, university departments style themselves variously, while still engaging in fundamentally the same activity.

2. A full record of the *Playwrights' Manifesto* may be found in *Théâtre International* (1981), no. 1, pp. 5–10.

3. D. Edgar (1981) *Théâtre International*, no. 1, pp. 5–10.

4. H. Pinter (1981) *Théâtre International*, no. 1, pp. 5–10.

5. T. Eagleton (1976) *Marxism and Literary Criticism*. Methuen, London, p. 67.

6. W. Benjamin (1977), *Understanding Brecht*, trans. A. Bostock. NLB, London, p. 87.

Part I

Empowerment

So often forms of pedagogy result in disempowering the recipients, rather than enabling them. The three chapters comprising this part of the book examine three contexts in which the aim is to empower those people engaged: the performer; the performers and the spectators; and the teachers.

Dorinda Hulton, clearly, in the 'Creative Actor' considers what may be seen as the enfranchisement of the actor/performer. In so doing, she raises not only the matter of the actor's relationship to a concept of text, but also focuses on the nature of what she means by 'training'. Her challenge is both to the 'text' and to institutional structures as the determining factors in the creative progression of the actor.

The praxis of this approach is to be found in the emphasis placed on an heuristic methodology of action derived from personal experience, more than on experience formulated through a written or recorded oral narrative. The tension that may exist between an idea of praxis as located in 'literary' dramatic narratives and what may be perceived as subjective experience, in this approach to theatre-making, is interesting. We readily accept the formalising of personal experience into the conventions of dramatic and theatrical narratives. Less readily are we prepared for the actor to work directly from her/his personal experience without the intermediary of the author or director as *auteur*. We are more familiar with the concepts of the personal and particular being articulated through the broader ideological schemes of literary conventions. Hulton's approach asks us to accept the validity of a more ontological reliance on a sense of unique personal experience.

11

The debate that arises from this methodology is further engaging when considered in relation to her quest to free the student from the demands of the institution. Her argument covers two aspects: the pressure on the student to conform to the institutional structure; and, particularly within the creative arts, the pressure to equip students to formulate artistic policies in line with the current market status quo – as she states, 'the impulse to align the self with material and methods which reaffirm the values of those in charge'.

Lesley Soule's concern in 'Performing Identities' addresses a discourse with specific attention to the narratives that are constructed through what she perceives as the three identities engaged in theatrical interaction: performer; spectator; and character (character being the text). These three identities (or how they relate) form the basis for a concept of praxis. This is a praxis that, while rooted in the practice of theatre, cannot be divorced from the complexity of the simultaneous differences and disjunctions that form what we call identity, an identity that cannot be discerned as singular or fixed. Through performance, a concept of identity as a fixed or singular concept is, in her words, 'unfixed'. She relates the constant state of flux in our perceptions of identity to the relationship between performer and spectator. The meaning of a performance is not fixed in the 'character' mirroring life, but the result of a plurality of readings located in the spectators' perceptions. The 'who' of a performed identity is not 'a state of being but a process of interaction, residing not in the subjective individual but in social behaviour'.

Stephen Cockett's argument, while developing the idea that we require stories in order to make sense of our lives, also addresses, indirectly, the relationship between the teacher and the taught. His focus, while being centred on the child in school, raises important considerations for university teachers, in particular the 'politics' of teaching within our discipline.

Harold Rosen, whom he quotes, argues that the purpose of storytelling is to create meaning – not necessarily given meanings as transcendental truths, but creating meanings out of our lived experiences: 'stories that characterise politics, institutions, the family, work, local community, history, the arts, education, advertising and sub-cultures'. The activity involved in creating, and articulating, meanings offers a potential for enablement, for developing the ability to ask, and answer, questions. The organising of our lived experiences, both in listening to and in the telling of stories, also leads us to reconsider the form and function of myth in our lives. Cockett refers to Roland Barthes in order to highlight a challenge to the accepted view of myth as untruth, 'myth as a language by which we perceive the world'.

This territory may also prove to be a veritable minefield. For no matter how we reconstruct a sense of the function of myth, there is always the problem of myth being employed in order to naturalise the existing hegemonic culture into a universally accepted status quo. The answer to this problem is, and I believe this to be intrinsic to Cockett's argument, in storytelling as praxis. First of all, if we take our lives, full of their contradictions, both within ourselves and between ourselves, we are taking the first steps towards a form of *Verfremdung*. Further, the fact that there is necessarily, in this context, a reciprocal inter-action between teller and listener (the location of the teacher/teller in relationship to those taught) means that there should also exist the potential for the empowerment of both listener and teller.

1

Creative Actor (Empowering the Performer)

Dorinda Hulton

'Creative Actor' is a Theatre Practice option which lasts for ten weeks at the start of the third year of the students' degree course. It is concerned with the question of how an actor might be trained in the making of plays rather than in their interpretation. The work has been an attempt to explore some of the processes and ways of thinking which might form part of such a training.

This exploration, or series of explorations, has extended over a number of years and has been marked by trial and error on my part and on the part of the student actors with whom I have worked. The directions in which the training has developed, however, have been guided by a dialogue between their interests and my own, rather than by the application of any one theory or practice. (In this work I understand the term 'training' as being concerned with the relationships which may be made between the mind and the body.) We have reached for many theories and practices and have, also, tried to reach for one at a time. Such inventions as we have come by have been brought about through connecting one with another or consciously allowing a lack of connection.

The term 'creative' is a broad one, with a good deal of mystique attached to it. For the purposes of this essay I would, therefore, like to regard creativity as being the result of two complementary types of thinking: lateral and vertical. 'Lateral thinking is generative. Vertical thinking is selective' (de Bono, 1977, p. 12).

The processes and structures within the work are intended to encourage ways of thinking that are either generative or selective or both. The student actors who engage in the training are, in a way, not called upon to be any more or less 'creative' than a child on a beach finding, selecting, arranging and then naming a collection of driftwood. A thing made is a thing made. Its value, within different contexts, is a question of perception.

I shall, therefore, as a means of attempting to make these ways of thinking clear, describe a few of the central processes and structures simply, without inflating or deflating them. A description of what happens within the work, or calling a piece of driftwood a piece of driftwood, must include examples of practical exercises: the work is, essentially, a training. I have, within this chapter, drawn these examples from various sources, but they are explained as briefly as possible (too briefly to be used as instructions), in order to give a glimpse of 'what happens'.

The work, also, is predicated upon 'experience'. I feel, therefore, that it is appropriate for me, within this chapter, to draw on my own experiences and observations, as a further means of describing 'what happens'.

There are three strands in the training.

The first strand proceeds as a series of *short compositions*, which are individually performed. These short compositions are intended to develop the physical, vocal and imaginative skills of the student actor, while attempting to order performance imagery in time and space in order to allow meaning to emerge and be shared with an audience. They are, in effect, a means as well as an end and blur the distinctions between process and product.

This first strand allows the student actor practice in the selection of her/his own objectives for each stage of the work, and practice in the selection of her/his own material and processes for making work. It follows the notion that it is practice determined by her/his own choices which will teach her/him, rather than a blueprint provided by the tutor.

The second strand engages the student in the development of physical, vocal and imaginative skills, which may be applied expressively or which encourage a sense of 'centring' in the actor, *a safe place*, in and from which to explore. The approach to making the short compositions presupposes a physical, vocal, emotional and mental flexibility, in order to be able to experiment, retain, discard, change and change again in the search to find a language of performance imagery which can hold the meanings the student actor is seeking to find and share. Such an approach may be a little alarming without a complementary training, in which there is an emphasis on research into the connections which may be made between the body, the voice and the imagination.

This second strand, therefore, calls upon forms of actor training as they might be taught in drama schools in England within the areas of 'movement' and 'voice'; on the practice of hatha yoga, which strengthens the connections between mind and body within a multiplicity of physical postures or *asanas*; and on other techniques, whose variety is intended to contextualise and broaden the students' own practice.

A third strand in the work, in which the group members act as a small audience for the developing compositions, aspires towards a training in *perceptions*, appropriate to a director who may be engaged, with the actor, in the making of plays rather than in their interpretation. This third strand engages the student in functioning as a member of a group, not in order, at this stage, to collaborate, but to provide, collectively, a pool of suggestions and responses intended to develop the theatre language with which the actor is working.

Within this third strand, there are also tasks which may be approached in pairs, with each student taking it in turns to act as 'composer' or 'director' in relation to performance imagery generated by her/his partner. These tasks or sequences of exercises are a further attempt to provide a means of developing the perceptual skills appropriate to the director, who may be engaged with the actor in the making of plays.

These three strands in the training interweave, complementing and contradicting each other. In the following sections of this chapter, I shall attempt to disentangle them and, briefly, to discuss each of them in turn.

The short compositions

A sense of purpose

The scale in which the student actor operates, within the short compositions, is tiny and her/his actions are always minor and subject to revision. Collectively, the work aspires towards being a celebration of the plurality of individualities, minorities and subcultures. If there is a confrontation implicit in the work, it is towards the confusion between the idea of community and that of conformity.

The pressure on the student to conform, within an educational context, is, in part, related to the power differential between the student and tutor. The temptation to formulate an artistic policy likely to secure funding or subsidy, which the professional theatre company in England currently faces, is paralleled in the student by the impulse to align the self with material and methods which reaffirm the values of those in charge.

The product of the training, however, is phrased as being 'a familiarisation of the individual with her/his *own* processes and ways of thinking for making plays'. The structures within the training, therefore, are intended to be provocative rather than prescriptive.

At the start of the work there is the invitation to review and take stock of the diverse range of forms and ideas of theatre which have been encountered in the first two years of the students' degree course, to list them and to select from that list directions in which to explore further. The work, in fact, is predicated upon and presumes previous investigations into various relationships between theory and practice within different forms.

Students, then, are asked to make a second list, which names different reasons for making theatre. Using this second list as an inspiration, and casting aside any fears of declaring their own aspirations to themselves, the students, individually, identify three reasons for making a number of small pieces of theatre. The intention is that these reasons will guide their own attempts; provide them with a reference point when they become lost, as lost they will surely become; and remind them, at the outset, of developing 'a sense of purpose based upon their own commitment', rather than upon one more pragmatically appropriate to the educational context within which they are operating.

Planning

A chart is used as a means of mapping the territory the student wishes to explore, with material s/he has chosen. It reminds her/him that the whole business of making pieces of theatre occurs within a finite timescale, and invites her/him to plan and name her/his objectives, for each week, at the outset of the work. These objectives are selected, by each student, both in relation to the development of performance skills and in relation to 'meanings' within the material to be shared with an audience. They are intended to provide a sense of focus and direction, in terms of both thinking and doing, to the short compositions and are tested, weekly, in 'presentation' classes, with a small audience. They are, in a sense, a method of applying the theory of objectives (Stanislavsky, 1967, pp. 111–26) to the role of 'actor as devisor'.

The acceptance that this planned route might change is implicit within adjacent columns in the chart. These allow space for the objectives to alter in response to the needs and interests within the work, as it emerges. The chart also allows space for the tutor to plan an order for the taught classes. The taught classes alternate with the presentation classes and attempt to suggest tasks or sequences of exercises the individual may select from in order to develop the work further.

The area that each taught class will explore is named on the chart and the sequence of titles gives a clear indication of a planned route. Again, adjacent columns allow space for the plan to change in response to the needs and interests within the work, as it emerges.

Starting points

In the first week of the ten-week course, the student is invited to select an event experienced by her/himself as a starting point for generating material for the short compositions. Four examples follow. The first records an experience which, also, contains 'public resonances':

> in October 1993 an event took place in Londonderry, Northern Ireland.... There is a village five miles from my home town of Limavady called Greysteel. It is a Catholic area lying on the banks of Lough Foyle. Southern Ireland or Eire lies just across the water and at night you can see the lights of Donegal. The distance between the two countries is only five miles by water.
>
> 31 October 1993 ... 10.30 p.m. two loyalist gunmen walked into the local pub *The Rising Sun* and opened fire on the people inside ... it was Halloween night and the people inside were wearing costumes, dancing, singing, drinking and celebrating the holiday atmosphere.
>
> The gunmen entered, also wearing costumes, shouted 'TRICK or TREAT' and began to shoot.... Amongst the dead were two old friends of my father and a young woman of nineteen who had attended my school. (Jeanette Hunter, 1995)

A second example gives a short list of possible starting points. In these the 'public resonances' are not so evident:

- moving to Wales
- man in Greece fell off balcony, fell into coma
- dream about UFOs
- something to do with short/tall people
- saying goodbye to my goat Lulu. (Marcus Blackburn, 1995)

In the next example, the student has made a spatial and emotional connection between a private experience and a 'public resonance':

the loneliness I experienced in the halls of residence in my first year at university. It was not the sensation of being isolated that interested me, but the irony of being excluded when surrounded by so many people. I had twelve people on my corridor but did not feel as though I could speak to any of them.

... I equated this experience to that of somebody living in a block of flats, without knowing the other people residing on the same floor. (Rachel Burney, 1995)

Finally, in the fourth example (which is part of a much longer account) the student has connected a small event with a more general perception:

We left the monastery, and headed for the bottom of the hill, where the village was. When we got there, we went into a small shop. A little boy popped up from behind the counter, and played a game of scaring me with his toy. His toy was a dead lizard. I laughed, and pretended to be scared.

It struck me that in my own culture, I would have played the same game, but the toy lizard would have been made from plastic. In Western culture, we sanitize, and package things – such as death – that we do not wish to address. (Beverley Slade, 1995)

So, the term 'experience', within the context of the training, refers to a period of time within a person's life in which connections have been made or in which they have been lost. These 'connections' or 'disconnections' may be between any of those operations we think of as being 'internal' or 'external' to a human being, such as perceptions, feelings, dreams, memories, ideas, actions and language.

Experience is thought of, therefore, as being no more inner than outer, 'not process rather than praxis, not input rather than output, not psychic rather than somatic, not some doubtful data dredged up from introspection rather than extrospection' (Laing, 1967, p. 17). It is, rather, a recognition of the interaction, or lack of it, between the realities these words represent.

Certainly, the aim in placing the starting point for generating material for performance within experience is not to lead towards some kind of subjective neo-expressionism or therapy. Rather, it is to provide a complement to other areas of the degree course which have their starting points in ideas, and which seek to locate the experience behind those ideas. This complementary approach chooses to begin, at least, by exploring an area, which in some senses is already known, in order to discover and uncover perceptions which are new to us, hidden within it, or staring us in the face. And to share our discoveries.

Developments

Having selected an initial starting point, the invitation to the student actor is towards a search to find forms which might contain these connections and disconnections. This search leads to experiment with a number of performance styles which may be juxtaposed in sequence or layered in order to allow connection and communication with an audience.

It begins with two collections, both supplemented by suggestions from other members of the group and myself.

The first is a collection of 'images' which may be enacted and which derive from the connections and disconnections within the event experienced. In order to help students to dream up images which may be enacted, rather than abstract ideas which then have to be translated into performance terms, I suggest the use of the terms *imitative*, *indicative*, *expressive* and *metaphoric*, as a means of categorising imagery and visualising alternatives.

Benedetti, in *The Actor at Work*, divides the language of gesture into four broad categories of gestural function which overlap, but which, for the purposes of study, he separates: illustrative or imitative, indicative, emphatic and autistic (meaning literally 'to the self'). In a 'Physical Gesture Scene' he asks the actor to select a simple but highly physical action and suggests that she perform it four times. Addressing the actor, his instructions read:

> if your action is pantomimically to lift a heavy box and move it across the room, you would:
> 1. Illustrate lifting it, as if you were telling us about how you did it without actually doing it. You may use words as well as gestures here.

2. Indicate lifting it. ('I'll pick it up from over there and carry it over here.')
3. Use emphatic gestures that are *symbolic* (rather than illustrative) as you tell us *how it felt* to lift the heavy box. See especially how your voice is affected.
4. Finally, perform the action symbolically and *secretly* using autistic gestures (for example, hitching up your belt as a substitute for lifting the box). (Benedetti, 1970, p. 57)

I have adjusted the terms which Benedetti used as a means of categorising gesture and applied some of their definitions to my own sense of performance imagery. There is, again, the sense that the separation between the categories is useful only as a means of generating alternatives. Thus, using (an account of) the event experienced as a starting point, I suggest to the students that they select the most important 'actions' within an event and think of different ways of communicating those actions to an audience. The 'actions' selected from the event need not be physical, but the aim is to try to imagine a means of physicalising, vocalising or verbalising them.

(1) Imitative imagery, when it relates to character, engages the student actor in naturalistic forms.
(2) Indicative imagery engages the student actor in showing an action, or part of it, clearly, without attempting to imitate it naturalistically. Gesture, for example, might be used as a means of showing or 'signing', rather than 'feeling', an emotion: within a particular cultural context the 'V' sign will indicate aggression, irrespective of the energy with which it is performed; within another context, the same sign, but with the palm facing away from the body, would indicate victory.
(3) Expressive imagery attempts to embody; that is, it seeks to find a physical or vocal form for emotions.
(4) Metaphoric imagery involves the student actor in finding a substitute action which might imitate, indicate or express an important element within the event.

The second of the two collections is composed of material which is in some way associated with, or expressive of, the event experienced. This material might include a painting, a piece of music, a poem, a song, a photograph, a story, a newspaper article, a biography, an autobiography or a novel. (There should be at least one substantial, non-dramatic, text in the collection for the student to work from, so that any writing s/he engages in will be seen, by her/him, as being a choice and not a necessity.)

These two collections provide a means of generating alternatives, deliberately. 'The most basic principle of lateral thinking is that any possible way of looking at things is only one from among many other possible ways' (de Bono, 1977, p. 58). And the intention is, through combining different forms and ideas, to provoke fresh insight into the ways in which performance imagery might be juxtaposed in sequence, or layered, in order to allow connection and communication with an audience. There is, however, at this stage, a daunting amount of material to work on and from, so that the difficulty in making the short compositions each week is located, initially at least, in the process of selection and reduction. (Practice in making choices seems to me to be, properly, part of a training in making work, as does practice in identifying which of those choices are the important ones.)

As I have said, during the Creative Actor training, a number of short compositions are made and performed by each student. Each week, then, a different process might be attempted, and a composition might begin again, in terms of content, with a different starting point. Alternatively, the student may choose to develop her/his work in a less fragmented, more sustained way. More often than not, sustained sections of work are interspersed with impulsive changes in direction.

After five weeks, the student is invited to consider various ways in which imagery from these short compositions may be selected, combined and transformed in order to create a new piece of work. This 'new' piece of work is shared with a slightly larger audience within an 'open class'. The process of selecting and combining imagery is indicated below in diagrammatic form:

Week 1 ~ ~ ~
Week 2 —/—/—
Week 3 •
Week 4 Ø

The work shown in Week 5 may, for example, be:

or   —•—•—•
or   Ø
or   ~ ~ ~——•

Later, after five weeks, the student actor is invited to select a second event which has occurred at a distance from her/himself, perhaps one s/he has read about in a newspaper article, biography or autobiography.

As I write this, Deng Xiaoping is dying and I am reminded of the Tiananmen Square protests and the young student who stood in front of the tanks. There can be no comparison between the action of that student and the action of a student actor operating in 'a safe place' with so much less at stake. There can be no comparison but there can be a connection.

The second five weeks follow the same basic pattern as the first five and in week 10 a second 'new' piece is created. This final composition may draw on imagery from some, all or none of the previous weeks' work and may as well be called an 'inter-play' as a play. It may, for example, attempt to explore a connection between the personal and the political; or to make visible a disconnection between the public and the private. It would, almost certainly, be no longer auto-biographical to the student. It would, also, aim to be no more than 20 minutes in length and to have a clear intention in relation to its meaning for an audience.

A safe place

As I have said, the weekly classes in which the short compositions are presented are alternated with taught classes which suggest tasks or sequences of exercises the individual may select from in order to develop the work further. Some of these classes comprise practical investigations into actor training, drawn from a variety of sources, whose range is intended to contextualise and broaden the students' own thinking and doing. These classes are supported, whenever possible, by documentation, in written or video form.

The taught classes, also, provide me with the opportunity of inviting students into the territory with which I am familiar (even if they enter it with their individual maps folded in their back pockets). This territory, which has been shaped by my own training, is in the areas of movement, voice and image work.

One path in my training, in the area of voice work, has led me towards certain broad principles which I use as guides within the processes of training (Andrews, 1994). I have interpreted and adapted the ideas within these principles freely and applied them to the processes on the Creative Actor course. They are intended to encourage *attitudes* and *activities* which operate below the threshold of any possible competition between group members.

A sense of purpose, clearly and simply articulated at the outset of the work, is applied to each stage of the training process, in the form of objectives. This sense of purpose or *clear order* is one of the four broad principles which I ask students to test in their work. The others are termed: *presence, reduction* and *relaxation.* The ideas that are associated with these terms, within the context of the training, overlap, and I will use brief descriptions of exercises as a means of indicating them.

A clear order

> Ask the participants to describe a circle with the right foot. They do it for a minute. They forget about the foot, still continuing to make circles. Then ask them to write their first name in the air with their right hand at the same time ... this is almost impossible. (Boal, 1992, p. 62)

Several ideas are inherent in this exercise:

(1) the participants are clear about what they are trying to do, even if they cannot do it;
(2) they are clear about the order in which they are going to try to do it;
(3) in order to have the best chance of doing it, they concentrate on doing one thing at a time, even if, at a certain point, that one thing amounts to doing two things at the same time;
(4) they accept the fact that activities which engage the body cannot, entirely, be solved by the mind;
(5) they experience the fact that nothing terrible happens if they fail.

Practice in 'giving up', in relation to an objective, seems to me to be an important element in the work, as well as practising the ability to recognise the right time to give up, for the time being. Any 'continuous' training operates in terms of stopping and starting; and it is so much easier, and so much less generative, to cling to what we cannot do.

In fact, the exercise, and others like it, is quite possible to achieve (assuming there is some point to them), with regular practice in a discipline such as yoga, which strengthens the connections between the mind and the body in precise and practical ways (Iyengar, 1977). This practice invites a sense of integration or 'centring' in the actor, between the body, the breath and the images within the forms of the *asanas*: the word *yoga*, in fact, in its Sanskrit root, means to 'yoke' or to 'bind'.

Paradoxically, I have also found that attentive practice in the *asanas* encourages a facility for carrying out two disparate sets of instructions simultaneously. I have long been interested in the idea of engaging the actor in doing 'two things at the same time', as a means of indicating two parallel or contradictory levels of experience. Some of the inside/outside exercises of the Open Theater (Pasolli, 1972) are formulated in relation to this technique (with the voice and body acting separately, but simultaneously, in different spheres). I would regard this area as being at the very centre of my interest: a fascination with the layering of experience or, even, the commonplace lack of integration within experience. And a fascination with the search to find a theatre language and forms to hold and share these.

The disconnection between feeling and speech or between rhetoric and action are, for example, commonplace recognitions. Less commonplace, perhaps, and possibly more interesting, are the connections which may be made when the same feeling is shared between different people. This emotional connection between people, when translated into performance imagery, invites a form in which empathy is implicit. In another example, a number of different emotional responses towards the same event suggests both connection and disconnection. In this instance, a form is invited in which irony and self-doubt are implicit. Either case might be termed a 'conjugation'. (I mean conjugation in the traditional sense of *amo, amas, amat.*) Either case, also, presents a possible alternative, in terms of form, to a linear use of narrative or to the sense of progression contained within the pattern of argument, conflict and resolution. In both of the examples related to a declension of emotions, there is a movement which radiates away from and towards a central point of connection and concern, rather than one which proceeds from A to B to C. In both forms, however, given the fact that performance imagery always operates in 'real' time, the question of 'order' is inescapable.

Presence

Exhale and, after exhaling but before breathing in, take 30 steps forwards. Stop and breathe in. Then exhale and repeat the sequence three times walking forwards and three times walking backwards.

The most important element in this exercise, which encourages the upwards and outwards swing in the ribcage, is for the student actor to remember that s/he has a choice in whether or not to follow, and how far to follow, an instruction. (The 30 steps can be treated as an aim and not a demand.) The distance s/he can travel will vary, from day to day, moment to moment, and be influenced by many factors. The invitation, then, within the training, is to practise measuring that distance, *moment to moment*, so that s/he is able to work more easily, at her/his 'present best', and not below or, by forcing her/himself, beyond it.

The presence of the actor, in my view, is related to an audience's perception of the quality of an actor's engagement with imagery; and that quality is, in part, determined by the actor's capacity to work within her/his own sense of 'present best'. This has little to do with any 'objective' measurement of skill or excellence. Neither has it to do with any subjective self-congratulation. It is, instead, the recognition of a *quality* of engagement between subject and object that is particular to both. Thus, the small child, with learning difficulties, performing in a school hall, may have as much 'presence' as the trained actor performing in a national theatre.

A second observation I would make is that, in my experience, there are more difficulties encountered in training and in performing that are associated with doing too much and trying too hard than ones that are associated with doing too little and being lazy.

Reduction

> Take any movement/action sequence and repeat it for ten minutes, while attempting to manifest an image of 'flight'. Begin vigorously, but if there is difficulty, reduce the size and speed of the movements; and be as specific as possible, imaginatively.

Practice in broadening the options and then seeking out the essential underlies many of the processes on the Creative Actor course. This practice presumes the capacity to recognise the 'essential', whether it be in relation to the telling of a story, the setting up of a dialectic within a story, the sharing of a feeling in relation to an event, or the finding of a form which might hold a number of different perspectives.

In accepting the principle of reduction, I risk association with the pejorative term 'reductive'. The risk is all the greater when the principle is applied to language, and there is a resistance to seeming and even being simplistic in, say, naming objectives or declaring a commitment. The shortcomings of simplicity, however, seem to me to be of greater generative value in the processes of making work than the virtues of complexity. At the very least, collaborative processes beyond the course are clearly facilitated by negotiating and naming shared objectives.

Relaxation

Vibrate the tongue, towards its back, while sustaining a vowel sound.

This exercise affects the resonance of the voice, by relaxing the tongue. The vibration, also, gives a gentle massage to the base of the brain via the inside of the skull. The gentle massage can occur only if there is an absence of tension in the tongue. It is, precisely, an absence, an absence of tension, which makes the action and its effect possible. The principle of relaxation tries to encourage the actor to allow, within any activity, an *absence* of tension or anxiety when those qualities are functioning restrictively rather than protectively.

There are so many causes of anxiety which are embedded in the structures supporting and surrounding the making of theatre, in England, at this time. The whole business of functioning within a timescale that is constricted and determined by funding or subsidy, for example, which the small companies face, creates a pressure. There is a real need not so much to get out of the kitchen as to open the windows.

Sometimes difficult to locate, these causes of anxiety seem to me, often, to be hidden behind the hot air of conceit and competition. The work in Creative Actor aligns itself with any attempt to challenge an environment which is governed by these energies. It also aligns itself with any attempt to create a safe place, in which to take more risks.

As a training, it hopes to affirm the recognition that supportive, playful and provocative energies are the starting points for creativity.

Perceptions

The strand in the work which aspires towards a training in perceptual skills (appropriate to the director who may be engaged, with the actor, in the making of plays) engages the student in the regular practice of acting as part of a small audience for the developing compositions.

This 'practice of acting' consists of four methods of responding to work with the intention of assisting in its development. These four methods are called, in the training, reading, affirmation, criticism and provocation.

Reading

The sense that an individual audience member makes of the imagery within the short compositions is a dialogue between the meanings contained within the material itself and the relevance of those meanings to her/his own belief systems: 'the brain has a powerful ability to put together and seek to coalesce into sense whatever is put before it'; and 'attention will move to those areas which trigger existing patterns' (de Bono, 1992, p. 79).

I have found that it is probably more useful to the actor to hear a number of 'readings' rather than one or two at length. In the class, a rotating one-to-one system is used, with a time limit. This allows every student practice in articulating responses briefly and simply, without the development of a hierarchy, which may be present in a discussion format; and without the student resorting to, and being dependent on, the overnight think. Reflection, which clarifies itself over a period of time, is often of value, but the intention, at this point, is to sharpen perceptual skills.

The audience member is not, at any stage, given an explanation of what the work 'means'. Instead, s/he feeds back to the actor her/his own perceptions rather than ones channelled by explanations. Her/his reading of each composition will, therefore, when added to the pool of responses made by the other group members, reflect a general impression of the sense that is being communicated by the material, as well as the perceptions particular to her/him. This kind of information can be extremely helpful in gaining insight into the way in which imagery may be revised and edited in order to communicate more clearly with an audience.

It is extremely hard for imagery to cut across established patterns of association and to effect the paradigm shift which would be necessary in order for a belief system to change. In fact, sometimes an incidental aspect of the work will trigger a series of associations irrelevant to the actor's intentions, as in the story of the man in the dark grasping an elephant's tail and thinking it (the elephant) to be small and tufty. In a sense, the audience member is as much a maker of the play as the actor.

There is, however, as well, the possibility of change: a paradigm shift can also be 'a thing made'.

Affirmation

> the readiness of the brain to receive and creatively use response and suggestion is dependent upon context and emotions. (de Bono, 1992, p. 79)

The one-to-one method relieves both actor and audience member from an inappropriate pressure of consensus in relation to these positive value judgements, which will have as much to do with an audience member's own belief system as with the work. If there is a consensus, it will emerge independently.

A recognition of the generative power of affirmation seems to me to be fundamental to encouraging growth. Even if there is nothing which is perceived to be positive about the work, analysis and criticism should always be made with respect. After all, a lack of perception could indicate just that: a lack of perception.

Criticism

Some attempt needs to be made to relate criticism to a sense of the actor's own objectives (as perceived by the audience member and not as explained by the actor). This is a difficult task, requiring, as it does, a shift in perspective. However modest the context, the making of a short composition is, in itself, a critical act: 'Be it realistic, fantastic, Utopian or satiric, the construct of the artist is a counter-statement to the world ' (Steiner, 1989, p. 11).

Provocation

Associated or seemingly disassociated ideas and practices, arising from interpretative, affirmative or critical perceptions, can allow fresh insight and help to develop the work.

I have found that it encourages greater freedom, both in giving and in hearing (though not necessarily accepting or following) these ideas, if the actor does not feel, immediately, compelled to assess the usefulness and, therefore, the value of these suggestions. Ideas which at first seem ridiculous might at a later point still seem ridiculous and, if so, at the very least, will prove valuable in determining the appropriateness of an original choice. Practice in listening seems to me to be an important part of the training.

Much reliance is placed on both provocation and chance as a means of finding the starting points for, and developing, the short compositions which act both as training exercises and as short pieces of theatre on the Creative Actor course. This reliance acts as a reassuring complement to the equal emphasis which is placed on the rather more earnest, but necessary, planning and naming of objectives for each stage of the work.

Any creative idea or form which is recognised as being of some 'value', within a particular context, will appear logical in retrospect, and this appearance encourages the unreliable sense that creative ideas and forms may be arrived at through logical thought. We know, now, that the brain operates as a self-organising patterning system and that, in order to cut across habitual ways of thinking, chance and provocation are as good a way as any of discovering fresh routes to follow in order to arrive at new perceptions (de Bono, 1992, p. 78).

Collaboration

A further aspect of the strand in the work, which aspires towards a training in perceptual skills, occurs within the taught classes. It takes the form of tasks or sequences of exercises which may be approached in pairs: the role of the composer within the exercises being, in one way, not dissimilar to that of a director engaged with the actor in the making of plays. An example of such a sequence of exercises, which incidentally also uses chance and provocation as tools for generating material for a short composition, is outlined below.

(1) Select three short fragments of text from a sheet of newspaper.
(2) Generate three different movement actions related to an image, say, 'chaos', which can be repeated.
(3) Generate three expressive sounds which are outside your normal vocal range.
(4) Sitting in a circle, pass one piece of text to the person on your right, one to the person on your left and keep one yourself. Do the same with the movements and then the sounds. Each person should now have an arbitrary collection of nine fragments of material. Show your nine fragments to a partner, who then acts as

a 'composer', selecting from and arranging the material, in time and space, in order to allow meaning to emerge. Images may be combined or extended, for example, over a long period of time; reduced so that they are barely perceptible; or the expressive energy which originally accompanied the sounds may be transferred to the words, which might be spoken at differing volumes in different parts of the space. Out of this play, the composer attempts to find a pattern or form for the material, which in some way contains an implicit, if not explicit, sense of meaning.

(5) Test the sense of emergent meaning on a small audience.

In this exercise, there is an interplay between the sound, movement and word images themselves. A second interplay is also at work in the selection and sequencing of the images by the composer; and a third between the imagery and the perception of it by an audience. The *sense*, in fact, of any of these three 'interplays' is dependent upon, and determined by, perceptual connections.

A second example of a task or sequence of exercises, which may be approached in pairs, with each student taking it in turns to play the role of 'composer' or 'director', is given below. In the taught classes I may combine elements from different sources in order to devise 'new' exercises. In the example given, I have experimented, in part, by combining methods derived from *The Actor as Storyteller* (Alfreds, 1980) with ideas adapted from *The Art of Fiction* (Lodge, 1992).

Write three texts:

(i)   In the third person, past tense, write a description of a character, possibly including a sense of where, when and why as well as who.

(ii) In the first person, present tense, write the story of a memory, possibly including direct speech and dialogue.

(iii) Write an interior monologue, which is related to the private sensations and thoughts of the character, reflecting the moment which is at the heart of the story. Alternatively, make a text composed of a definition or analysis of an object in the story, information about which may be used metaphorically, in order to indicate a feeling at the heart of the story.

Explore three physicalities:

(a)   Make a list of key physical features for your character, for example: eyes, mouth, jaw (three related to the face); and shoulders, spine, feet (three related to the rest of the body). Select an expressive adjective to describe each feature. Work physically with a sense of these features and try to retain as many of them as possible, while speaking a text. See how this affects your speech rhythms and tone of voice. Try, also, taking on the characteristics, one by one, as you speak a text, so that a sense of the character's presence gradually emerges.

(b) Make a list of the important physical actions within the story. Select from these and explore them physically in different ways, for example: as a series of freeze frames, slowed down, speeded up, as repeated actions, enlarged, reduced. Again, select from among these attempts and try working with the text at the same time. Try to avoid merely illustrating the story through actions, but rather use the actions to indicate behaviour or express feeling more clearly.

(c) Extend, enlarge, shorten, reduce or repeat a naturalistic expressive gesture. Alternatively, explore ways of 'becoming' the object within the metaphor you have chosen, creating it in the space or interacting with it using movement or materials.

Explore three kinds of sound-making:

(A) Make a list of the character's vocal qualities, for example: a tendency to boom, gabble, drawl, speak in a high-pitched voice. Select from this list and experiment with extending or enlarging certain characteristics. Use a piece of text and play with changes in pace, pitch, power and rhythm. Try not to confine yourself to the naturalistic. You could, also, try this with a key phrase for your character, for example 'Get out of my life'.

(B) List the sounds which occur within the story. Think of them as images in themselves and work on them vocally. Try speaking part of a text with the quality of the sound effect you are imitating.

(C) Work on an expressive sound, for example: sobbing, gasping with surprise, laughing. Again, try speaking part of a text with the same sound quality. You could also try working with a sound associated with the metaphor.

Try different combinations of (i), (ii), (iii), (a), (b), (c) and (A), (B), (C). Order your attempts in order to allow meaning to emerge, or work with a partner, taking the role of composer. You could try repeating the sequence with a second or even third character. This possibility leads to a form containing a story within a story. Either story might involve shifts in perspective between the 'outer' and 'inner'.

Such exercises are, in themselves, intended as provocations rather than as prescriptions. As I have said, I plan and name these areas of exploration at the start of the work: for example, 'Time and Space', 'Song', 'Poetry, Painting and Music'. This plan, however, may change and the classes are, in a way, a means for the tutor to suggest sequences of exercises in response to the work *as it emerges* within the short compositions.

I try within each taught class to include some element of risk, both in order to avoid prescription and, also, to learn myself. The collection of material from different sources that each student makes at the beginning of the Creative Actor course acts as subject matter and springboard for this experimentation.

Occasionally, I invent an approach for which I can find no source, other than my own imaginings, only to discover, once I have 'invented' it, a network of connections. I have, for example, devised a short sequence of exercises, using a newspaper article as a starting point, which asks the actor to act as 'reactor' to the language used within the article. The actor speaks the text very softly, listening to the sounds within the language, through the inner ear, via the inside of the skull. At the same time s/he performs three arbitrary gestures very slowly, with the quality of being moved (physically that is) by another person. In a sense, the audience members are invited to look through the body and voice of the actor, as they might through a stained-glass window, to the bodies and voices in a landscape beyond. Within such an exercise, the actor intends to be neither a reflector nor an interpreter of reality, but a medium through which it is possible to sense other realities.

A piece of driftwood is not, in the end, 'a piece of driftwood': it is a collection of words. (Magritte, 1969, p. 33)

There are, therefore, three pressures upon the material within the short compositions which encourage its development. The first is from within the material itself (that is, the work will develop according to its own internal logic) and the other two are external interventions. The actor/reactor in play with the material will try to impose meaning on to it as much as recognise meaning inherent in it; and an 'active' audience who propose alternatives, criticisms, interpretations and who offer affirmations will have a provocative, mediating and creative function.

The four ways of responding to work, and the tasks suggested in the taught classes, place the individual actor within a welter of responses from which to make her/his own choices. Crucial to this process, however, at this stage, is the idea that the choices s/he makes are in relation to her/his own passion and perspective, so that response is seen as part of a dialogue intended to test communication, and not as a driving force.

Within the Creative Actor course, choice ultimately remains with the actor in relation to the selection of material and methods. Beyond the course, the thought is that the actor, empowered by practice in making work, is better placed to share, genuinely, in a collaborative process with a director, writer and other actors rather than being a means (through improvisation within one process of devising) by which the director and writer develop their own ideas. In such a model, beyond the course, the choice of material would most naturally lie with the actor, responsibility for its development would be shared between the actor, director and writer, and responsibility for its meaning in relation to an audience would lie with the director. There would also be, within such a model, a sense of fluidity between these roles so that, for example, an actor/writer for one project might act as a director in another.

> This ordering of responsibility, and shifting hierarchy between, but not within, each project, is also distinct from the one in which the choice of material lies with the writer and its interpretation by actors is mediated by a director. (Schechner, 1985, p. 230)

There is the thought, finally, within the training, that playful experimentation with a number of forms might help with the development of the theatre language that allows and invites fresh insights: not only those of the play-maker, for they will always entail a kind of sensitive and sensory propaganda, but also, more deliberately, rather than incidentally, those of an audience.

In such a theatre language there would be a plurality of approaches and a multiplicity of forms; and Stanislavsky would get his street name back. In 1905, betraying his cultural context, he wrote:

> realism, and [depicting] the way of life have outlived their age. The time has come to stage the unreal. Not life itself, as it occurs in reality, must be depicted, but rather life as it is vaguely perceived in fantasies and visions at moments of lofty emotions. This is the spiritual situation that must be transmitted scenically, in the way

that painters of the new school use cloth, musicians of the new trend write music, and the new poets poetry. The works of these painters, musicians and poets have no clear outlines, definite and finished melodies, or precisely expressed ideas. The power of the new art lies in its combinations of colors, lines, musical notes, and the rhyming of words. They create general moods that carry over to the public unconsciously. They create hints that make the most unobservant person create with his own imagination. (Kirby, 1995, p. 28)

Joseph Chaikin (1992), in *The Presence of the Actor*, noted that 'reality' is not a fixed state: the word 'reality' comes from the Latin word *res*, which means 'that which we can fathom'. Perhaps Stanislavsky would accept a revision of his vision: one in which 'lofty' emotions might be created within an audience, through a recognition of the extraordinary within those he terms 'unobservant'.

Works cited

Alfreds, M. (1980) *The Actor as Storyteller*. Theatre Papers, Dartington College of Arts, Devon.

Andrews, G. (1994) *Gael Andrews*. Arts Archives, Exeter.

Benedetti, S. L. (1970) *The Actor at Work*. Prentice Hall, New York.

Boal, A. (1992) *Games for Actors and Non-Actors*. Routledge, London.

Chaikin, J. (1992) *The Presence of the Actor*. McClelland and Stewart, New York.

de Bono, E. (1977) *Lateral Thinking*. Pelican Books, London.

de Bono, E. (1992) *I'm Right You're Wrong*. Penguin Books, London.

Iyengar, B. K. S. (1977) *The Art of Relaxation*. Theatre Papers, Dartington College of Arts, Devon.

Kirby, M. (1995) 'Happenings', in *Happenings and Other Acts*, ed. M. R. Sandford. Routledge, London, pp. 1–28.

Laing, R. D. (1967) *The Politics of Experience*. Penguin Books, London.

Lodge, D. (1992) *The Art of Fiction*. Penguin Books, London.

Magritte, R. (1969) 'L'air et la chanson', in *Magritte*, ed. D. Sylvester. Arts Council, London, p. 33.

Pasolli, R. (1972) *A Book on the Open Theater*. Discus, New York.

Schechner, R. (1985) 'Performer Training Interculturally', in *Between Theater and Anthropology*. University of Pennsylvania Press, Philadelphia, pp. 213–60.

Stanislavsky, C. (1967) *An Actor Prepares*. Geoffrey Bles, London.

Steiner, G. (1989) *Real Presences*. Faber and Faber, London.

I also wish to acknowledge extracts from the Creative Actor portfolios (1995) of the following student actors: Marcus Blackburn, Rachel Burney, Jeanette Hunter and Beverley Slade.

Other sources

Feldman, P. (1977) *The Sound and Movement Exercise as Developed by the Open Theatre*. Theatre Papers, Dartington College of Arts, Devon.

Meckler, N. (1994/5) *Ways of Physicalizing Thoughts, Feelings and Text*. Arts Archives, Exeter.

Oida, Y. (1979/80) *Shinto Training of the Actor*. Theatre Papers, Dartington College of Arts, Devon.

2

Performing Identities (Empowering Performers and Spectators)

Lesley Wade Soule

Re-invention is a seductive notion, currently applied to the 'self' and to the body. It is also a premise which underlies the teaching of theatre. The primary way of learning how to re-invent theatre is to make performances, a process which necessarily involves the material body and therefore provides an opportunity for its re-invention. Generally speaking, making theatre in order to re-invent it means getting ideas from physical practice. It is also helpful to study theatre practices from other contexts: how they were done and what the ideas behind and around them were. During practice, this knowledge can then be appropriated (without being merely reproduced) as part of the process of re-invention.

While practice is central, it is impossible without theory. As theatre-makers we constantly get ideas from our own (and others') practice and put our (and their) ideas into practice. 'Theater is theory, or a shadow of it,' writes Herbert Blau. 'In the act of seeing, there is already theory' (Blau, 1982, p. 1).

The idea of theory, however, indeed the very word, gives us difficulty. Traditionally, to theorise means to summarise or abstract. Theory can provide a generalised account of past or current practice (for example Aristotle) or an imaginative description of possible practice (for example Artaud) or a set of general rules about what practice ought to be (for example almost any Renaissance neo-Aristotelian). Excitingly, however, theatrical theory, since it is in an immediate compound with practice, cannot be easily defined. The giddy interdependence of theory and practice in the theatre spirals around the notion of the inseparability and interpenetration of the physical and the cognitive.

It is my premise that for theatrical theory to be fully productive it should be organically linked with the physical practices of performance. There is a kind of theoretical understanding in theatre-making which can be explored and expanded only through using the body (including voice) in space. It can be talked about, although a fully workable vocabulary for doing so still needs to be developed. The greater the development of physical skills and awareness of performance, the more flexible and diverse invention and theoretical understanding can be. In theatre, as in life, physical and intellectual skills are inseparable. Theory and practice in theatre-making can be seen, then, to be bonded in organic interaction, so much so that if at some point in the process we try to disassemble the activity into these two ostensibly individual parts, both theory and practice stop growing.

In university drama departments, there is sometimes a dissonance between those for whom theory is the end and practice the means, and others who take the opposite view. Since theory and practice are inseparable, however, such arguments may boil down to whether you prefer practical chickens or theoretical eggs.

Blau's association of seeing with theory, cited above, reminds us of useful analogies between the theory–practice compound and the relations between the senses of seeing and hearing. Vision, being more focused and directional, leads more directly to perception and conceptualisation. Hearing, with a large component of sensation, tends to create more immediate bodily experience and ambient physical awareness. A performance, too, is composed of such complementary dimensions. It is a fluid, public interaction of a number of bodies, performers and spectators, whose multi-dimensional physicality is both theoretical and practical, a viscous, unfixable process.

In recognising the importance of the spectator in the performance (particularly in the university context) we must remind ourselves that the spectator's functions in the theatre are more than and different from those of the reader. In the first place, a theatrical spectator is one of a group, whereas a reader is solitary. Secondly, there are many elements in a performance besides language with which a spectator will interact. Giving insufficient weight to these non-linguistic elements tends to lead to a theory separated from practice. Such theorising can become in some degree de-socialised and disembodied: at its most extreme a kind of private solo performance.

Another problem that can arise from theory that fails to take physical practice sufficiently into account is that it tends to lose touch with the specific problems of practice as it occurs. Such theory may be difficult to pitch at an appropriate level for the practice to which it is to be related. Just as over-abstract acting theory can mislead performers into enacting 'generalised emotion', so over-scaled theory can produce its directorial equivalent, 'staging ideas'.

In teaching theatre, the theoretical terminology used should be accessible and relevant to the practitioners and their work. As Stephen Lacey and Doug Pye have written, 'One of the central difficulties we face is that ... the languages in which critical and practical work are conducted are often different, sometimes radically so' (Lacey and Pye, 1994, p. 21). Much of the theory used in theatre studies has been borrowed from literature, philosophy, linguistics and psychiatry. The problem cannot be solved by supplementary lectures or students acquiring specialised dictionaries. Of course theatre, as a healthy mongrel, has for centuries cross-bred with other disciplines and continues to appropriate theory from other fields. Caution is needed, however, in making this sometimes treacherous translation into a new context. Such non-theatrical theories sometimes tend to encourage an approach to performance that is too logocentric and which lacks a sufficient understanding of the range and complexity of its immediate physicality. They may admit an assumption that the only significant functions of performance are mimesis and the creation of conceptual meanings.

In a university context, there are bound to be pressures to change the nature of theatrical performance to suit the backgrounds, education and perspectives of academics. Theatre is a kind of practice in many ways alien to the traditional university. Research and teaching in the humanities and social sciences, for example, tend to be based on individual study rather than group laboratory work with bodies. Many academics are not comfortable with the physicality of theatre. 'Those trained in philosophy,' Judith Butler remarks, 'are always at some distance from corporeal matters' (Butler, 1993, p. ix). Traditionally, even dramatic criticism has been based far more on the reading and interpretation of written texts than on making or attending performances. As Marianne Novy has reminded us, 'In approaching other literary forms, we confront a text; in approaching drama, we confront human beings in performance' (Novy, 1984, p. 19).

The goal being re-invention and the method practical experimentation, a kind and scale of theory is required that will make these possible. I will be describing here a theory of theatrical performance helpful in meeting this need. Underlying this description is a set of premises, all of which have to do with bodies.

The first is the familiar Deweyan idea of learning by doing: what is performed by the body and experienced through the senses will be more usable and readily accessible than other kinds of learning. This is basic educational theory. I assume, too, that what is learned in this way will stimulate greater flexibility in its application: while all learning will contribute to re-inventing theatre, that which is learned bodily is likely to contribute more than that learned only cerebrally. Sessions in theatre practice can function as early rehearsals for as yet unconceptualised performances, although one has to accept the validity of an argument that states that such rehearsals may be seen as coercive.

A second, and possibly to some a radical, premise in this work concerns the three identities which engage in the interaction we call theatrical performance: performer, spectator and character. The spectator is the most important, followed closely by the performer, with the character (that is, the text) third. This is because only the spectator and performer are present at the point of direct interaction. I also assume that staging written texts is by no means the sole or even primary purpose of performance. Performance is moving presence; theatrically speaking, a text is fixed and absent. Catherine Elwes says, 'Performance is about the "real-life" presence of the artist' (quoted by Forte, 1990, p. 257). (Some may detect a feminist perspective here. Certainly feminism has sometimes identified women seeking freedom as the potential 'ruin of representation' (Forte, 1990, p. 252) and thus of the hegemony of the text in the theatre.)

The third and most obvious premise is that the material of which theatre is made is physical presence, that is bodies in dialogic interaction, and that the language of bodies is polyphonic and not only significative. The bodies of theatrical performance of course include the bodies of the spectators. In stressing bodily presence one is reminded of the ephemerality of performance, but the bodies who create theatre are always political: they remain responsible for their actions. The body meant here is of course more than material, corporeal, moving and sounding flesh, and more than object image. By body is also meant a processual complex of internal and external action, enacted, perceived and responded to. Perhaps the more appropriate term is 'presence', since it primarily denotes identified energy.

The concept of theatrical identity that I am working with embraces a number of questions: what kind of thing is it that we think of as 'who'; who is in control of what we call 'who'; how is this 'who' made; does the 'who' exist only in action, or is there a 'who' that is a state of being? An identity is commonly perceived as singular, its sometimes widely scattered components integrated by the perception of 'identity', that is sameness/likeness. Perceiving identity means emphasising the similarities and connections of its parts over their differences and disjunctions (even while acknowledging the latter): therefore, we can have an identity made of a diverse single body or of more than one body.

It soon becomes apparent that, though we try to conceive of the identity of a person as a singular entity in mental space, it will not hold still in time, for it goes on living. This becomes clear when we try to act out a conception of an identity (for example a character, or 'oneself'). We discover that we are performing a memory, which through enactment ceases to be past and becomes the ongoing present. Performance always unfixes.

This lack of definition has another cause: the creation of a living identity always involves a spectator. It is useful here to ask how personal identities are formed. The ethologist Thomas Luckmann states:

> Reciprocal mirroring is an elementary condition for the formation of personal identities.... Personal identity ... does not develop from 'within' as does the biological individual; it comes from 'without'. (Luckmann, 1979, p. 66)

The idea of mirroring has been fundamental in early theories of child development. Our first thought here is of children's frequent imitations of adults and each other. But the child is not actually mirroring other people's behaviour. In copying (re-enacting) it, s/he assimilates it for her/his own purpose, which is 'to act out her/himself'. This contributes to a feeling of self, rather than to an awareness of personal identity. (The same is true when this is done by students.) More important in the creation of identity is the later kind of mirroring, which occurs when the child (and of course the adult) does not copy the other person but uses her/him as a 'mirror'. By performing an act and then observing the 'mirror's' response to that action, the child/ adult forms an idea of what s/he has done, and thus of who s/he is. The other person does the same thing ('reciprocal mirroring') and the interactive exchange continues. Identity, in other words, is who one is in terms of the effect of one's actions on others and the interaction that evolves out of that. This 'who', therefore, is not a state of being but a process of interaction, residing not in the subjective individual but in social behaviour, as Luckmann, Goffman and many other writers have pointed out (including Judith Butler in the context of gender identity: see Butler, 1990, 1993). Reciprocal mirroring is also the means by which identity is created in the theatre. For centuries the stage has been regarded as 'a mirror of custom' (Donatus, 1965, p. 34). It is a commonplace that audiences look at the actors and actions on the stage as a mirror image of themselves and their world. In 'identifying with' the actors, the spectator is 'identifying' her/himself. This process might be described as mediated one-way mirroring, rather than reciprocal mirroring, for the performers' representation of human behaviour (that is mimesis) is taken by spectators to be an interpreted 'mirror response' to their behaviour in life from which they can 'identify' themselves. Direct, unmediated reciprocal mirroring between the spectator and the performer is limited in illusionistic performances because the fore-grounding of fictional identities significantly interferes with direct reciprocity between performer and spectator. In the non-representational components of performance, however, reciprocal mirroring does occur, for example when the performer responds directly to the spectator, who by this means perceives her/his own identity as a collaborator in the theatrical transaction. Performers create their identities by the same kind of process: through the audience's responses. As in life, theatrical identity is created by social interplay, the processual interaction between performer and spectator.

The idea of identity as interaction is inherent in the theatrical. History can be of use in understanding theory: the Elizabethan theatre provides an invaluable paradigm of the basic nature of performance identity. 'Renaissance art,' says Philip Brockbank, 'was very sensitive to the relationships between structures of society and structures of the "self"' (Brockbank, 1985, p. 4). The difference between internal/subjective 'self' and external/objective 'identity' (or 'individuality') was marked in the Elizabethan theatre. Edward Burns describes the distinction:

> Individuality ... tends to be presented as 'outside', as 'character' written in 'fame' – character, as depending on an idea of con-struction and perception ... is, according to this model, 'external'. This does not mean that these texts function without an idea of 'interiority', but it does mean that such a thing is essentially discrete from character, and that it is in character, not in the sense of an inner self, that our 'individuality' inheres. (Burns, 1990, p. 139)

Such an understanding of identity has considerable consequences in how we approach the creation (or re-invention) of theatrical performance. The identities we create may well have much less to do with inner feeling and 'truth of motivation' than nineteenth-century romantic realism has led us to believe. Robert Weimann sees the idea of identity as:

> reflecting and inspiring the theatrical transaction itself, whereby images of identity and relationship are seen as structured and evaluated through the way in which they are conveyed to, and received by, an audience of spectators. (Weimann, 1981, p. 30)

The creation of this kind of identity in the theatre depends on the equal empowerment of performer and spectator, both understanding that they are jointly engaged in the creation of identities.

Here we should also distinguish between identity and character. Identity that has been fixed into the permanence of a fictional dramatic character is no longer identity as a processual, changing social interaction. Illusionistic staging, which presents performers primarily as 'characters', that is significations of absent 'identities', disempowers both performer and spectator and makes their free participation in the joint social creation of performance identities almost impossible. It is also important to note that the reciprocal mirroring necessary for performer and spectator to create an interactive identity is hampered by the interposition of a character, a fixed identity that cannot, of course, engage in any such reciprocity. Character tends to create physical alienation between performer and spectator.

In the modern illusionistic theatre, the text and its fictional 'identities', as well as the many theatrical arrangements and conventions that have developed to strengthen the illusion, have made the interaction of performer and spectator in large degree indirect, with the result that both are significantly disempowered in the theatre. Actors are compelled to devote their main energies to impersonating fictional characters, while spectators are expected to concentrate their attention and responses on 'identifying' with these representations. As a result, the interaction of actors and audience is largely shaped by the ideological creations of absent 'artists'. There is, therefore, little opportunity for performer and spectator to collaborate directly in creating immediate and physical performance identities.

The theory I am describing here is based on the practices of pre-modern popular comedy and on twentieth-century reader theory and deconstructionism, in both of which the interest is not primarily in the text but in what the performers and spectators do with the text as a site of collaboration. 'Character' is therefore seen as a secondary, imaginary identity, often only a pretext or perhaps a theme for performer–spectator interaction. If character ceases to be the main or only focus of the performer's and spectator's attention and becomes instead a framework for their interaction as performer and spectator, then the performer's approach to character will no longer follow the traditional Stanislavskian, subjectivist model. The performer's own subjectivity need no longer be put mainly at the disposal of the text, but can also be employed as a source for her/his interaction with the spectator: subjectivity is socialised without being reified. This does not mean any lack of interior feeling, only that self-reflexive feeling no longer rules the performer's work. Action becomes the main element of performance. There is no loss of individuality, however, for as Burns has reminded us it is action that individualises, not feeling. Our feelings are very much alike; it is our actions that are unique.

What is central to this view is the process of discovering and creating in the course of the performance progressively complex and processual interactive identities. As this process develops, both the individual and social perspectives on identity creation are explored. The process of physical responsive interaction between performers and spectators becomes a shifting collective enactment of subjectivity as well as of social identity. Such a communal experience is very different from the fixed and reified representation of subjectivity in a written dramatic character. Performance identity is the creation through play of a lifelike model of identity as cultural interaction. Parts of it will inevitably be taken as significations and meanings will be constructed around them. Like the textual character, however, these will be fragmented by-products, just one group of components in the overall identity process. Any initially fixed fictional identity ('character') is bound to be destabilised by the multiple interplay of performer and spectator. Complexities like this take performance into the realm of chaotic systems.

While a performance identity is a collective, interactive creation, it still possesses the singularity of any identity. In most cases, this singularity derives from the centrality of the performer's body, which usually remains – though not in all performances – the seed of the interaction, the centre of conscious attention. The actions most basic to the performer are, therefore, the first aspects of presentation to be considered.

Since in this explanation I am holding any theory of an innate basis of fixed essential identity to be extraneous to the work, I will begin not with the actor as a person, but with the 'corporeal style' or 'act' (Butler, 1990, p. 139) that is commonly known as an actor's persona. Because the performer her/himself is usually framed in some way in the theatre and therefore perceived as aesthetic/public rather than as mundane/private, s/he acquires very quickly for the spectator a performance personality, or persona, which inspires some kind of belief and which the performer her/himself also effectively believes in. This persona is a mode of self-presentation which can be voluntary or imposed by the director or spectator. A striking example of an imposed persona is found on the Restoration stage. When women began to act female roles, every actress was given a persona of sexual availability, which remained an active ingredient of her impersonation of character (see Howe, 1992, pp. 32–6). This persona was taken by the (male) spectator to be her real (and appropriable) 'self'. Another very different kind of performer persona is seen in the clown (for example Grimaldi or Chaplin), where it often becomes a quasi-fictional character (for example Joe or the tramp) without a specific story locus. The range of non-dramatic public personalities that the word persona may describe emerges, then, at one end of the spectrum from the (inferred) personal identity of the performer and, at the other, merges into dramatic character. Wherever it may lie on this spectrum, it is taken as an authentic theatrical identity and evokes appropriate belief. This means that, corporeally, the persona can be identified with and become part of a reciprocal mirroring process.

The common desire to stabilise human identity leads most spectators to give importance to dramatic character as an element of definition in the performance. Character appears to have an independent existence, since it is corporeally absent. Because it seems unchanging it is felt to have greater authority: this is the source of the power of the absent playwright. The authority of character, however, actually derives not from its fixity but from our belief. If we examine the theatrical event more closely, we find that ultimate power lies with the performers and (especially) the spectators. Popular theatre has always recognised this, and uses dramatic character as a convenience, with little more than a name and a few broad traits to provide a frame within which performer and spectator, ignoring the supposed authority of mimesis, can create a collaborative performance identity.

When performance breaks away like this from systematic and coherent representation of a dramatic text (as in the work of the Wooster Group, for example), it facilitates the re-invention which is the aim of teaching theatre. Since the previous theatre work of most students has often been focused on producing and performing dramatic texts, however, it is probably necessary at some point early on to deal with the matter of text. After exploring the performer and her/his relation to the spectator's participation, therefore, one can usefully turn to the element of character. The purpose of doing this is not to explore character but rather to make clear to students that the performance of a play is not, at root, the faithful representation of the fictional action of the text but something very different. They may also begin to discover that texts and performances are not made of the same kinds of material. David Cole describes the performer's encounter with text in this way:

> In the last analysis every script leaves the actor in the lurch: it sets him down before an imaginative structure fashioned out of materials not his own, which he must somehow re-imagine and recreate in his wholly different medium of gesture and sound. (Cole, 1976, p. 33)

Only through such discoveries as these can students become free to explore the fluidity that analysis of the interactions between performer, character and spectator makes possible.

In using the theory of performance identities I have described as the basis for teaching theatre practice, there are a number of central objectives. One is to establish the obvious and crucial fact that the performer is never alone. To do this one must overcome the assumption, common to many approaches to theatre practice, that the performer (or performers) functions separately from the spectators, who are there to watch and listen to her/his creations. In the approach I am proposing here, the performer is never regarded as an isolated subject or object. Everything s/he does is seen not simply as an individual's action but as part of a collaborative interaction with spectators. Since a performer's action is always part of an interaction, it is studied and practised as such *from the beginning*.

In order for this objective to be achieved, of course, the spectator must become an active collaborator rather than an essentially passive consumer of the performer's performance. It is essential that students recognise as early as possible in the work that performer and spectator must be equally empowered. Acceptance of this view is hampered by the common feeling that, in the theatrical situation, performer and spectator are somehow 'different'. The otherness of performer to spectator and vice versa relates interestingly to the question of gender.

Marianne Novy comments on the analogies between gender relations
and audience–actor relations:

> Though stage conventions circumscribe the interaction of audience
> and actors, nevertheless their simultaneous presence across from
> each other is an important part of the theatrical experience. It
> involves the audience directly in confronting human beings who
> belong to a group defined as other – an experience in some ways
> rather like that of the social relations of the sexes. Parallels are not
> simple: from one point of view, the actors act or take initiative, in
> the conventional role of men, while the audience is passive or
> responds, in the conventional role of women. But the actors' acts
> are, by the nature of theater, apart from the larger world; actors are
> more like women if the audience considers them either trivial or
> mysterious and itself, like men, the norm. These analogies, however,
> model actor–audience relations on gender relations of patriarchy; a
> less hierarchical view would emphasize mutual dependence and the
> audience's active, intimate involvement in the experience of the
> theater. (Novy, 1984, p. 19)

To achieve such 'active, intimate involvement', the traditional uni-
directionality of performance must be replaced by something nearer to
circularity, a reciprocal flow of interaction between the acting and
spectator areas, however they may be spatially distinguished.

A corollary objective is to help students get as free as possible from
an over-dependence on written text and its representation (with all the
accompanying assumptions and conventions). To do this requires 'the
acceptance of the performance as the actual site of the meaning (not
as the translation or decoration of a text)' as Bernard Dort has
pointed out. 'The progressive emancipation of the elements of theatrical performance,' he continues, 'implies a change of structure in the
performance – the abandonment of an organic unity laid down in
advance and the choice of a meaningful polyphony open to the
spectator' (Dort, 1982, pp. 63–4).

As the work develops, clusters of performer–spectator collaborations will emerge, as a variety of performance identities are
developed, which then can be brought into interaction in many and
various ways. Along the way, close attention has to be paid to what
specifically each of the contributing identities – performer, spectator,
character – brings to the interaction. Each act by one of the collaborators should be judged not by its apparently intrinsic value or meaning,
but in terms of the reaction it provokes in the collaborative creation.

As with all workshop teaching, the development of the right kind of group ethos is vitally important. The central factor in this case is the awareness that interaction means cooperation. As the premise is that a performer never performs an action alone, then the assumption that a performer should rehearse alone, though understandable if one wishes to preserve a presumed-to-be fragile essential individuality, may be unhelpful. Individuality consists not of separateness but of difference. The development of 'individual' skills and powers occurs through students' collaborations. This includes the skills and powers of witness. Enacting and interacting, the students build their own performer–spectator identities by the process of reciprocal mirroring.

To restore the extemporaneous physicality of the spectator's participation is perhaps the most difficult and essential task in this kind of work. Much has been said in the context of actor training of liberating the actor's basic instincts, freeing her/him from constraint. It is equally important to de-civilise the spectator, to overcome the deeply ingrained social and theatrical assumption that when a performer starts to speak or move we should become politely, attentively silent. Such silence may be helpful to a performer who is trying to 'express' some inner subjective state or perhaps attempting to concentrate her/his attention on a difficult skill: in such cases it might be called a collaborative silence. But once a performer performs an external action on a stage, it becomes a social action and as such calls for a reaction in kind. Only rarely is polite silence the most genuinely collaborative or even supportive response. More often it represents yielding to the performer all responsibility for what happens. One reason for such repressions of physical response may well be a tradition of literary *politesse*, which values 'good listening' and respect for the authority of words more than spontaneous dialogic interaction. The effects of literature and illusionism have tended to make spectating more like reading than conversation.

The aim of the approach I am suggesting is to help spectators to enter into physical dialogue with performers, that is to enact outwardly those responses they have been trained from childhood to repress. In learning to break free of this constraint, students can benefit from observing audiences of children upon whom such training has not yet taken hold. Studying available evidence of audience responses at historical performances even in Britain (for example medieval drama, early Renaissance popular comedy, nineteenth-century melodrama and pantomime) as well as at contemporary street and cabaret performances can also help students to realise that polite inaction has by no means been the historical norm for theatrical witness.

Students need to rediscover how to act out responses physically, even if sometimes this must begin with simple responsive exclamations. In work of this kind, we are handicapped by two centuries or more of romantic individualism among actors and controlled, internalised response in the audience. The conventional illusionistic theatrical relationship has involved a repressive distortion of the physical relationship between performer and spectator. In focusing on the ideas and feelings of art we have unlearned the actions of physical community.

Workshop practices: the enhancement of performance identities

I would also like to stress the importance of parallel work in skills and research. Students must be helped to develop the powers of body and voice that will help them be more interesting and effective collaborators with spectators. Equally important, of course, are the skills of the spectator, which can be improved by training in careful observation and spontaneous responsiveness. Student performers and spectators can develop their creative and re-inventive capabilities by studying the work of innovative practitioners whose experiments relate to each step of their own exploratory practice. They can bring in theoretical and historical material and report on it to the rest of the group. Areas of research and practice are then brought together through shared performances and in analytical writing.

Those who teach theatre at university and who might want to explore the practical implications of the theory outlined here will want to develop their own exercises and workshops. The following are brief descriptions of a number of particular experiments which might suggest ways of approaching this kind of work. I have listed them in a developmental order – the progression being from simple individual performer–spectator interactions to more complex group interactions – with the thought that under some circumstances the whole sequence might provide an experimental model of the making of a full production. From a more individualistic perspective, this sequence can also be seen as a model of the evolution of a performer from individual body/presence through the creation of persona to performing masks, roles and dramatic characters. The main intention is to provide examples of some exploratory exercises, with a few suggestions about detail that might be of practical help.

Perhaps it should also be made clear that in the following exercises, while I speak throughout of 'the performer' and 'the spectator', it is assumed that students will interchange these functions among themselves and that the numbers of each will vary. While it is sometimes helpful to work with a ratio of one performer to one (or very few) spectators at first, the numerical ratio of performer(s) to spectator(s) can be changed as one goes along, from the familiar model of one performer to a group of spectators along the whole range to a single spectator with a large group of performers. It is perpetually interesting, for example, to explore the effects of such changes on the relative authority of performer and spectator.

(1) The single body as focus for performer–spectator interaction

A single person, in uniform movement clothes and a faceless mask, is observed walking across a space to a chair, sitting for several moments, rising and walking away. The first objective is to move through the almost inevitable initial phase: 'We are all watching this body' (and the performer's 'They are all looking at me'). If spectators are strongly encouraged – repeating the exercise as necessary to voice and act out any and all perceptions and responses evoked by the presence of the performer's body – the event will effectively cease to be 'a performer doing a simple action' and become instead 'a group of people reacting physically to a performer's presence'. While the performer's body presence may continue to be the focus around which the interaction develops, the performance identity (a group one in this case) consists almost entirely of spectator actions.

If this becomes clear, then the exercise will have achieved its primary aim. It is, of course, possible, and very profitable, to develop it further by substantially elaborating the actions performed by the performer and the reactions of the spectator, developing the two into more complex interactions. Keeping the performer's acts simple is very helpful in reminding students how little 'stage action' is necessary in a performance to make a great deal happen.

(2) Voice as physical interaction

Work in this particular exercise is most effective if it excludes the use of language. The same basic process of a simple action (in this case a vocal sound) by the performer leading to reactive vocalisations from spectator(s) can be used and, of course, developed in complexity to

articulated speech, though without any intelligible language. The
emphasis throughout is on the physicality of voice, helping students to
realise that it is a kind of bodily movement and has strong tactile and
spatial qualities. It is essential to develop dialogue between performer
and spectator, of course, but not dialogue in the usual sense of
exchanging linguistic meanings. Voice as physical interaction is
explored as a kind of interactive touching of spectator and performer.
It is well known that voice is best taught as an outcome of movement.
In the present context, too, this connection is invaluable. Obvious
examples include such actions as a performer vocalising as s/he moves
and evoking not merely vocal but movement reactions from spectators. The reverse can also be experimented with, as in a performer's
moving gesturally and spatially in reaction to spectators' vocalisations.
A group of performers and the group of spectators then converse in
movement and sound.

Probably the single most important kinds of exercise in vocalisation
as theatrical physical interaction involve the exploration of laughter.
Laughter is one of the most powerful physical interactions possible
between human beings sharing a space. Laughter can abolish the
separation of performer from spectator. Forms of 'laughter dialogue'
can be explored as one of the most dynamic and exciting of communal
performance-identity creations. (The ideas of Bakhtin and Weimann
are both helpful in stimulating this kind of work: see, for example,
Bakhtin, 1984, pp. 11–12, 90–4; and Weimann, 1969, *passim*.)

(3) Space as a variable of physical interaction

Exercises with space might consist of holding other variables of
performer–spectator interaction steady while changing the spatial
relationships between performers and spectators. Perhaps the most
obvious variations worth exploring are those of scale and distance.
This can involve working with movements (and vocalisations) between
performers and spectators at different scales: from tiny gestures or
whispers to large-group movements or sounds. Comparably, the same
physical interaction can be tried with varying distances between
performer and spectator.

Performance interactions can be created with students playing
groups with special needs, such as the visually disabled, where there
can be a highly innovative use of space.

More qualitative alterations of space can, of course, be explored
through variations in lighting, for example changing the relative

amounts of light on performers and spectators. It is important here to keep attention focused on the performer–spectator interaction, trying not to let the lighting changes become effects for their own sake. It is also interesting to note how lighting, by emphasising the visual, tends to encourage the assigning of 'meaning' to interactions.

A third aspect which can be profitably explored is what may be called social space. A whole range of experiments is possible in which the social character of the space is altered and the effects upon interactions tested. A particularly interesting one consists of having groups of students enact responses appropriate to different kinds of audiences, such as commuter or café. Another way to explore social space is to create a 'marketplace' where both performers and spectators are varied and multi-focused, and where interactions can multiply to the point of seeming chaos, yet a composite social identity can still be felt that partakes of carnival.

(4) Physical performance skills as parts of interactions

The development of specific performance skills (simple tumbling or juggling) by both individuals and small groups can form a part of the parallel body training I have previously mentioned. As these skills are developed, they can also be brought into play in the kind of marketplace or carnival context mentioned above.

Such skills will have both subjective and objective dimensions. The subjective entails the performer's own awareness of the skill as a development of bodily power, as well as manifesting to the spectator the difficulties and satisfactions of exercising the skill by means of accompanying vocalisations, breathing and facial gestures. The objective dimension includes the spectator's recognition and admiration of the extended powers of the body as a physical instrument, and the expression of that awareness through immediate visible and audible responses to the performer's act of skill.

Perhaps the most interesting and valuable part of this experiment comes when the skill action has a developed sequence so that the spectators' reactions become part of the structure of the skill performance, which then ceases to be only a display and becomes part of an interaction. Models of such collaboration can be seen in extended acts in cabaret (magicians) or the circus (aerialists or tumblers). When skilful performer(s) and responding, prompting spectator(s) produce a shaped, dynamic interaction, then a one-way 'show' has become an interaction.

(5) Body images as visual/conceptual performance identities

The work with skills will have begun the process of moving away from
an emphasis on auditory and kinaesthetic responses to a greater
awareness of the body as a visual presence. In using the body to create
images or forms, students will become aware that vision is a far more
'mental' sense than hearing, touch or the kinaesthetic sense. Working
on images results in an increased emphasis on the conceptual for both
spectator and performer. Body images, even those involving movement, tend towards fixed forms. Movement patterns sometimes even
begin to be seen as a series of stop-frames. When we see it used to
make images, we begin to 'read' the body. Such visual formalisation
leads to the creation of what are in effect body masks, visual forms
used to 'define' body presence, to give it 'a meaning', even if not
always one that can be verbalised. (At this point students may well
want to digress into a study of the purposes and effects of costuming.)

The tendency to attach meaning to the performer's body involves
seeing it as a signifier. Among other things, this raises the question of
authority between performer and spectator, a question that becomes
increasingly important in their interactions. In this case, the question
arises of whose meaning or signifier is referred to by the performer's
body, that intended by the performer or that inferred by the spectator? The interaction between performer and spectator loses some of
its physicality at this stage. When s/he presents her/his body as an
image, the performer is on the way to becoming a fictive identity:
persona, role, or character. Correspondingly, the spectator moves
towards becoming an interpreter (even a reader) more than a responder. A crucial point has been reached, where it is important to
make every effort to keep some part of the performer–spectator
interaction as immediate as possible: immediate both in the sense of
being unmediated by signification and in the sense of being direct,
quick and spontaneous in its physical manifestations.

It is likely that, at this stage of the work, the performer will become
aware of the process of creating her/his own stage persona (especially
after the preceding work on skills). Having explored their interactions
in terms of body presence, voice, movement, skills and now body
masks, both performer and spectator will increasingly perceive their
interactions as in some sense aesthetic. They will perhaps tend to see
themselves more than previously as 'making theatre', and the dangers
of becoming unduly influenced by the conventions and clichés of
contemporary theatre will increase. The persona a student develops
may well show signs of such influences. It will, however, have had the

advantage of having been developed in continuous interaction with collaborating spectators, rather than in bedroom-mirror fantasies. This may well have the additional advantage that a performer's new-found persona will be less likely to remain rigidly fixed. It could be helpful that the next stage of work, with face masks, will quite probably re-open the question of choice of persona.

(6) Face masks as components of performance identities

The use of face masks is one of the most ancient of theatre practices and possibly the one most studied in theatre research and explored in theatre practice. Their use in the present explorations cannot hope to cover all the dimensions of the practice and its theoretical impli-cations. That being said, it is interesting that the two basic functions of masks correlate with the interactions upon which this work is focused.

A mask is obviously a performer action which evokes a spectator reaction, and it is significant that one way of distinguishing types of masks is between those which are assumed (or performer-chosen) and those which are imposed (or spectator-chosen). This distinction may also be described as one between mask as concealment and mask as control. A performer wearing a mask may be using it either as a means of conveying and confirming accepted social attitudes (as with the masks of known social types in Hellenistic comedy, for example) or as a representation of hidden, threatening powers (as with the demonic masks of some Asian and African rituals). The interaction provoked by the performer's use of a mask will take very different forms, depending on these locations of authority in the performance. It should be added that, with almost any mask, whatever the original source of its authority, the location of power can shift during performance between performer and spectator. For example, a mask imposed by spectators (or an ideology) to exert social control over the expression of the demonic can be used by the wearer as concealment (for example Iago). While the very definition of a mask can give it apparent power, it can also make it subject to appropriation as an instrument. As will be seen later, the same is true of character.

The interaction of mask-wearing performer and responding spec-tator will vary considerably with the nature of the mask and its source of authority. For control (social) masks, the performer's actions may be primarily validated by a positive interactive response from the spectator: that is their interaction enacts agreement with the ideology represented by the mask. For concealing (demonic) masks, on the other hand, the nature of the performer–spectator interaction may be led by the performer, with the spectator often voluntarily enacting play forms of fear or submission (for example with Halloween masks). In the course of developing these interactions, whatever the nature of the mask, any number of shifts of authority can occur and thus many kinds of identity interactions can be developed.

Specific areas of experiment may include the creation of a 'character' by mask alone, by the mask augmented by movement and gesture, and by breathing and/or voice (not language). Communally orientated work on social roles may also be explored, using stereotypical masks, as well as group masking experiments, as in the traditional masked ball, where social relationships are deliberately rendered liminal.

Probably the most important phase of work with masks occurs when discrepancies between mask and wearer begin to be explored. By such simple means as using a mask with a stick handle, it is possible for a performer to put on and remove a mask quickly: that is, to alternate rapidly between her/his actions as performer/persona and as mask-persona. This marks a decisive step in the development of performance identities, a change from what can be called the dialectic interaction of performer and spectator to what can be termed the trialectic interaction of performer, mask identity and spectator. A whole new set of interactions comes into being: performer–spectator, performer-mask, spectator–mask, each providing an active context for the others. Specifically, the performer and the spectator are each engaged now in two interactions, which can be played against each other in infinitely varying ways. This is a paradigm of the actor–spectator–character trialectic in the performance of drama. Clearly, the mask phase of this kind of project can involve the greatest leap forward in understanding how performance identities are created.

(7) Gender roles as components of performance identities

Among the stereotypes or social roles referred to above, gender could take a prominent position. It is a level of identity that can be usefully focused on at this stage of performance identity work. As a culturally created typing of human beings, gender (as distinguished from biological body differences) can be regarded as a category lying somewhere between mask and character. I choose here to call it a role because it involves so many predictive stipulations about behaviour. Because of its relative definition, a gender role can also be regarded as a kind of behavioural mask. To view gender in this way is to assume that there is a difference between, as it were, the mask and the wearer of the mask (that is between the role and the player of the role). This is a question on which there is some disagreement: is there an essential female identity to project (see, for example, Cixous, 1984, *passim*) or is it impossible to distinguish between the subjectivity and the projected role (see Butler, 1990, p. 142 and *passim*)?

The parallels between the performance of and response to gender roles and the theatrical interactions between performer, mask/character and spectator are striking.

Many of the possibilities for experimentation in this area are being explored by feminist teachers and performers. In the context of the present project, I believe that investigating possible variations of the performer–gender/role–spectator interaction can be very useful. A point of departure is provided by the work with masks just discussed.

Viewed as a behavioural mask, gender can be considered in terms of assumption versus imposition, concealment versus control. It is possible to explore the conflict between these dimensions: for example, while the mask of female gender role is generally imposed by male-dominated ideology, it can come to be viewed – by those who imposed it – as a mask assumed by a woman to conceal and better implement her demonic power. What started as control can thus become concealment, without ceasing to be – for the female obliged to wear the mask control. Somewhat comparably, the machismo mask of masculine gender role, assumed as an expression of power and security, can sometimes become, for the wearer, an imposed control, while still being seen perhaps by a female spectator as assumed and threatening. In both these cases, experiments in varying the inter-actions of performer (mask wearer) and spectator, as well as their respective interactions with the mask, can open up a whole variety of possible performance identities extending well beyond those offered by cultural conventions. It is obvious that the key to such possibilities lies in the distinguishing of mask and wearer. Since gender roles are rarely available with stick handles, it can be useful to devote sessions to 'putting on' and 'taking off' gender masks. Such masks may be made of painted fabric or papier-mâché; of facial gestures; of particular patterns of physical behaviour. It might happen, for example, that a female spectator could be engaged in an interaction with a threatening behavioural mask of male gender and simul-taneously with a gentle male performer wearing it, whose actions as a performer are very different from those of his role mask. The three of them might create a complex interactive identity which could be a significant model of both life and theatrical performance.

Such interactions, while trialectic in their basic structure, become even more complex in practice. Just as a spectator can enact a multiple set of responses to a performer's action, thus effectively creating a composite, multiple interaction (and fragmenting the supposed 'meaning' of the performer's precipitating action), so also the performer can enact a composite set of varied actions within the performance framework of the same mask/role action, thus also creating a multiplicity of performance interactions. The actions of performer and spectator are never as fixed and rigid as those attributed to mask/role/character. It is in the context of creating gender performance identities that the enormous multiplicity of subjective actions and reactions available to performers and spectators can begin to be appreciated (even within supposedly defined and restricted types and roles). We begin to see how little our common terms of identity – 'woman', 'you', 'I', 'he', and so on – actually tell us of the interactions they supposedly designate.

(8) Character as a component of performance identity: 'regulatory fiction' or 'prétexte'?

I hope it is clear from the foregoing that the series of explorations sketched out here, entailing a progression from single-body presence to image to persona to mask to gender role to character, has embodied a kind of evolution of performer action and performer–spectator interaction. From the point of mask use onwards (if not earlier), performers will have begun to play with fictive identities. With the introduction of masks and certainly with gender roles, students will also have begun to work with identifying actions explicitly originating outside the performer–spectator encounter. This process develops further when work with a dramatic character text begins and the tendency towards conceptualising physical behaviour becomes even greater. While gender roles are fictions created and performed in a real (though ideologised) world, dramatic characters (also products of a cultural matrix) are openly acknowledged as fictions supposedly functioning in another place and time. Both, of course, are to a substantial extent the creations of persons absent from the performer–spectator physical context. Some crucial questions face the performer and spectator. How much authority is to be given to these absent creators? How much and what kind of belief should be given to this character? The traditional choice in modern European/American illusionistic theatre has been to treat the character as what Judith

Butler (speaking of gender role) calls a 'regulatory fiction' (Butler, 1990, p. 141), one which creates tracks and boundaries for the performer–spectator interaction. An alternative is epitomised by the nineteenth-century French actor Mounet-Sully, quoted approvingly by Meyerhold, who maintained: 'Chaque texte n'est qu'un prétexte' (Meyerhold, 1969, p. 209).

An important key to carrying on the kind of explorations which are the purpose of this whole exercise lies in the notion of removable/replaceable masks. If dramatic character is treated by the performer as a *'prétexte'* (and by the spectator as an object of playful and voluntary belief) then it is possible to continue to build complex and interesting performance–identity interactions in the course of performing a dramatic text.

If the implications of performance/identity theory are to be dealt with adequately, it is necessary for students at some point to work with a written text. Several criteria enter into the choice of text. The best for the purpose may be one that does not require any very high degree of illusionism. Texts drawn from pre-modernist popular theatre could be particularly well suited. The very alienness of an old or foreign text can make it more suitable for appropriation as an experimental *prétexte*: students may be less likely to feel a misplaced responsibility to literary or historical 'faithfulness'. Some texts offer an additional dimension by including characterisations not only of fictional characters but also of theatrical spectators. Such meta-theatrical texts provide particularly illuminating opportunities for performers and spectators to play 'performers' and 'spectators', adding another set of dimensions to the complex of interactions. Any dramatic text which explicitly incorporates spectator presence and response is likely to lend itself more readily than others to this kind of work. Taking such criteria into account, the most important consideration remains: to use a text that will as much as possible allow and empower both performer and spectator to interact and create collaborative performance identities, stimulated but not constrained by considerations of dramatic character.

Conclusion

What might be gained from such an exploratory project? A deepened awareness of the richness of theatrical performance, of the staggering complexity of its physical presence. A better understanding of how the identities created in theatrical performance are not fixed, readily describable 'persons' or 'characters', but collaborative, processual identity interactions, which, because they belong to no individual writer, actor or spectator, possess a life that is the very life of the theatrical event. It might also be noticed that when theatre practice, deeply engaged in, gradually grows into an advanced form of collective life, and the theoretical egg out of which it developed seems to have disappeared, the theory is found to be still somehow present, like a developing skeleton underneath the muscles and sinews that have grown around it, an internal structure which, while it may be invisible, nonetheless enables the practical chicken to stand and walk by itself.

Works cited

Bakhtin, M. (1984) *Rabelais and His World*, trans. H. Iswolsky. Indiana University Press, Bloomington.

Blau, H. (1982) *Take Up the Bodies: Theater at the Vanishing Point.* University of Illinois Press, Chicago.

Brockbank, P. (ed.) (1985) 'Introduction: Abstracts and Brief Chronicles', in *Players of Shakespeare: Essays in Shakespearean Performance by Twelve Players with the Royal Shakespeare Company.* Cambridge University Press, Cambridge, pp. 1–10.

Burns, E. (1990) *Character: Acting and Being on the Pre-Modern Stage.* Macmillan, Basingstoke.

Butler, J. (1990) *Gender Trouble: Feminism and Subversion of Identity.* Routledge, London.

Butler, J. (1993) *Bodies That Matter: On the Discursive Limits of 'Sex'.* Routledge, London.

Cixous, H. (1984) 'Aller à la mer', trans. B. Kerslake. *Modern Drama*, vol. 27, pp. 546–8.

Cole, D. (1976) 'The Visual Script: Theory and Techniques'. *The Drama Review*, no. 20, pp. 27–50.

Donatus, A. (1965) 'On Comedy and Tragedy', trans. M. Rogers, in *European Theories of the Drama*, ed. B. Clark. Crown, New York, pp. 34–6.

Dort, B. (1982) 'The Liberated Performance', trans. B. Kerslake. *Modern Drama*, vol. 25, pp. 60–8.

Forte, J. (1990) 'Women's Performance Art: Feminism and Postmodernism', in *Performing Feminisms: Feminist Critical Theory and Practice*, ed. S.-E. Case. John Hopkins University Press, Baltimore, pp. 251–69.

Howe, E. (1992) *The First English Actresses: Women and Drama 1660–1700.* Cambridge University Press, Cambridge.

Lacey, S. and Pye, D. (1994) 'Getting Started: An Approach to Relating Practical and Critical Work'. *Studies in Theatre Production*, vol. 10, pp. 20–30.

Luckmann, T. (1979) 'Personal Identity as an Evolutionary and Historical Problem', in *Human Ethology: Claims and Limits of a New Discipline*, eds M. von Cranach, K. Foppa, W. Lepenies and D. Ploog. Cambridge University Press, Cambridge, pp. 56–74, 83–5.

Meyerhold, V. (1969) *Meyerhold on Theatre*, trans. and ed. E. Braun. Methuen, London.

Novy, M. (1984) *Love's Argument: Gender Relations in Shakespeare*. University of North Carolina Press, Chapel Hill and London.

Weimann, R. (1969) 'Laughing with the Audience: The Two Gentlemen of Verona and the Popular Tradition of Comedy'. *Shakespeare Survey*, vol. 22, pp. 35–42.

Weimann, R. (1981) 'Society and the Individual in Shakespeare's Conception of Character'. *Shakespeare Survey*, vol. 34, pp. 23–31.

3

Drama in Education: Learning Through Story (Empowering Teachers)

Stephen Cockett

Storytelling with children is an act of enchantment. The teacher telling a story in the classroom creates focus by determining the pace of the narrative, creating a sense of mystery and working on the imagination to visualise character and situation. The listeners, caught up in the flow of events, want to know what happens next and to see tensions resolved. They surrender to the narrative. In the drama class, many of the same elements of story are present: there are beginnings and endings, characters and issues, but the relationship between audience and 'storyteller' rarely aspires to a state of enchantment. The class is busy and frequently noisy; the activity is unpredictable, demanding initiative, collaboration and experiment; the teacher works as an enabler, adopting an oblique approach, drawing on the pupils' ideas. Teacher and pupils act as partners in the making of the story.

A linear narrative may move with agility across time and place, reveal the inner thoughts of the characters, add commentary and set new scenes with only a few words. By comparison, drama is sluggish, demanding time for everyone in the group to become involved, express their thoughts, listen to and understand each other, and agree on a course of action. For students preparing to be teachers and anxious about maintaining discipline, storytelling is by far the safer option, especially in the primary school, where children are familiar from nursery-school days with the cosy informality of the story corner and the relief it offers from the hurly-burly of classroom business. Drama is altogether more risky. It may take place in a hall with a variety of extraneous noises, or in a cramped classroom with the furniture piled up at the sides. The classroom routines and external controls do not apply, discipline and order depend on trust and cooperative spirit. Using only the children's imaginations and skills, the teacher must try to build a fictional world in which each person has a place and purpose.

It is not surprising that many student teachers feel a little unnerved by the prospect of delivering their first drama lesson. Survival seems too closely tied to the quality of the drama they teach, and if the children fail to become involved, chaos may threaten. Responding to these pressures, the student may be inclined to reduce the risks by keeping a tight grip on the lesson, eliminating all creative space, or by choosing the easy option of drama games.

Preparing for school placements

In the term before each school placement, students in the English and Drama Department in the School of Education at the University of Exeter follow a course in classroom practice which includes methods of drama teaching. Most anticipate the challenge with a mixture of enthusiasm and anxiety. Some of their concerns can be addressed by helping them to build a resource of drama strategies, but although a file heavy with lesson material may be a great reassurance as the placement approaches, the weight of prepared material can itself give a false sense of security. When they start teaching in school, students may find themselves expending ideas like rapid machine-gun fire, shooting away till all are spent. In the aftermath, they then face an unnerving void. A basic collection of resources is useful, if only as a scaffold on which to build practical experience, but students gain a firmer sense of purpose in their teaching if, while developing teaching strategies, they also clarify the aims and objectives involved in teaching drama to children. In this respect, the course preparing students for school is not wholly separate from other parts of their studies. This chapter looks at one way in which the students' academic course supports their professional preparation in drama.

Story: narrative and drama

The first year of the English and Drama course is built around the
theme of story and storytelling. An examination of the functions of
story in a broad context provides a valuable route into understanding
the dramatic approach to narrative. To most students, the notion of
story in education means stories that teachers have read to them, the
class bookshelf, writing stories (usually from their own experience),
and in later years novels, silent reading in class and at home. They are
among the people who, as Harold Rosen (1985, p. 12) suggests, are
predisposed to see stories as 'autonomous islands, becalmed in books'.

The work in the first-year course encourages the students to reach
outwards from this notion and look at stories as products of the way
the human mind tries to understand experience by shaping it into
narrative. The starting point is Barbara Hardy's notion (1987, p. 1) of
story as a 'primary act of mind':

> We dream in narrative, daydream in narrative, remember, antici-
> pate, hope, despair, believe, doubt, plan, revise, criticise, construct,
> gossip, learn, hate and love by narrative. In order to live, we make
> up stories about ourselves and others, about the personal as well as
> the social past and future.

By placing events in a narrative sequence we begin to make sense
of them. Harold Rosen (1985, p. 13) pursues the notion in his article
for teachers, 'The Nurture of Narrative':

> The unremitting flow of events must first be selectively attended to,
> interpreted as holding relationships, causes, motives, feelings,
> consequences – in a word, *meanings*. To give an order to this
> otherwise unmanageable flux we must take another step and invent
> beginnings and ends, for out there are no such things. Even so stark
> an ending as death is only an ending when we have made a story
> out of life.

Through story we gain a sense of reality, an understanding of the
world we live in. Events and actions must be sequentially ordered.
Only by managing experience through the time-frame of story can
children, as well as adults, identify attitudes and ideas, beliefs and
values. None of these has an existence independent of manageable
form. Similarly, we clarify purpose, aims and a sense of mission by
placing them in structures implying time past and time future. Story

enables us to work out what we should do next, as well as to discover values which transcend immediate, day-to-day circumstances.

Following this initial focus on how we think in story, the students do some actual storytelling. Some of the stories they use are real, drawn from experience, others are fictional, selected from the library. In workshops the students look at ways of dividing the story into narrative segments, visualising key images, incorporating different character viewpoints and telling the story with a sense of drama. Then they go out into schools to tell their stories to audiences of children.

Students find this approach to story as organised narrative of real and fictional events straightforward. More difficult to grasp is the link between stories and everyday life, and the notion that stories are woven into the fabric of the culture that permeates their lives: stories that characterise politics, institutions, the family, work, local community, history, the arts, education, advertising and subcultures. Alan Sinfield (1989, p. 24), following the line of Raymond Williams' cultural analysis, makes the point that these stories are *lived*:

> They are not just outside ourselves, something we hear or read about. They make sense for us – of us – because we have been and are in them.... They become common sense, they 'go without saying'.

How stories exist but 'go without saying' is puzzling. Part of the problem may be the word 'story', which implies a structure with some sort of planned organisation, but cultural stories have no underlying purpose in this sense, they just evolve, and that is why we take them for granted. Students tend to categorise story as either real or fictional, so a concept of story that blurs the distinction between what is actually true and what is fictional demands a difficult shift of perspective, especially for those who prefer to think of truth in more absolute terms.

Roland Barthes (1973, pp. 117–74) uses the term 'mythologies' to describe the signs embedded within common cultural forms. This raises another complication: in common usage, the word 'myth' denotes an untrue idea or explanation; Barthes, however, sees myth as a language by which we perceive the world: myth communicates realities with a 'naturalness' which makes them 'go without saying'. John Crossan (1975, pp. 53–4) says that the power of myth lies in the ways it offers to each individual living the myth possibilities for *gain*, ways of enriching the experience of life through the reconciliation of natural oppositional elements:

It is much more important to believe in the possibility of solution than ever to find one in actuality. The *gain*, or advantage of myth, and its basic function, is to establish that possibility itself.

We live in a continuous state of becoming, and our ambitions, investments and endeavours can function only within the framework of myth. When myth has lost the prospect for gain, it ceases to function as myth. Modern myths change ceaselessly – what was important a few years ago may not be seen as valid today. Values change as myths change, but some values are more constant than others.

Each of us lives in a number of overlapping myths or stories at the same time – myths of work, home, politics and religion. Together they form a hierarchy in which some stories are dominant, others sub-sidiary. We function better in some stories than in others: an unsatisfactory work situation may be compensated for by a greater degree of gain in another structure, say sport or music. If we wish to do so, we can opt out of the dominant stories of our mainstream culture into an alternative culture with its own network of myths. Whatever stories we live in, they matter fundamentally, because they tell us who we are, and what we should do, and what is of worth and value. Over time, however, myths are adapted in response to natural dynamic forces and in their use to us for making significant meaning and action. In the ebb and flow of dynamic change, it is wise periodically to test the strength of our stories, for by testing their strength we know better their usefulness. Drama and the arts are ways of testing the stories by which we live.

Students preparing for a school placement require some practical strategies for initiating dramatic activity in the short term; to survive in the longer term, however, they require a more sustaining theoretical framework. This purpose, of creating a link between theory and prac-tice in the students' teaching, underlies the study of drama and cultural stories. The notion of developing a detached, critical perspective through drama is at variance with early theories of drama in education, which valued qualities of absorption, sincerity and spontaneity in the children's responses, as indicators of subjective understanding. But dramatic activity which promotes personal, self-authenticating creative expression, far from developing learning, actually inhibits it, for it fails to give the child a critical standpoint, or a framework for making objective, evaluative judgements. Learning in drama, as in all other areas of the curriculum, draws on individual differences and viewpoints, but is both rational and objective. A more fruitful dramatic process is that in which the children and the teacher move back and forth across the threshold between the real world and the fictional world of the drama, at the same time involved and detached, committed and critical. In this respect, the drama class reflects the objectives of Brechtian theatre: the participants work towards a change in understanding by shifting between inside and outside viewpoints, faithfully creating aspects of human social life while keeping a critical view on what they are doing.

The degree of critical detachment varies with different types of drama. At one end of the range, where drama moves closer to ritual, objectivity diminishes. Some drama celebrates, and has the important function of confirming, existing beliefs. In fact, we probably use drama, more than we care to admit, to confirm existing value structures and the securities they afford. But at the other end of the spectrum, drama has a more challenging function: to test the mettle of our stories, put them under stress and seek out their weak points.

Crossan (1975, p. 59) identifies a spectrum of story types which places myth at one end and parable at the other. On this spectrum myth establishes the world, parable subverts it. Myths, particularly the old ones, have an extended life, binding together disparate cultural elements, whereas parable is a one-off event. A parable repeated to the same audience loses some of its power and begins to move closer to the area of myth; it may retain its force only with a new telling to a new audience. The story of the good Samaritan, one of the best known of all parables, no longer functions as parable; over time it has become distanced from its context and now, paradoxically, it occupies a fixed place in Christian mythology. Virtually all well known parables have become myths and, consequently, have lost their initial driving power to make us question. But while parable subverts myth, it can work only in relation to myth; parable is rooted in the established culture, testing the strength of its stories and the values within them.

Most drama teachers would regard the terms myth and parable as somewhat remote from the day-to-day realities of managing drama in school. In their practice, however, they work through story structures with a similar dynamic relationship: they create fictional frameworks which focus on the tensions between continuity and change, established values and new attitudes, and the 'go without saying' aspects of culture and critical viewpoints. They work, in fact, in the space in the story spectrum between myth and parable, using the special flexibility within the drama to exploit the tensions connecting both story types. A good proportion of the time in drama lessons is taken up by establishing situation and background, drawing from the pupils' own experiences and their knowledge of cultural stories. Past discourse between teachers emphasising exploration leading to change of understanding through drama has tended to obscure the fact that most lesson activity is founded on the stories and patterns of behaviour that act as forces of stability in our culture. For the pupils, the most immediate satisfactions in drama derive from simply creating a fictional world and moving around within it in the guise of character. Creating the world and building belief takes time, and often spreads over more than one lesson; at some point, however, the teacher seeks a point of intervention with a question, incident, character, that forces reappraisal of the established dramatic context; the teacher has a double intention – to facilitate the invention of the fictional world and then to 'subvert' its structure by introducing new issues. Resolution of the tensions that emerge may not be simple, but resolution may not be the purpose of the exercise. Teachers often refer to drama as a problem-solving activity, but more important than the task of resolving problems is seeking knowledge of what creates them, learning how tensions are rooted in the dynamic forces between competing stories. Drama is more about problem-knowing than about problem-solving and, in that spirit, I will now explore a series of practices in the classroom concerned with the perception of problem-knowing. The explorations are not models of procedure, but critical comments upon proceedings.

Drama in the primary school

The most challenging components of the students' course are the terms they spend in school. While courses preceding the school placements can never fully prepare students for the experience, they offer some time for the students to explore the principles and methods of good practice, free of the burdens of classroom management.

In the primary classroom, the student teaches across the curriculum and has the flexibility to integrate elements of different subject areas. In the core curriculum subjects, the school usually defines the areas for the student to cover during the placement, but will allow a freer hand in drama.

If the drama can be located within a topic involving work in a number of subjects, then a two-way benefit is gained: classroom work saves time in the drama lesson by setting the context for it, and the drama adds stimulus and purpose to work on the topic.

The main method of preparation with the students is to take simulated situations and develop them through collaborative discussion and practical experiment. One such simulation for student work might be the following:

A year-4 class (eight-year-olds) working on the topic 'Castles'

- *In classroom work*, the children are looking at how and why castles were built; the castle and the surrounding community; and castles under siege. Their work includes writing, drawing and diagrams, and is supported by visual resources displayed in the classroom.
- *At story time*, the teacher reads from legends about giants and dragons, knights and castles.
- *In art,* the class are creating a large mural of a dragon which they have named 'FIRE' in red letters as bright as the flames from its jaws.
- *Drama.* Capitalising on the groundwork of these lessons, the teacher has devised an outline plan based on a community of people living in and around a castle a time long ago. In that place there is a dragon called Fire. Unlike the terrorising dragons of myth and legend, Fire has for many centuries been the protector of the castle and the community of people living in the town around it, keeping them safe from invading armies. But now Fire is old and unable to fly, or even breathe the flames for which it was once renowned. The community reveres and cares for the dragon, for without it they would surely have perished. Now the threat of attack has passed and the community can look forward to a more peaceful life.

The situation suggests a time past, a time future and a present which is suspended at a point of change between the two. Its symbolic folk/fairy structure allows a freedom for the imagination, which may be less easy to achieve in a naturalistic drama based on an actual situation, and it offers scope for raising questions about values: what matters is not the dragon but what it represents. Using this framework with the students, the first task is to identify possible issues and questions that might give the drama a direction, such as:

- Fire has been strong but is now old and vulnerable, like many old people in any community. How is Fire valued?
- What are the problems of looking after Fire?
- What is the community's responsibility towards Fire?

- What are the community's rituals and traditions?
- What might happen in the future?
- What changes might occur that would alter the community's attitude to its past?

Planning the lessons

Lesson planning must move from the level of the abstract to the specific. Creating drama is a partnership between teacher and pupils: the teacher must decide how much detail to provide and how much space and flexibility to leave for the children's responses. Students can develop themes and ideas in the abstract, but to build the fictional world with the children through action, they must take a series of practical steps:

- *Establish the context* – the class sits in a circle and through narration the teacher creates a picture of the castle, the people who live there and of Fire's brave deeds in the past.
- *Define the children's roles.* Drama is built on what the children *do*. With young children it helps if they can all play similar roles within the same context. In this situation they could be the citizens employed as carers for the dragon, involved in a variety of tasks as part of a daily treatment routine. Without their work, Fire would have no hope of surviving.
- *Develop the children's understanding of the roles through open-ended questions.* A useful strategy is to make the children experts; the teacher can then ask questions from a lower-status position – what are the special tasks they have to perform? What are the risks to a dragon of this age? Ideas offered in return must be valued in discussion and, where possible, be included in the story.
- *Define the space.* How big is the dragon? Where does it live? How far does it stretch? Whereabouts is the head? The tail? How can the scales at the top of its back be reached? What happens if someone walks 'through' the dragon?
- *Choose your own role as teacher* – to stay outside the action or to move within it perhaps as a supervisor asking questions, checking on the quality of the work, helping with problems.
- *Choose a particular starting point* – the citizens prepare for the daily treatment routine. Together they take up a rope attached to the tail and heave Fire into the castle yard. From this point the action can develop freely and interactively, each pupil with a

specific job: cleaning, scrubbing, putting on dragon grease to prevent scales cracking. Through action the children work their way into the role and the situation, which then provides the springboard for further development of the story.

In their first lessons, students tend to move the drama forward too quickly, cutting short the time for children to build belief. They need strategies for consolidating the story. In this situation, Fire's history and place in the community could be developed through:

* eyewitness accounts of famous events handed down through the generations;
* ceremonies and rituals celebrating key moments in the history of the castle and the dragon;
* demonstrations of skills connected with the task of caring for Fire;
* interviews in pairs about the work with Fire;
* meetings to discuss problems arising.

The flexibility of the primary school timetable makes it possible for work and activity between drama sessions to form part of the development of the story; the pupils may:

* illustrate key events in the community's past;
* display them on the walls of the classroom in the form of a 'Bayeux tapestry' narrative;
* write accounts of each illustrated incident;
* create news reports, maps of the castle and community, diagrams of famous battles;
* write an instruction manual for the treatment and care of Fire.

The purpose of the lesson plan up to this point is to establish the dramatic context using both characters and action, which will then be challenged by the introduction of a new dramatic element. This intervention could be planned before the lesson starts, but what happens after it will be less predictable. In the story of Fire, the teacher may stop the drama, or move it forward a little in time, then intervene in role as a new manager who has been appointed by the castle authorities. The manager's task is to look at ways of improving the efficiency of the castle and its community now that they face a more peaceful future.

The technique of working in role, particularly with younger children, is one of the most useful strategies at the teacher's disposal. It allows the teacher to control the drama from the inside while keeping the momentum flowing and, when necessary, to introduce a new and challenging direction which demands a response within the fictional framework of the drama. First, a convention must be agreed with the children to indicate when teacher is teacher and when in role. For example, the teacher puts on a jacket or a pair of glasses, or walks to the side of the room and returns as the character. The choice of role will depend on dramatic circumstances. In this situation, the manager could be a go-between, an agent rather than the figure of authority who is simply doing the job; this would allow him/her to avoid confrontation by deflecting the citizens' concerns and to leave issues unresolved by stepping out of the drama to report back, to gain more information, or to find answers to the citizens' questions (as well as giving him/herself more thinking time). The teacher must also decide how much information to give in role and how much to hold back. The manager's first appearance may be deliberately uncontroversial: s/he asks the citizens if it may be possible to witness the daily routine of caring for the dragon; the treatment routine may then be repeated with the manager listening, asking questions, taking notes. Afterwards, the teacher could step out of role and stop the drama to allow time for reflection with the citizens – who is this manager? What do you think the manager was wanting? Slowing the drama allows time for ideas, attitudes and opinions to take shape. Children have no difficulty in accepting quick shifts in the teacher's role if each change is clearly signalled.

The teacher, as manager, may then move the drama forward by calling a meeting of all citizens to explain a new plan for developing agriculture in the fields around the town (based on the maps and diagrams created by the children in the classroom). It is a new and exciting plan, though some economies will have to be made, as well as changes in employment and in the pattern of castle and community life; but all will benefit from the scheme, which will make far better use of available resources. It will, however, require the support and effort of every member of the community, who must be prepared to learn new ways of working. By deliberately *not* mentioning the dragon, the manager creates space for a response from the citizens. This is a deliberate risk, with the purpose of moving the drama closer to unpredictable territory. If/when the children's 'voices' in role begin to shape the drama, the teacher from then on must think on his/her feet.

Students, learning how to plan lessons, can generally grasp the practicalities of the drama up to this point; the problem then is how to prepare for the next stage, which moves beyond the planned structure. Some students may be tempted simply to trust their skills to work spontaneously on the children's ideas, but a wiser course of action is to try to anticipate some likely directions in the story. Many children will have constructive contributions to make, but will express them tentatively, and it is the teacher's task to draw them into the drama. Planning for possibilities makes the student more alert to the ideas offered by the children. Simple solutions that offer no scope for exploration should be avoided: a polarised confrontation between the citizens and the castle manager may be exciting but will soon burn out. The more sustaining tensions will be those giving rise to a wider diversity of questions and viewpoints in situations which allow the citizens to voice their thoughts within the community's power structure and to play a direct part in the process of change:

- A visitor arrives from another community some miles away which has adopted a policy similar to that advocated by the manager. They have prospered, though some members more so than others; but they did not have the problem of looking after a dragon.
- A meeting with the castle authorities is arranged to seek opinion about the future of Fire the dragon; the authorities have no particular desire to be rid of Fire, but a dragon is very expensive in terms of material and labour (a willing teaching-practice tutor can be invaluable in one of these additional roles).
- The manager, shifting to the side of the citizens, tries to persuade them that this is a chance to break the pattern of the past and reduce their work load. Wouldn't they prefer more freedom and independence?
- The citizens meet in family groups to discuss the best way forward.
- A whole group meeting is organised in which each family group contributes its ideas and opinions.

The final stages of the drama may not reach a resolution and the students should avoid fixing the story in order to round things off neatly. If the characters have expressed a wide range of viewpoints, a more satisfactory conclusion may be to freeze the action and ask each character in the drama to speak his/her thoughts in turn.

Drama in the secondary school

The teacher in the primary school monitors the structure of the drama while providing space for the children's ideas and creative action. The children take part in the teacher's 'play' and through their contributions influence its development but without taking 'directorial' responsibility. Teachers working at the primary level generally believe that the children's learning within the fictional world of the drama is more important than learning about the form of drama. In the secondary school, drama teachers give high priority to de-mystifying the dramatic process: pupils must gain control over their learning through knowing *how* drama is made.

Over the years there has been intense debate, mainly in the secondary field, about the value of drama as an agent for change in moral attitudes and social behaviour, as against drama as an art form with its own intrinsic value. In the early years, the drama-in-education movement built its identity on conceptual dichotomies separating theatre from drama, and work in process from acting and performance. More recently, however, secondary teachers have moved in their practice towards teaching drama as an art form, while recognising its adaptability and use for different educational purposes. The core syllabus is teaching the form of drama, with the aim of enabling the pupils to think and communicate through the language of drama. This means that pupils must be taught to use dramatic form as a way of thinking and of developing ideas, also to understand how the material for drama is rooted in the stories we live by, and the tensions that occur between different story structures as part of the natural dynamic process of change.

These principles shape the work with students preparing to teach in secondary schools. Structures for drama at secondary level have a more open-ended design, giving the pupils greater control over the creative process. As poetry forms an important part of the English and Drama course, students frequently choose poems as starting points for drama. One such poem may be 'Dick Lander' by Charles Causley (1988), which could form the basis of a four-week drama project leading to a performance:

> When we were children at the National School
> We passed each day, clipped on the corner of
> Old Sion Street, Dick Lander, six foot four,
> Playing a game of trains with match-boxes.

> He poked them with a silver-headed cane
> In the seven kinds of daily weather God
> Granted the Cornish. Wore a rusted suit.
> It dangled off him like he was a tree.

My friend Sid Bull, six months my senior, and
A world authority on medicine,
Explained to me just what was wrong with Dick.
'Shell-shopped', he said, 'You catch it in the war.'

We never went too close to Dick in case
It spread like measles. 'Shell-shopped, ain't you, Dick?'
The brass-voiced Sid would bawl. Dick never spoke.
Carried on shunting as if we weren't there.

My Auntie said before he went away
Dick was a master cricketer. Could run
As fast as light. Was the town joker. Had
Every girl after him. Was spoiled quite out

Of recognition, and at twenty-one
Looked set to take the family business on
(Builders' merchants, seed, wool, manure and corn).
'He's never done a day's work since they sent

Him home after the Somme,' my Uncle grinned.
'If he's mazed as a brush, my name's Lord George.
Why worry if the money's coming in?'
At fireworks time we throw a few at Dick.

Shout, 'Here comes Kaiser Bill!' Dick stares us through
As if we're glass. We yell, 'What did you do
In the Great War?' And skid into the dark.
'Choo, choo.' Says Dick. 'Choo, choo, choo, choo, choo, choo.'

The poem offers an outline story but leaves most of its content unsaid. As in primary-school drama, the area for exploration lies in the space defined by the given story outline, but in this project the pupils can exercise more creative control over the development of the story. The setting of the poem locates the drama in the cultural stories of the period, the values and commitments which shaped people's lives, the tensions between dominant stories and personal realities, and the changes in social patterns.

The first practical question for the student is how to make best use of the poem itself as a stimulus for drama. One of the most common mistakes is to assume that the poem will automatically trigger imaginative responses which will flow directly into dramatic action;

more frequently, however, the reading evokes uncomprehending stares. In most cases, an oblique approach works more effectively than a straight reading of the poem. The advice to students is to prepare the pupils for the poem with a more concrete starting point. In this situation it could simply be the matchboxes 'shunted' by Dick Lander: the class sits in a semicircle in the drama space while the teacher, in silence, lays out a row of matchboxes on the floor. The teacher then invites a member of the class to be Dick Lander, dresses him in jacket and scarf and puts a cane in his hand, thus creating a still image of Dick with his 'train' of matchboxes. The still image itself implies a story: the figure is a person with a history and a future. The teacher then narrates some details about Dick: his name, age, when he went to war, his brigade, regiment, rank and where he now lives. The class walks around the figure, working out other details prompted by questions from the teacher. Returning to the position around the character they then share their thoughts and questions.

This exercise may lead naturally to a reading of the poem. During the reading, the class keep watching the figure of Dick Lander and afterwards reflect on the poem (ideally using a printed copy), the teacher prompting responses with questions. What other clues does it suggest about Dick's life? What do they think about Dick? This initial stage of the lesson should proceed slowly in order to engage the imagination. In the ensuing discussion, the teacher may draw out different areas of the story suggested by the poem and the pupils' responses to it, for example:

- Dick's life before the war – his relationships with people, his achievements, ambitions, how other people see him, key events in his life;
- the context of war – propaganda, the pressures to enlist, patriotism, jingoism, what people thought about the war, how it affected life at home;
- Dick's private story – Dick's attitude before enlisting, the attitudes of his family and friends;
- the generation after the war – the prejudice towards Dick as a war victim and the cruelty of the children's games.

The class may then work in separate groups, suggesting ideas for developing each area of the story and recording them on large sheets of paper. The sheets then together provide a plan for the next stage in the project.

Research by the pupils

Whether they work as a whole group on each story in sequence or in separate groups, the pupils need to undertake some research. The drama must be informed by an understanding of actual events. The scale of the topic highlights the secondary drama teacher's problem of having to establish a knowledge base on which to construct work within the dramatic form. Though the First World War forms part of the history syllabus (at 'key stage 3'), teaching in parallel with the history teacher, though desirable, may not be possible. The drama teacher must provide whatever contextual information and resources are needed for the drama and, unlike the class teacher in the primary school, has no scope for maintaining interest and continuity between the sessions, which fall only once a week. So it helps to remember that:

• while some research can be done between lessons, it is also essential to have resource material available during the lesson;
• the selection of material is itself a framing device – the pupils need material which allows scope for their exploration, but too much material becomes an obstruction;
• the manner of presentation of the resource material is important – a specially designed drama space can be transformed into an exciting 'hands on' exhibition with pictures, posters, books, video extracts, objects and music of the period.

Action strategies for developing character and story

The momentum of the process must be maintained through action. Students need strategies to help the pupils create ideas in 'first draft' form, to experiment with character, situation and incident. Judging the pace of a lesson can be difficult; students often allow activity to run on until creative energy is exhausted, or allow groups to polish to perfection one or two scenes before a sense of the overall story has emerged. An experienced drama teacher keeps the lesson moving forward by making continuous evaluations of the pupils' work and quickly employing strategies for particular purposes.

Each structure applied has the function of a 'holding form', moving the dramatic action a step forward. The students' repertoire of strategies include those discussed under the separate headings below.

Still images

Pictures can be created in groups representing attitudes, ideals, as well as particular moments depicting the realities of war. In this project, the pupils could:

*   create idealised images of valour, patriotism, images with captions, for example 'It will all be over by Christmas';
*   consider Dick's family's idealised picture of him as a war hero;
*   examine propaganda posters and photographs to find out how their messages were constructed and communicated;
*   invent posters and pictures of their own;
*   place still images in a sequence, to tell a story in a simple form of animation;
*   juxtapose still images with actual oral accounts from the war front and at home, some showing humour and irony;
*   present the images with music.

Developing the story from a group of objects

Objects themselves imply stories; while touching and examining them the pupils develop associations with character and situation. The objects should be set in a context connected with the character to whom they belong and suggest a story rather than tell it, for example a small army bag belonging to Dick and containing a shaving mirror and brush, writing paper, and perhaps other more enigmatic items – a treasured object suggesting a particular moment in time past, a letter from home, or a postcard with a short, cryptic message. There may be some things that give clues to the state of Dick's mind – jottings, an attempt at a poem, or the start of a letter with numerous crossings out, an extract from a book with a sentence encircled by a pencil. The introduction of the bag should be set in a story context – where was it found and by whom? Then in response to questions about the objects, the pupils make connections, find explanations and build a background story.

Scene 'clips'

The class divides into small groups. Each group targets one important moment in Dick's life and creates a scene lasting no more than 15 seconds. The groups can work on clues in the poem or from their research work: Dick's work, relationships, his family and their feelings about the war, Dick going to war. The scenes may pose awkward questions: could Dick have been a conscientious objector? He may have been given the 'white feather' denoting cowardice. Perhaps Dick sees the war as an opportunity to escape from his surroundings and he confides this to a friend the night before they enlist together. Each scene must establish a time and place and capture the 'essence' of the moment.

Hot-seating: creating character and story

Individual characters from Dick's life respond in role to questions from the class. As well as developing character, the dialogue opens up the story through individual viewpoints. Characters may be drawn from the short scenes from Dick's life – a fellow soldier in the war; Dick's younger sister who is still alive today; his mother on the evening of the day Dick has told her he intends to enlist, or that he does not want to take part in the war; Dick as himself, not shell-shocked, but able to speak and comment on what happens around him. The exchange between characters and class may be built around original documentary material – a letter home, a commendation from the commanding officer, a quotation from an oral account of life in the trenches.

Teacher in role

The teacher uses a new role to move the drama in a new direction, add tension, or to provide unexpected information. The effect will depend on when the character enters: if the work has been making easy assumptions about Dick as victim, a new character and 'story' could alter the way the pupils relate to Dick. For example, the teacher, through narration, creates a setting of a room with old furniture and pictures, s/he then enters and sits in a chair. S/he is the sister/brother of a soldier killed at the Somme. The class has the opportunity to ask questions. The character could at first be reluctant to reveal information, as if there is something to hide, so that the class must tease out the story: his/her brother had been wounded early in the Battle of the Somme and Dick Lander was acting as stretcher-bearer, but he panicked before he reached the safety of the trench, leaving the brother to die. While running away from the front line, Dick was severely wounded by a stray shell.

Or perhaps Dick deserted and the incident was reported to the commanding officer, but the officer was killed and the matter went no further. The character could be holding an old envelope containing a copy of a letter written to him/her by another soldier who witnessed the incident.

Using text as model

Pupils can learn about the language and form of drama directly from play scripts. At one time, drama teachers would have thought it heresy to mix the study of text with the pupils' spontaneous improvisations; in this project, however, a play such as *Oh What a Lovely War!* offers a 'workshop manual' of techniques on how to:

- turn documentary information into dramatic scenes,
- create different locations through action,
- communicate horror through humour,
- create ironies through the juxtaposition of scenes and images,
- use music to heighten dramatic effect,
- incorporate factual information as a backdrop to particular experiences of the war.

Secondary teachers use a range of strategies to open up the routes across the territory defined by the story framework, but when using them they pursue the parallel objective of helping the pupils gain a detached, critical understanding of the dramatic process in which they are involved. As the drama develops through successive stages of thought and action, the pupils take increasing responsibility for making evaluative judgements and practical decisions, and exercising directorial control. Their critical understanding develops with their ability to handle the form, to sense the tensions, motives, causes and consequences inherent in human problems, and to talk constructively about what they are doing. This learning is continuous, but in an extended project it comes into special focus at particular points:

When pupils come together to share work

Through sharing work created in small groups, the class gains a fuller picture of the range of dramatic elements. But to avoid it becoming a routine of mini-performances with no critical reflection, the teacher must focus the pupils' thinking, encourage evaluative comment by throwing questions back to the class. What is the drama communicating? Which issues/questions in the scenes can be developed? Can ideas be expressed more simply, be improved by removing certain elements? By engaging the class in critical discourse, the teacher demystifies the drama with the pupils and enables them to take a greater degree of control, to make decisions and live with the risk.

When creating the form of the drama for performance

At a certain stage in the project, the class will need a structure for building towards performance. In the Dick Lander project, the objective could be to create a 'living documentary' to mark the anniversary of the Battle of the Somme. The central theme of the documentary would be the life of Dick Lander, created as a montage using elements of all four story areas developed by the class. The framework is intentionally simple in order to focus the pupils' attention on what they want to communicate, and on selecting and building a dramatic sequence, using what they have created so far: the scenes and characters, images, 'talking heads' including members of Dick's family past and present, music, extracts from the news, extracts from letters, information about the war and the Somme, flashes of memory in Dick's mind, as well as the image of Dick and the matchboxes, and the boys' treatment of Dick.

This is a critical stage in the pupils' learning which is dependent on the pupils being able to keep close contact with the feelings and issues in the material, while viewing them with an objective eye. Here, too, the principles about learning through drama and story come into focus.

The point was made earlier in this chapter that the drama teacher works in the space between myth and parable, between cultural stories that establish the world and those that subvert it, the space where story boundaries overlap, exposing diverse viewpoints and ideals, and creating tensions and ironies. The new 'holding form' which aims at building a coherent shape and purpose in the drama, in a sense, invites the pupils to occupy the same space in the story spectrum and assume a greater measure of control and responsibility for the development of the drama. They can do this, however, only if they have reached a level of autonomy in their skills and knowledge of drama enabling them to make critical evaluations and objective decisions. With a more detached view of their work on the Dick Lander story within its historical context, they can address, with greater independence, the critical questions about the way cultural stories shaped and shape attitudes, ideals, commitments and values, how new stories arose out of the experience of war, and the subversive threat from competing viewpoints, realities and experience. The pupils manipulate the form, select and refine the scenes, characters and images that contribute to the complexity of Dick Lander's situation, and create tensions and ironies through juxtaposition of elements in a dramatic sequence.

Conclusions

Both primary and secondary drama teachers enable their pupils to make stories with dramatic form. The primary teacher exercises a greater degree of directional control over the form than the secondary teacher, who aims to enable the pupils to work autonomously by teaching them to control the form for themselves. In both age phases, the raw material for the drama is the stories of ordinary life and culture, and teacher and class work to create drama with a unity between the form and the issues and tensions in the material. The pupils' learning in drama lies at the core of this integration of elements. Drama teachers often define their purpose as helping the pupils to 'find the form to fit the feeling'; the difficulty with this notion, however, is that it assumes that the feeling is known and understood before the form to express it has been created. Rather, the feeling comes to be known *through* the form: the form *identifies* the feeling. The same principle applies to story and to drama. Participants in drama do not so much seek expression for pre-existent inner stories, as make new structures from the raw material of known stories within cultural contexts. In this way they gain access to new awareness, new forms of knowing. So it is with all art forms, including stories, either told or read. Different forms create access to different types of knowing. The distinctive nature of learning through dramatic story lies in the distinctive nature of the dramatic form.

Works cited

Barthes, R. (1973) *Mythologies*. Palladin, Collins, London.
Causley, C. (1988) *A Field of Vision*. Macmillan, London.
Crossan, J. (1975) *The Dark Interval. Towards a Theology of Story*. Argus Communications, Illinois.

Hardy, B. (1987) 'The Nature of Narrative', in *Stories and Meaning: The Collected Essays of Barbara Hardy.* Harvester Press, Sussex.

Rosen, H. (1985) 'The Nurture of Narrative', in *NATE Papers in Education.* National Association for the Teaching of English, Sheffield.

Sinfield, A. (1989) *Literature, Politics, and Culture in Post War Britain.* Blackwell, Oxford.

Part II

Dialogues With Texts

As Peter Thomson states in his chapter, 'An Approach to Play-Reading', 'It is no longer axiomatic in drama departments that play texts take priority over all other subjects of study'. As we may observe in the preceding chapters of Part I, much of the impetus of our pedagogy is directed towards the many other factors that exercise teachers of drama. However, we have no reason to add fuel to the sense of disenfranchisement, felt by many playwrights, when they see the writer's position marginalised within the greater scheme of drama work.

Thomson offers a pedagogy of 'active play-reading' that challenges the once uncomplicated belief that drama departments are distinct from English departments only because they study plays through performing them. The idea that our *primary* task is to study plays in performance perpetuates the argument that, ultimately, the play (the literary text) is the fixed point of meaning by which a performance is measured. Here, Thomson's praxis refers to the employment of a physical action as part of a dramaturgy distinct from *dramatic literature*. It is a praxis that has more in common with the principles of Brecht's *Lehrstück* than with any concept of performance as a fixed cultural commodity.

Let us consider, first of all, the mode of teaching suggested and the subsequent implications for the social relationship between teacher and student. Subsequent to these considerations, we then need to consider the relationship of those two elements to the text. How do we teach a play? We may read it together. Do we then allot parts to the 'best' readers, or do we ask the students to read speeches around the group and, by so doing, possibly lose the comprehension of sonority? Do we give lectures on the subject? This latter procedure may offer the opportunity for students to experience a great and witty performance by an erudite scholar. Or it may be a dull reading from notes, which, anyway, could be accomplished with more efficiency, and comfort, in the library. Whatever the quality of the lecture, the teaching method supports the idea of a fixed point of (superior) knowledge disseminated 'down' to the students. If the two former methods are employed, the reading, as Thomson points out, is 'prefatory or illustrative to the lecture'.

Alternatively, the argument that performing the play is the only way by which we may fully understand it cannot be taken entirely seriously. Within the university context, this approach may so often prove to be a practice beleaguered by a 'paraphernalia' of theatre that, in the 'amateur dramatics' of universities, causes pragmatics to take precedence over understanding. This is not, in itself, an argument against fully staged productions of plays. However, it recognises the danger that such productions are as likely to impede as to facilitate serious study of dramaturgy – because their focus is on appearance and time is their enemy.

Thomson's 'active proposal' suggests much more, involving a consideration of the individual's status within the physical and social learning space and, perhaps of greatest importance, the student's active involvement in the learning process. The student, within this context, is facilitated in her/his capacity to perceive the words of the characters as *Gestus*. The different social configurations constructed for the students within the classroom are only in part concerned with the pattern or shape of the play. More, they are indicators of a reading that leads the student to *an* experience of the play's *Gestic* textures. Unlike the imperative stance of the polemical director or the authoritative lecturer, this approach does not seek to colonise the play, but builds a praxis in its relationship with the play.

Continuing to trace the possible dialogues we may develop with texts, Graham Ley focuses on the specific problem of plays that are not only far removed from us historically, but also removed by language. As an area 'foreign' to many drama students, the subject of ancient Greek drama has often been seen as the province of classical scholars. His argument starts from that perception, but then outlines what he terms the democratisation of the processes by which we may become familiar with that particular dramatic culture. The idea of democratisation comes from two sources. The first is the availability of good translations of the plays, allowing access to the work for drama students without linguistic ability in ancient Greek. The second source for his concept of democratisation is to be found in the work of Harold Kitto in the 1930s and 1950s, 'who was resolute in his efforts to make a Greek play a recognisable moral action, comprehensible to human beings who were susceptible to both thought and feeling'.

Ley's texts (and therefore his dialogues) are many layered and, in order to understand his basic premise of democratisation, we need to perceive the 'maps' he employs. In one sense the clue is in the subtitle of his chapter: 'problems of study, reception and understanding'. So often the learning process is one that implies study in the conventional sense of literary scholarship and, while this methodology is not to be cast out, his chapter recognises the multiplicity of ways by which we create a fruitful relationship between ourselves and the texts.

Broadening the possibilities for the ways by which we may study Greek play texts leads directly to the terms *reception* and *understanding*. Ley's dialogues are rooted in the material, social, political conditions of the culture that produced those plays. This awareness of the material conditions of the productions of a particular culture may be taken on a broad social level, but may also be directed specifically at the social relations embedded in the moment of theatrical production. Further, we may discern information within the plays that leads us, in a direct and concrete fashion, to perceptions that may hitherto have been thought of only in the abstract terms set out in lectures. Ley describes the potential for Euripides' *Women of Troy* to be seriously described as a 'lecture on war', while doubting that a lecture could reproduce the effects of Hecuba's attending of the body of her grandson in the compass of his father's shield. The layers and maps of Ley's dialogues lead us through the texts to the culture itself, in all its strangeness and complexity, and beyond, to new forms of reception in the ways by which these plays may touch our lives through theatre. In essence, the teaching of the play as literature, removed from a material context, then and now, can deliver only a small part of the story.

James MacDonald develops the dialogue between text and performer in adaptation. The emphasis of the chapter is on a potential pedagogy for drama within the context of a public celebration of the process, rather than on what we identify as the professional theatre production. However, we would be guilty of a monadic myopia if we were to seek an exclusive division between those two levels of activity. Our purpose might be expressed as the intention to educate people towards a theatre that might be, as opposed to the training that leads the student/actor towards an assimilation into the established theatrical professional status quo. MacDonald highlights the former orientation when he declares that his emphasis is on what is learned by the student, rather than on the performed product. The texts for adaptation were chosen, in this context, in order to challenge individuals in a manner appropriate to their development, rather than according to any perceived extrinsic criteria.

The initial challenge in this argument relates to the ways by which we, culturally, locate the author of a text. Admittedly, the examples employed are largely concerned with prose writers (novelists) well removed from the theatrical activity in question. However, MacDonald, himself a playwright, is engaged by his role in the performer's praxis. This is a well trodden path and we may recall other such engagements: David Edgar with Charles Dickens' *Nicholas Nickleby*, or, in a slightly different vein, Caryl Churchill's collaborations with the Joint Stock Theatre Company.

The focus of this example of adaptation of and collaboration between texts is on the *process* of production, rather than on the *outcome*. It is the linked material and cultural factors that create opportunities (and constrain them) in the learning process. What we may be certain of, and what most challenges us in MacDonald's position, is the constantly shifting location of author and text. Given that the declared primary intention is the learning process, a sense of performance is still involved, albeit viewed from an unfamiliar perspective. Clearly, in his attempt to establish an active relationship between thought and action, MacDonald is prepared to shift the location of a given text's cultural resonance and meaning.

4

An Approach to Play-Reading

Peter Thomson

It is no longer axiomatic in drama departments that play-texts take priority over all other subjects of study. But that was the presiding assumption in the 1960s, when I first became anxious about what was meant by 'reading a play'. Hugh Hunt, my professor at Manchester, brought to the job an uncomplicated belief that drama departments were distinct from English departments because they studied 'plays in performance', but the indistinctness of that distinction was already clear by the time the first cohort of students had graduated. That was when, fresh from postgraduate study in English, I arrived in Manchester to take up my first real job. Harold Pinter was the hottest property for up-to-date students, who were already finding Osborne and Wesker old-fashioned. During my first year, there were extra-mural undergraduate productions of *The Dumb Waiter, A Slight Ache* and *The Lover*, all underwritten by a conviction that the *avant-garde* was embodied in these enigmatic pieces. Beckett was reverently performed, too: *Endgame, All That Fall, Come and Go.* Esslin's *The Theatre of the Absurd,* published in 1961, seemed to be dictating to the decade. Rather than challenging incomprehensibility, the student productions embraced it. Ionesco was an exotic drug, learned by heart in preparation for hastily mounted studio production. But when did the thinking take place? Since I had been allotted a course on contemporary drama (despite the fact that my research was in the nineteenth century), I had some catching up to do. It would be a good start, I reckoned, to read some plays in class. And that was where I discovered something I should have known.

We are going to read, let us say, *Waiting for Godot*. Next week I will lecture on it. The reading, that is to assume, is prefatory or illustrative. There are 20 students in the class, each (days of luxury) with a text. The lecture-room has fixed seating, the empty drama space being largely a thing of the future and the students are spread around in clumps of friends or friendlessness. How do we start? 'Who'd like to read Vladimir?' Democratic, but stupid. It is not the done thing, among British students, to appear to be keen. So I distribute the parts – all four of them. Sixteen students feel disengaged, Pozzo and Lucky spend the first five minutes thumbing through to find their entrance (I daren't give anyone the part of the boy, so I'll read it myself when the time comes), and Vladimir and Estragon avoid reading well, even if they could, for fear of making a spectacle of themselves. If I interject too much, the reading will go on for ever. If I say nothing, the dispiriting encounter with language will be mercifully abbreviated. I can, of course, redistribute Vladimir and Estragon at various intervals. But on what principle? And how do I retain the attention of those who have had their turn?

Even if this picture is exaggeratedly gloomy, there remains a danger that the reading of plays in class will be disappointingly inert. There will almost always be students for whom the sound of the words is a kind of 'muzak', a background for creative doodling or unfettered mind journeys. I found myself searching for a more active style of reading. The first experiment was with Pinter's *The Collection*, a play in which the author's insistence on the unverifiability of intimate memory supplies both subject and method. One part of the divided stage represents the Belgravia home of a homosexual couple, Harry and Bill, another part the Chelsea flat of James and Stella Horne. The couples are connected by a common professional interest in dress design and, perhaps, by the fact that Bill and Stella slept together while they were attending a dress collection in Leeds. The status of that 'fact' is as uncertain at the end of the play as at its beginning. Our whole attention is focused on the sequence of competitive dialogues of which the play is composed. These are not so much conversations as they are the verbal equivalents of rallies at tennis, with each play seeking to produce a winning stroke, either by word or action. Thus, when James forces his way into the house to confront Bill, he begins the rally aggressively and, having dealt with Bill's counterattacks, wins the point:

JAMES:	Got any olives?
BILL:	How did you know my name?
JAMES:	No olives?

BILL: Olives? I'm afraid not.
JAMES: You mean to say you don't keep olives for your guests?
BILL: You're not my guest, you're an intruder. What can I do for you?
JAMES: Do you mind if I sit down?
BILL: Yes, I do.
JAMES: You'll get over it.

JAMES sits. BILL *stands.* JAMES *stands, takes off his overcoat, throws it on an armchair, and sits again.*

BILL: What's your name, old boy?

JAMES reaches to a bowl of fruit and breaks off a grape, which he eats.

JAMES: Where shall I put the pips?
BILL: In your wallet.

JAMES takes out his wallet and deposits the pips.

(p. 129)

I brought to the class four hats and four long scarves. I then set out four chairs, two each side of the space, and called up four students to fill them. They were each given a scarf and hat and asked to place the hat on the floor beside their chair and let the scarf hang loosely round their necks. They were then asked to read the play, winding the scarf round and round their necks if they thought they were winning the conversational rally and donning the hat if they thought they had won it. The quality of the reading soared and the non-readers were critically engaged by the scarf-and-hat business. Thus, in the section quoted above, if Bill begins triumphantly to wind his scarf on 'What's your name, old boy?' and dons his hat on 'In your wallet', what does he do with the hat and scarf when James actually deposits the pips in his wallet, donning his hat as he does so? Surely Bill has to throw his hat to the floor and unwind his scarf in a hurry. And what frenzy of physical action should accompany Harry's jealous quizzing of Bill?

HARRY: Oh, by the way, a chap called for you yesterday.
BILL: Oh yes?
HARRY: Just after you'd gone out.
BILL: Oh yes?
HARRY: Ah well, time for the joint. Roast or chips?
BILL: I don't want any potatoes, thank you.
HARRY: No potatoes? What an extraordinary thing. Yes, this chap, he was asking for you, he wanted you.
BILL: What for?
HARRY: He wanted to know if you ever cleaned your shoes with furniture polish.

BILL: Really? How odd.
HARRY: Not odd. Some kind of national survey.
BILL: What did he look like?
HARRY: Oh ... lemon hair, nigger brown teeth, wooden leg, bottlegreen eyes and a toupée. Know him?
BILL: Never met him.
HARRY: You'd know him if you saw him.
BILL: I doubt it.
HARRY: What, a man who looked like that?
BILL: Plenty of men look like that.
HARRY: That's true. That's very true. The only thing is that this particular man was here last night.
BILL: Was he? I didn't see him.
HARRY: Oh yes, he was here, but I've got a funny feeling he wore a mask. It was the same man, but he wore a mask, that's all there is to it. He didn't dance here last night, did he, or do any gymnastics?
BILL: No one danced here last night.
HARRY: Aah. Well, that's why you didn't notice his wooden leg. I couldn't help seeing it myself when he came to the front door because he stood on the top step stark naked. Didn't seem very cold, though. He had a waterbottle under his arm instead of a hat.
BILL: Those church bells have certainly left their mark on you.

                                                 (pp. 1399–40)

Insofar as *The Collection* has a plot, this interchange is peripheral to it. It is an exercise in the technique of harassment, reminiscent of Goldberg's quizzing of Stanley in *The Birthday Party*, although Bill is a much better-equipped victim. Indeed, the scarf-and-hat reading of Pinter exposes much about his compositional method. The unexpected revelation of this particular reading of *The Collection* was that the true victor is the almost wordless Stella. It is her pre-play confession, fact or fiction, that precipitates the jealous crossfire that is the total action of the play. We see her, generally fondling a kitten, more often than we hear her. But at the end of this reading, while the hatless Harry and Bill gazed dumbly at each other on one side of the room, James posed the unanswered question, 'That's the truth ... isn't it?', and lost his nerve. While he unwound his scarf and finally discarded it, Stella wound hers more and more tightly, fondling it as if it were her kitten, her feminine strength, her 'pussy'. There was a long silence and the reading ended when Stella smilingly put on her hat.

Pinter's evident nervousness of female potency is a notable feature of *The Homecoming*. Ruth, the lone woman, has to answer to the familial roles of mother, wife, sister and daughter and to the extra-familial roles of mistress and whore. Her instability is a mirror image of the unstable male context into which she is imported. I attempted a reading of the play that would honour its muted narcissism. The idea was that each of the six reader characters would have a silently active responder, charged with acting out the concealed physical implications of the laden dialogue. These physical responses to impulses from the language should be stylised, closer to dance than to realistic mime. The important thing was that the responder should be sensitive to the sexual and familial nuances out of which Pinter builds the play's tension. I was hoping that the responders would evolve increasingly subtle methods of presenting images of gender roles rather than literal bodily transcriptions. The mutations from mother to mistress to rapist to child to sado-masochist in Lenny's first contest with his unknown and unannounced sister-in-law seemed like a segment of a savage dance drama, as I envisaged them in my study:

LENNY: And now perhaps I'll relieve you of your glass.
RUTH: I haven't quite finished.
LENNY: You've consumed quite enough, in my opinion.
RUTH: No, I haven't.
LENNY: Quite sufficient, in my own opinion.
RUTH: Not in mine, Leonard.
Pause.
LENNY: Don't call me that, please.
RUTH: Why not?
LENNY: That's the name my mother gave me.
Pause.

    Just give me the glass.
RUTH: No.
Pause.
LENNY: I'll take it, then.
RUTH: If you take the glass ... I'll take you.
Pause
LENNY: How about me taking the glass without you taking me?
RUTH: Why don't I just take you?
Pause
LENNY: You're joking.
Pause.

    You're in love, anyway, with another man. You've had a secret liaison with another man. His family didn't even

know. Then you come here without a word of warning
and start to make trouble.

She picks up the glass and lifts it towards him.

RUTH: Have a sip. Go on. Have a sip from my glass.

He is still.

Sit on my lap. Take a long cool sip.

She pats her lap. Pause. She stands, moves to him with the glass.

Put your head back and open your mouth.

LENNY: Take that glass away from me.

RUTH: Lie on the floor. Go on. I'll pour it down your throat.

LENNY: What are you doing, making me some kind of proposal?

She laughs shortly, drains the glass.

RUTH: Oh, I was thirsty.

(pp. 49–51)

In the event, the most positive outcome of this reading was the
recognition of the insistent activity of the responders during the Pinter
pause. They embodied the mental movements of an engaged audience.
But the brief was too demanding for a first reading. I later developed
the method over a longer investigation of Congreve's intricate *Love
for Love*, culminating in a performance of Restoration sexuality which
mingled speech and choreography. Even so, I believe that a teacher
with a stronger command than I of physical language might make
something of this crude scheme for an active reading. As class sizes
grew, I found myself drawn to slightly safer ground.

The Pinter readings were, in effect, explorations of the texture of
his writing. They had little to say about the pattern or shape of his
plays. That is not, in itself, a matter of concern. The wish to say
everything about a play is an expression of the urge to colonise it. The
fundamental aim of the kind of reading I am concerned to develop is
that the reading should be *an* experience of the play – not *the*
experience of the play, and certainly not simply a preface to a possible
subsequent experience of the play. The manner of the reading, its
devising by the teacher, should make its own comment. It is neither a
simple speaking aloud of the text nor a lengthily illustrated lecture.
Examples from Shakespeare may help to make the point.

Macbeth

It is an uncontentious view of the play that Macbeth, having murdered
his way to the throne, becomes progressively isolated as he endeavours
to secure his seat on it. The process can be readily illustrated in a

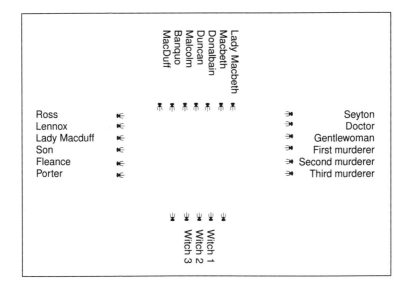

Figure 1. Suggested seating arrangement at the start of a reading of *Macbeth*.

two-hour reading of the play. In advance, the teacher needs only to set out chairs in an otherwise empty space. The casting is then determined by the chair in which the incoming students elect to sit. The initial lay-out might be as shown in figure 1.

The 24 chairs (the two flanking the witches are initially empty) are set out in a square, with the 'top table' of king and nobility facing the witches, and Duncan's adherents opposite those who will be retained by Macbeth. It is never the intention to read the whole play. An alternative is to give each excerpt a title on which to hang a brief, introductory observation. The *Macbeth* reading comprises:

I.1	'Fair is foul'.
I.2.1–45	'Brave Macbeth'.
I.3.69–106	'Can the Devil speak true?'.
I.5.28–end	'Make thick my blood'.
II.2	'I have done the deed'.
	(At the end of this scene, Duncan leaves the square, with his chair.)
II.3.1–48	'Here's a knocking indeed'.
	(After this excerpt, the Porter leaves the square, with his chair.)

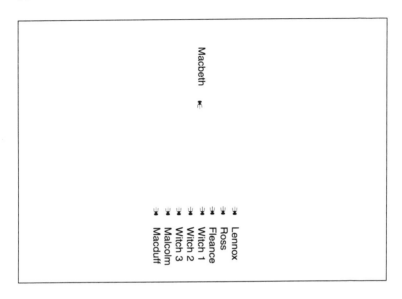

Figure 2. Seating arrangement left after V.5 of *Macbeth*.

II.3.94–end	'There's no mercy left'.
	(After this scene, Malcolm crosses to the empty chair beside the first witch. Donalbain leaves the square, with his own chair and Malcolm's.)
III.1.1–10	'Here's our chief guest'.
III.3	'To be thus is nothing, but to be safely thus'.
	(After this scene, Fleance crosses to the empty chair beside the third witch. Banquo leaves the square, with his own chair and Fleance's.)
III.4.108–end	'Blood will have blood'.
IV.1.132–end	'Macduff is fled to England'.
	(After this excerpt, Macduff crosses, with his chair, to sit beside Malcolm. Macbeth and Lady Macbeth are now alone at 'top table'.)
IV.2	'Where is your husband?'.
	(After this scene, Doctor and Gentlewoman, and Lady Macduff and her son, leave the square, with their chairs.)
V.3.30–end	'the thanes fly from me'.
	(After this excerpt, Lennox and Ross carry their chairs to sit beside Fleance.)

V.5   'She should have died hereafter'.
             (After this scene, Lady Macbeth and Seyton leave the
             square, with their chairs.)

All that remains of the square of chairs now is shown in figure 2. The
reading is completed by two short excerpts:

V.6.42–73   'Turn, hell-hound, turn!'.
             (After this excerpt, Macbeth leaves the square, and his
             place is taken by Malcolm.)
V.6.93–end   'By the grace of grace'.

I make no critical claims for this reading of *Macbeth*. It is included
because it shows the method at its simplest. Twenty-two students are
automatically involved in the reading, and the structure is clear
enough to allow for easy substitution. Most significantly, an interpretation of the play is physically enacted by the class and debate
encouraged on the place and purpose of the witches, the significance
of Fleance and the graciousness of Malcolm. That, as Beckett might
say, is enough to be going on with.

Hamlet

This reading presents an argument for the meta-theatricality of
Hamlet. Shakespeare is here peculiarly excited by the double challenge
of the dramatised fiction and the fact of its dramatisation. In their
different ways, and using the same cast of characters, Polonius,
Claudius and Hamlet try to fashion the future along the lines of
acceptable dramatic conventions. Polonius was an actor once –
ironically, he will re-enact his student role of the murdered Julius
Caesar, this time behind an arras rather that 'i' th' Capitol' (III.2.96).
To an extent, he is an actor still, playing the good father to a decidedly
histrionic family and playing the loyal chamberlain to a player king.
His performance is comic partly because it is unvarying. He is a single-
style actor in a multi-styled play. But Polonius is not self-aware as an
actor. His preference is to compose, or at least to stage manage, the
play of state. And the plot of his play, tragically wide of the true mark,
is a familiar tale of blighted love. Hamlet has been driven to
distraction by his passion for Ophelia. Twice Polonius attempts to set
up controlled improvisations. For the first, he and Claudius will be the
unobserved judges of Hamlet's performance, while Ophelia's task is to

provoke that performance. Polonius places her with an almost directorial concern for detail:

> Ophelia, walk you here. Gracious, so please you,
> We will bestow ourselves. – Read on this book,
> That show of such an exercise may colour
> Your loneliness.
>
> (III.1.44–7)

For Polonius, though not for Claudius, the ensuing scene confirms
the truthfulness of his 'play', and he volunteers to set up another
improvisation, this time with the Queen:

> He will come straight. Look you lay home to him.
> Tell him his pranks have been too broad to bear with,
> And that your grace hath screened and stood between
> Much heat and him. I'll silence me e'en here.
> Pray you be round with him.
>
> (III.4.1–5)

When Polonius is provoked into attempting a personal intervention
in the scene, his 'play' comes to a sudden end. There are seven scenes
in it and six characters (in search of an author?) – Polonius, Hamlet,
Ophelia, Claudius, Laertes and Gertrude – although the teacher will
need to make reference to Polonius's attempt to 'write' Reynaldo:

I.2.42–63
I.3.55–end
II.1.75–end   (Note the histrionic Ophelia's miming of Hamlet.)
II.2.86–170   (At which point Hamlet displaces Polonius's play with
                  his own.)
III.1.44–56 and 89–end
III.2.355–69
III.4.1–34

Hamlet's play, predictably, is much more complex than Polonius's.
Its central character is not the 'real' Hamlet, but the 'acting' Hamlet,
costumed in his 'antic disposition'. By substituting for himself, in a
play of his own devising, a madman, Hamlet the protagonist exploits a
dramatic fiction in order to test the accuracy of a historical 'fact'. His
play ends, properly, with the death of Claudius. It has eight scenes and
eight characters – mad Hamlet, Horatio, Ophelia, Gertrude, Polonius,
Rosencrantz, Guildenstern and the First Player:

II.2.171–216

II.2.290–325   (Shakespeare is surely here introducing his own company, the Lord Chamberlain's Men.)

II.2.364–413

II.2.525–end

III.2.86–126   (*The Mousetrap*, too, is strictly a part of Hamlet's play.)

III.2.255–354

III.3.73–96   (The scene that ought to end Hamlet's play.)

III.4.169–end

From this point onwards, Hamlet loses control of events. Even the necessary killing of Claudius is not so much the climax of Hamlet's play as an explosive reaction to the recognition that he has been fatally plotted into Claudius's play. It is Claudius who is the arch play-maker, the inventor of Rosencrantz and Guildenstern, expert in courtly procedure and himself a supreme actor. Like a master improviser, Claudius thinks on his feet. When Hamlet and Laertes scuffle in Ophelia's grave, he performs an act of mediation, already discerning a distant advantage. Working at his best, as in the preparing of Laertes for the duel, he is actor, director and dramatist in one. The duel, as Claudius intends it to be played, is his own creation:

> And for his death no wind of blame shall breathe;
> But even his mother shall uncharge the practice
> And call it accident.
>   (IV.7.67–9)

It is the intuitive timing of a master plotter that inspires him to interrupt the scheming by posing a question designed to allay Laertes' qualms: 'Laertes, was your father dear to you?' (IV.7.93), and it is accurate observation that underlies the prediction that Hamlet:

> Will not peruse the foils; so that with ease,
> Or with a little shuffling, you may choose
> A sword unbated, and, in a pass of practice,
> Requite him for your father.
>   (IV.7.112–15)

The mastery of detail, and the precision of the venomous phrase 'with a little shuffling', are in a different theatrical class from Polonius's simple disposing of Ophelia with a book. As author of the duel/play, Claudius may not have anticipated much help from his leading actor, but he welcomes Laertes' addition of the poisoned blade and compounds it with his own proposal for a poisoned drink. The scenario improves as it is devised. Hamlet, though, is an elusive adversary. Once Polonius's clumsy attempts at intervention have been terminated, the real battle between Hamlet and Claudius can be joined. Rosencrantz and Guildenstern are incidental victims, as Hamlet explains to Horatio in an image significantly foreshadowing the duel:

'Tis dangerous when the baser nature comes
Between the pass and fell incensed points
Of mighty opposites.

                                    (V.2.61–3)

The official adversary is Laertes, the real one Claudius. It is a confrontation that both men relish. Although bearing in mind a scenario of his own contriving, Hamlet's immediate, and fatal, agreement is to participate in the climactic scene of Claudius's play. It is a play with six scenes and eight characters – Claudius, Hamlet, Gertrude, Polonius, Laertes, Rosencrantz, Guildenstern and Osric:

II.2.1–39
III.3.1–35
IV.3.39–end
IV.3.39–end
IV.7
V.2.171–256   (At which point, Gertrude falls to the ground.)

Ophelia's death is a fortuitous external aid to Claudius the playwright and an insufficiently heeded reminder to Hamlet of the limitations of his art. But the death of Gertrude is in neither man's plans. It was, perhaps, hubris for them to suppose that the ordering of events was in their hands. With the death of the queen, we are left with an awareness that even Hamlet and Claudius have been unwitting collaborators in a greater play, one in which their parts were written beyond their knowledge. This reading of *Hamlet* ends with the hundred lines that follow Gertrude's fall. These clearly belong to no one's play but Shakespeare's. Meta-theatrical invention is over and the catastrophe is played through by a theatrical cast of eight – Claudius, Hamlet, Gertrude, Laertes, Horatio, Osric, Fortinbras and an ambassador. Grouped in four discrete areas and with their roles in the reading determined by the chair they elected to sit in, 30 people have taken part in what is, essentially, a critical approach to *Hamlet*.

Twelfth Night

This reading takes its theme from Feste's Latin warning to Olivia that appearances are not to be trusted: '*cucullus non facit monachum*' (I.5.50–1, 'the cowl does not make the monk'). This is a play in which people are constantly misread and almost as frequently rejected. Olivia rejects Orsino, Sir Andrew and Malvolio. She misread and is rejected by Viola/Cesario. Also rejected by Olivia, Sir Andrew is spurned by Sir Toby and Malvolio by 'Sir Topas', whom he misreads. Antonio is rejected by Viola/Cesario, whom he misreads as Sebastian. In this context of rejection, Sebastian's three-word acceptance, 'Madam, I will' (IV.1.64), has the dramatic force of a peripety. From now on, a happy ending is plausible.

Like so many of Shakespeare's comedies, *Twelfth Night* is set primarily in two contrasting locations, Orsino's court and Olivia's household, although, after the second act, it is Olivia's household that dominates while the idea of Orsino's court retains its dramatic tug. For this reading, a central area is divided into three sections by a narrow, central aisle, which will represent sea coast and street. There is a single chair in the middle of each of the larger sections (figure 3), but the 20 readers cast themselves according to the chairs they select on the periphery of the space. The teacher has the opportunity to comment on their roles as, in sequence, they take their place in the action.

Olivia's chair will remain empty for some time, but she is already a powerful presence before she makes her first appearance. The direction of the readers' gaze will be significant throughout this reading. Orsino's eyes are fixed on Olivia's empty chair from the moment he enters with Valentine for the first except (I.1.24–end). Like the other readers, Valentine brings his chair on with him. A possibly epicene attendant at Orsino's probably epicene court, he looks towards, but not directly at, the duke. Direct gaze is reserved for lovers. The reading proceeds as follows:

I.2.   The Captain, a sketched-in adorer of Viola, in parallel with Antonio's adoration of Sebastian, looks towards Viola, who stares vacantly into an uncertain future. She, like Olivia, is bereaved of a brother.

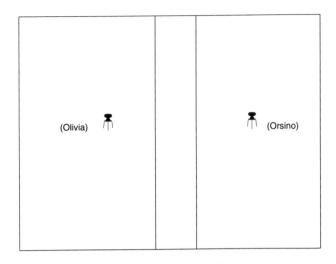

Figure 3. Suggested seating arrangement for a reading of *Twelfth Night*.

I.3.41–107   While Sir Andrew gazes at Olivia's empty chair, Sir Toby and Maria look, for amusement, at him. The stage is now peopled as in figure 4.

I.4   Having presented herself as a eunuch at Orsino's court, Viola is now steadfastly in love with him. Her female self remains in abeyance. Whatever happens to her through the rest of the reading, neither her chair nor her gaze will shift. Though the various courtings of Olivia are the dynamic of most of the play's plot, Viola's love for Orsino is its stable, emotional centre.

I.5.29–end   There is much stress on eyes and vision in this important scene. Olivia's gaze is initially as vacant as was Viola's on her first appearance. Captivated by Cesario, she turns her eyes suddenly on him/her at 'You might do much' (line 265). She has now her romantic focus, and the anxiety that accompanies it:

> I do I know not what, and fear to find
> Mine eye too great a flatterer for my mind.
> (298–9)

Feste's eyes are, by contrast, always unfocused. When

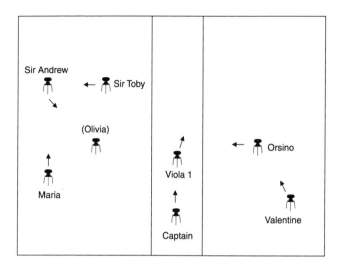

Figure 4. Seating arrangement at the end of Act I Scene 3 of *Twelfth Night*. (Arrows indicate direction of gaze.)

	he is with Olivia's household, he looks towards Orsino's court; when he is with Orsino, he looks towards Olivia. Malvolio stares towards, but not yet at, Olivia.

he is with Olivia's household, he looks towards Orsino's court; when he is with Orsino, he looks towards Olivia. Malvolio stares towards, but not yet at, Olivia.

II.1 Our first impression ought to be that Viola has entered with a strange man. Antonio re-enacts the rapt attention of Viola's captain and Sebastian her vacancy. The positions now are as shown in figure 5.

II.2 Recognizing the implication of the ring Olivia has sent Malvolio to give her, Viola feels the force of Feste's tag, *cucullus non facit monachum:* 'Fortune forbid my outside have not charmed her!' (line 18).

II.3.85–end Sir Toby and Maria now look to Malvolio for their fun, while Sir Andrew still dreams of Olivia.

II.4 Valentine is indistinguishable from Curio and can read his part, but the enigmatic Feste can be played by a second reader when he is in Orsino's court. Feste is not, perhaps, single. Trapped in the appearance of Cesario, though, Viola can make nothing of her duality.

II.5 Fabian joins Sir Toby and Sir Andrew to watch the outcome of the practical joke Maria has played on

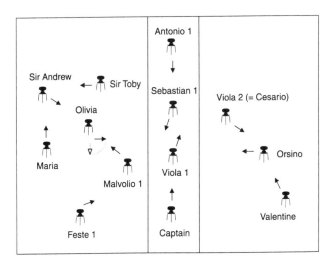

Figure 5. Seating arrangement at the end of Act II Scene 1 of *Twelfth Night*. (Arrows indicate direction of gaze.)

	Malvolio. The transformation of Malvolio is represented by the introduction of a second Malvolio, whose gaze, from line 154, is fixed on Olivia. The first Malvolio now turns his back on Sir Toby.
III.2	Sir Toby and Fabian set up the duel between Viola and Sir Andrew.
III.3	Antonio and Sebastian decide to part briefly.
III.4.253–end	There is no need to read the discomfiture of Malvolio. It can be represented by the turning of his chair away from Olivia. The crucial event in this scene is Antonio's nick-of-time arrival to rescue, as he thinks, Sebastian. The confusion caused by the twins is here figured by the introduction of a second Antonio, with his gaze fixed on Viola/Cesario. It is, however, the first Antonio whom the officers surround and arrest. The positions on stage are, by now, as shown in figure 6.
IV.1	To emphasise the confusion, a second Sebastian is added here, his chair placed beside Viola/Cesario's but his gaze initially towards the first Antonio. At line 64, 'Madam, I will' his eyes swivel towards Olivia, and remain fixed on her for the rest of the play.
IV.3	For the first time in the play, the course of true love runs smooth. Sebastian is the fifth person with whom

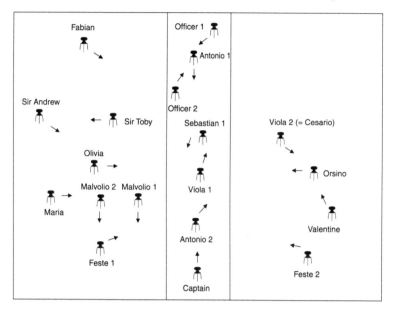

Figure 6. Seating arrangement at the end of Act III Scene 4 of *Twelfth Night*. (Arrows indicate direction of gaze.)

Olivia has been associated. She has rejected Orsino, laughed off Malvolio and scarcely noticed Sir Andrew. But Cesario is another matter altogether and this, she thinks, is he. *Cucullus non facit monochum* takes a sexually benevolent twist.

V.1   The key moment in this final scene is Sebastian's entrance, one of the most extraordinary moments in the history of comedy. Viola/Cesario is at great risk from both Orsino and Olivia, and the intervention of Sir Andrew and Sir Toby does little to distract from the hostile focus on her. Must this be the moment of shameful confession? There is no way in which Viola can satisfy both master and mistress – until Sebastian provides it. On stage, there is a multiple adjustment, a mass double-take. In one way or another, all those present must temper their gaze. For the first time, they can see straight. For the final tableau, Sir Andrew has gone. So have Viola/Cesario and the first Sebastian, a bachelor – his married alter ego remains. The officers have been dismissed and Antonio relieved of his

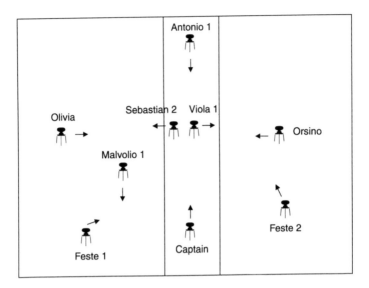

Figure 7. Seating arrangement at the close of *Twelfth Night*. (Arrows indicate direction of gaze.)

confused second self. Like Viola's captain, he remains in waiting, unrewarded by Sebastian's committed love, but less vengeful than the lingering Malvolio. The reported marriage of Sir Toby and Maria is of marginal significance, and Fabian and Valentine altogether ir- relevant. The stanzas of the final song can be shared between the still-unfettered Feste. The closing pos- itions, then, are as shown in figure 7.

Conclusion

These examples have not been chosen entirely at random, but the method can be randomly applied and adapted to suit the purposes of the individual teacher. Working at its best, it offers to the class a satisfyingly complete single-session encounter with a play, and to the lecturer a common focus for detailed commentary and discussion. If I have concentrated on Shakespeare, it is only because his plays are the commonest currency. I have described ways of approaching the texture of a script (*The Collection*), a writer's obsessive themes (*The Homecoming*), the shaping of a dramatic narrative (*Macbeth*), metatheatrical devices (*Hamlet*) and the significance of the truth-seeking gaze (*Twelfth Night*). The general aim has been to complete the readings within a two-hour slot on the timetable, but it is comparatively easy to abbreviate as well as to lengthen them. In straightforward readings, the text tends to dictate inflexibly. In active readings, there is a flexible relationship between the play and its readers. Better still, there is interaction.

Works cited

Line and page references relate to the following texts:

Harold Pinter (1977) *The Collection*, in *Plays: Two*. Eyre Methuen, London.

Harold Pinter (1978) *The Homecoming*, in *Plays: Three*. Eyre Methuen, London.

William Shakespeare (1967) *Macbeth*, ed. G. K. Hunter. Penguin, Harmondsworth.

William Shakespeare (1987) *Hamlet*, ed. G. R. Hibbard. Clarendon Press, Oxford.

William Shakespeare (1968) *Twelfth Night*, ed. M. M. Mahood. Penguin, Harmondsworth.

5

Ancient Greek Theatre and Society: Problems of Study, Reception and Understanding

Graham Ley

As things were...

In the last 50 years the study of Greek drama has undergone many changes, of which the most important might be described – loosely, but perhaps evocatively – as demographic. From being a relatively privileged subject, dependent on the pain and often the expense of language learning, it has become increasingly democratic.

In part, this major change is institutional and takes its minor place alongside that shift in the concept and practice of culture that is one of the dominant characteristics of the twentieth century. But access to the subject through educational institutions has plainly been dependent on the existence of accessible and attractive translations. In the post-war period, the initiative lay in the first instance with the American translations pioneered by David Greene and Richmond Lattimore in particular, whose combined editorship produced a vernacular series for the University of Chicago Press that was acclaimed almost universally. For Britain, the appeal of the 'classics' in general was consolidated by translations in the Penguin Classics series, in which Philip Vellacott played an important role. Admittedly, early translations of Sophocles in that series, made by E. F. Watling, carried rather too many of the resonances of the verse drama revival to be very successful after the mid-1950s and the revolution in the language and forms of the British theatre. But the example of the Chicago series was enduring and it has provided the stimulus to a vast variety of initiatives in the translation of Greek drama, to the present day. Institutionally, the emergence of drama departments has also had a major influence. Although members of drama departments have been responsible for remarkably few translations of Greek plays until recently, attention to Greek drama in translation and to medieval drama in particular undoubtedly expanded in tandem with the new subject area. But while medieval theatre became almost a hallmark of the new scholarship, and theatricality as much a subject of study as the traditional text, the profile of criticism in relation to Greek drama remained distinctly literary. To view this as a disappointing conservatism would, however, be mistaken, since, within the mainstream discipline of classics, literary criticism was still a novelty, a status to which some elements of classical scholarship would happily resign it even now. Modern appreciation of Greek drama owes a great deal to Harold Kitto in particular, who was resolute in his efforts to make a Greek play a recognisable moral action, comprehensible to human beings who were susceptible to both thought and feeling (Kitto, 1939, 1956). Kitto's moral humanism offered a rubric for all kinds of appreciation and had a firm appeal to what has been, somewhat nostalgically, called the post-war consensus. The term may in itself be a trap, an invitation to exercise a selective memory which ignores confrontation, but Kitto's readings could rely on a relatively stable view of 'human' nature which was only too content to relegate tragedy to the past, whether mythical or, for the readership, historical.

Nothing could better express the divide that existed in the mid-twentieth century than a comparison of Kitto's persuasive and encouraging, democratic criticism with the impressive theatrical compilations of Pickard-Cambridge (Pickard-Cambridge, 1927, 1953). These proved to be invaluable source books on the origins and development of the genres of tragedy and comedy, and on the organisation of the dramatic festivals. Yet, with the crucial evidence fixed with scholarly precision in the original Greek, and a documentary format for highly fragmentary information accessible only to dedicated scholars, these tomes acted like an anchor-stone for most reading lists, rather than a practicable resource for incoming attention.[1] For Kitto, the theatre was simply the 'natural' place for drama as a specific genre, while for Pickard-Cambridge documentation was an admirable enterprise that need look no further than its self-fulfilment in scholarly accuracy and comprehensiveness. If there was a meeting place for drama and theatre studies in the minds of students or other interested parties, it was likely to remain unsatisfied, unless a teacher with initiative chose to combine both elements.

A personal involvement

This brief and rather patchy retrospective can be no more than a rough guide; but it does provide an introduction to my own involvement with teaching the subject, which began in the late 1970s in the Drama Department of the University of London. I have since taught Greek drama in a very large number of different situations, mostly through translation but also in Greek, and mostly, but by no means exclusively, to drama students. Historically, if that is not too grand an idea, I would see my involvement as part of an extraordinary movement that has carried the Greek theatre into the contemporary repertoire. I recall reading somewhere, in the 1970s, that at least one leading director in the Royal Shakespeare Company considered Greek tragedy unperformable. By the end of that decade and at the very beginning of the next, there had been four productions in Britain which broke that impasse for the foreseeable future, or until the theatre forgets once again what it can do. These were the production of Rudkin's version of Euripides' *Hippolytos,* which I saw at the Donmar Warehouse in London; John Barton's 'epic' *The Greeks* for the Royal Shakespeare Company; Peter Hall's production of Tony Harrison's version of Aeschylus's *Oresteia,* performed in the Olivier auditorium at the National Theatre; and the television production of the same trilogy, in the version by Raphael and McLeish called *The Serpent Son.* What was significant about these productions was not only their relative simultaneity, but the fact that three major institutions had acknowledged the viability, and even the commercial value, of the performance of Greek plays.

There is no obvious, single change that can account for this revolution in attitudes and assumptions. Greek plays had, of course, been produced in Britain, Europe, and North America intermittently throughout the century, and Gilbert Murray's translations still exist as a record of one major movement. But the regularity and spread of productions of Greek drama in the last 15 years have not previously been equalled and comparisons with the Renaissance are not facile. Greek material is used for productions of every kind, from those that allow it to conform to existing presuppositions about staging and the 'dramatic text', to those that challenge all kinds of assumptions about theatricality or cultural identity. More to the point, a theatre-goer or a student is as likely to confront or be involved with a Greek play as with the work of any other historical convention, with the obvious exception of Shakespeare, to whom an industry is dedicated.

I have no wish to exaggerate my own influence here, which has been minimal; but I have felt, from the beginnings of teaching, that I was part of a movement that, in my own particular terms, was attempting at the least to offer an alternative vision of tragedy to a resolutely English tradition. The merits of doing so, apart from the absolute artistic claims of variety, were to my mind principally those of tractability. It seemed to me that Greek plays lent themselves to almost any kind of realisation at almost any level of activity, and so might contribute to the exploration of practice or to work on the audience in a manner that could sustain the development of almost any practitioner.

The nature of the problem

When I first started teaching I was determined to do something just right and thoroughly appropriate to the situation. In a department with a relatively strong bias towards practice, it seemed self-evident that theatre practice should be the keynote, and I was imbued with Wickham and Southern to the extent that I felt a model was at least available. I was certain that drama students should not be encouraged to fall back on the kinds of analysis they had practised at school and I could not face reading endless essays on characters in Sophocles. I was determined to teach 'theatre', but almost immediately encountered problems. In the first place, this was the era of Taplin, whose immensely influential and scholarly study of 'entrances and exits' in the tragedies of Aeschylus had been followed by a handbook for students and by close involvement with the production by Peter Hall (Taplin, 1977, 1978). The immediate reaction might be that this was a pedagogic gift. But closer inspection revealed that it was exceedingly difficult, in practice, to teach only 'entrances and exits', and the momentary tableaux that were the principal focus of his handbook. The second major problem was that, apart from a natural inclination to study whole plays, the students proved to be vastly more interested in Euripides than in any other dramatist. There was, and is still, aside from helpful contributions by Hourmouziades (1965) and Halleran (1985) in particular, no theatrical study of Euripides suitable for students, or none that I found successful. The third problem was not a problem but a delight, which was that the majority of the students I was teaching were women. This led almost automatically to a complete reversion of my initial assumptions, because the plain demand facing me was that I should introduce and explain Greek, or Athenian, social values.

Now there was nothing of that in Wickham or Southern, and very little in Taplin, and not much at all in Diana Rigg's sword-licking sleekness in *The Serpent Son*. What I did have to compose from was a consistent and inquisitive attention to the familial and political structures of Greek life. Once grasped in their essentials these led through to a potential diversity of practice. I found, in other words, what I had not expected and probably had not wanted: as a newcomer, I had to start from the beginning.

Mapping out Greek culture

It is a funny thing when you start to talk in your own voice, after trying to talk unsuccessfully in those of others. There is this strange stirring of interest among people who had looked politely bored before and had laughed quietly at your postgraduate beard and umbrella. Nightmares of alienation can easily exist before you accept that people actually want to hear what you most naturally have to tell, which is a matter of democracy, patriarchy and slaves. It is curious how subversive the revelation can be that democracy means 'power to/of the people', and how the notion of enslavement aligned to democracy provokes wider reflections. Over these years an agenda formed, which was nothing like what I had imagined, and which I still see as current. I shall attempt to describe it, in the hope that it will stimulate thoughts about what on earth does go on in the reception of a foreign and historically remote theatre.

My teaching practice had to clarify the following points, in the first instance, because there were misconceptions and large areas of ignorance, despite some acquaintance with the material: first, that the plays were Athenian and of the fifth century (I still find it a regular misconception that the Greeks were an amalgam and that they were all – audience and characters – in some way 'heroic'); and second, that the fifth-century Greek world was not all Athenian, but that Athens was predominant and imperial is also a necessary statement about the formation of a culture. I find it most useful to point out that the pillars of the Parthenon were built with tribute money; it speaks by analogy to the 'sympathy' engaged by tragedy and of the context in which that can afford to appear. Before I had read it in any prominent publication, I used to point – and still do – to the analogy between the democratic assembly on the hill called the Pnyx and the *theatron* in the precinct of Dionysos. I would also point to the circuit walls of Athens and Piraeus, and the connecting long walls, mention triremes, and establish that Athens was secure from attack by land or sea, and secure from the effects of siege. I had never thought that this information would be useful to, or even tolerated by, drama students. But it says a great deal about the security that gives rise to a stable convention of performance. The stability of the athletic contests, notably the Olympic Games, was assured by armistice, not by the power of an individual state. That the shape of the theatre recalls that of the political assembly in a direct-voting democracy; that both depended on the use of the human voice and gesture; that the audience capacity for the theatre exceeded that for the assembly: all these points establish or suggest a series of relationships between political life and the theatre which haunts people. I would then confirm this picture by observing that the audience was used to sitting or standing in judgement on political or judicial speeches; that the art of persuasion was the democratic art, or technique; and that artistic 'art', or theatre, made use of that art, or technique, and drew attention to its operation. These are all maps, in which rhetoric, of one kind or another, walks and talks.

Silent women and unhappy families

Pitiful as it may sound, it took me quite a while to put together the teaching materials for that mapping. For social history, the task was a great deal easier, notably because Lacey had already done much to gather the evidence and place it in an accessible form (Lacey, 1968). His informative work on the family, and the prominence in law and everyday authority of the *kyrios*, or male head of household, was duly expanded and variegated by feminist scholarship, with the study by Pomeroy (1976), followed by the excellent resource material compiled in translation by Lefkowitz and Fant (1981).[2] Women's studies were, by definition, not prepared to be confined to linguistic competence, and women students and those men who have been willing to follow them have generally found the resources they required. I tended from the earliest days to add to that list various works on death and burial practices, largely because I found that these illuminated the action of Euripides' *Alcestis* in particular, a play which, despite its anomalous

character, seems to encourage as much attention to the household or
oikos as any can.[3] Dramaturgically, I found that the details of the
prothesis, or 'laying out', of the corpse showed Alcestis herself treating
her still-living body as if it were already dead and that the procedures
of the *ekphora* or 'funeral' helped to clarify a central portion of the
play.[4] There is here, as in other plays such as *Antigone,* a distinct
alertness to the parallel with the processional arrival of the bride at
the house of the husband.[5] In *Antigone* the passage of Antigone out to
death is given, grotesquely, some of the characteristics of a wedding. It
is, of course, of the greatest significance that the death of Oedipus
(*Antigone,* 49f.) and then of his sons has presumably left Creon as an
unwilling *kyrios* for both Antigone and Ismene, and not just as the new
political and military leader (*strategos*) of Thebes. On the day after the
death of her brothers, Antigone would assume in the minds of the
audience the status of an *epikleros,* an orphaned heiress, which might
enhance the urgency of her prospective marriage to Haemon.[6] These
important components of the legal position of women render the
crises of affiliation and obligation all the more complex.[7] The
Hegelian antithesis between the rights of family (Antigone) and state
(Creon) is far too crude as an analysis of the play: the contemporary
social context of the play and its audience, if you like, strongly resists
its incorporation into a transcendental scheme of social development.[8]

The general subordination of women which the evidence demon-
strates allowed me to emphasise that the leading male characters are
culturally of greater significance to the dramatist and audience in
tragedies such as *Antigone, Hippolytus, Women of Trachis,* because the
tragedies demonstrably continue or end with their agonies. The
silence of Athenian citizen women in our written evidence obviously
draws attention to the eloquence of women characters in both tragedy
and comedy, and in particular to 'their' assumption of rhetoric in acts
of decisive persuasion. That the actors and the writers were male has
rarely, in my experience, deterred women students from interest,
because the assumption that (Athenian) women could or did not argue
cannot be drawn from their lack of access to literary presentation. As
so often, the concept of 'representation' (here, obviously, of women by
men) can lead to the nullification of a modern response, which may
then bear no useful relation to a response in the original culture.
There is clearly no absolute conclusion to be drawn. Where women
characters concentrate on their reputation (e.g. Phaedra), on questions of duty in relation to the imposed male order (e.g. Antigone), or
on their affections (e.g. Medea), there is no particular reason to
suppose that every value mentioned or indicated is 'simply' a male

fiction. The prominence of dilemma in many vocal women characters may be the result of the dramatisation of familiar conflicts embedded in social structure; but there is no reason to suppose that these structural conflicts were never vocalised by women within the hearing of men. In contrast, the silence of women characters in moments of crisis and recognition, notably exploited by Sophocles (Jocasta in *Oedipus the King*, Eurydice in *Antigone*) may be identified by criticism as emblematic. That it must be so is confirmed by the submission of women to suicide or ritual death in the dramatised myths, which direct reference to domestic or social practice or documentation will only marginally help to explain.[9]

In other words, the pedagogic moral is that the relationship between theatre and society is problematic, which is hardly surprising. What an attention to social structure does reveal is that the world of the plays must be considered as a world for the audience and that dramatic myth operated, most plausibly, on two competing levels: that of recognition (or similarity), and that of disjunction (or difference). For students, accustomed to the promotion of the 'otherness' of myth, antiquity and tragedy (in particular), beginning to have some under-standing of the audience liberates the texts from their aloofness and isolation, and acts against their unmediated appropriation by modern feelings and assumptions.

Aristotle and social theory

In the beginning, I was determined to keep Aristotle at a considerable distance from the immediate tasks of teaching and reception. It was self-evident to me that nothing more arid could be advertised than a course in theatre studies which depended on a philosopher for its bearings. In addition, I was conscious that Aristotle was writing long after the major period of Greek drama and that the temptation to regard him as a 'contemporary' of the dramatists was a major obstacle to an appreciation of the conditions and resources of fifth-century performance. What, after all, was the value of theory if it almost inevitably prompted a misreading of its subject and created a dis-tortion which only far greater reading than was likely could rectify?

In the event, this preliminary caution proved pointless. I was amazed how attractive students found the *Poetics*, perhaps not in all of its detail, but in the aphorisms which seemed both more challenging and more simple than standard criticism. Admittedly, there was prob-ably included in this a degree of admiration and respect for an 'authority', felt to be culturally so close to the material that any minor adjustments supposedly required by the lapse of a century could be happily ignored. In particular, there was the remarkable appeal of the subordination of 'character' to 'action', an observation that seemed to confirm and at the same time partly explain doubts felt about the dramaturgy of tragedy. This was an intrinsic value, not one justified by prior reference to a Brechtian scheme, and it may be worth commenting here that I have found students in general more willing to trust Aristotle than Brecht, and rarely capable of relating the two. There may be many reasons for this, but I should correct any impression that it has been the result of my own priorities, predisposition, or arguments. What irritated Bertrand Russell about Aristotle, namely his philosophical ordination of suggestions that belonged more properly to an archaic common sense, clearly constitutes part of the appeal (Russell, 1946).[10] I also suspect that Aristotle's willingness to believe that plots operate best in a mechanical way, with a kind of hinge in the middle, gives a meaning to the 'middle' that divides beginning from end without demanding too much affective attention. It is of little importance, for students, whether *hamartia* is taken to mean sin or a 'mistake', or whether 'reversal' and 'recognition' are the suggestive concepts: all are hinges to an action that might otherwise obsess, with disturbance and potential upset on offer throughout. In this respect, the *Poetics* operates on readers rather like Bergson's suggestion that human beings are funny when they are seen or portrayed like machines, which palliates any worries about the quality of humour, or the vulnerability of its objects.

I have been content, in general, to let students take from Aristotle what they will, since this is preferable to letting them hear from others what 'the authority' says. It has been difficult to extend attention to Plato and to the origins and development of the concept of *mimesis,* partly because – in my experience – drama students are far less interested, and very little read, in criticism of the fine arts. Similarly, interest in the related distinctions between epic and drama is almost non-existent, because students have read very little epic, or none at all, and Brechtian use of the term does not mean it is any better understood. Many students are drawn to propositions about the origin of drama, in the hope of an explanation; but the kinds of performance to which Aristotle alludes are substantially hidden from them and they make little progress. *Dithyramb* is as difficult to spell as Nietzsche, and the latter's inspired prose as awkward to read with confidence as the later chapters of Aristotle on language. It is possible that some students gain an insight from Freud and Nietzsche: I often direct attention to a few pages in *The Interpretation of Dreams* because I think they can help with an understanding of mass reception and perhaps with Aristotelian 'fear' and 'pity'. Nietzsche's polarities are hard to grasp, possibly because 'individuation' is an apparently redundant concept in a culture which assumes the inalienability of the 'individual'. Some sense of Dionysus may come through, but it is usually applied to the figure in Euripides' *Bacchae,* while the 'community' remains as plainly obvious and thoroughly uninspiring as it does in contemporary British political propaganda. Indeed, the political definition of the community is the approach to the chorus most frequently chosen by students, in a manner which would have infuriated Nietzsche, but which serves him right for his debt to Hegel.

In writing of teaching, I am not writing of the ideal, and my practice and pedagogy have been concerned almost without exception with undergraduates, and rarely with third-year undergraduates. A secondary course on the theory of tragedy could well be operated in the final year; but I have found that in drama departments the third year tends to be a climax of practice and realisation, rather than an expansive plateau of intellectual aspiration and achievement. My compromise in these circumstances has been to draw attention to those aspects of Aristotle's theory which I can plausibly align with an interest in the theatre and society. The focus here has been on *katharsis* and its association with the emotions. It is reasonably possible to draw attention to the presence of a theory of the emotions in Aristotle's view of rhetoric, to their manipulation by the speaker and to their significance in achieving sound decisions in public debate.[11] The idea that a democracy meant that matters of life and death, personal and public security, were decided and voted on by citizens has curiously not been occluded by representative democracy. The idea of 'purification' or 'purging', whether given a ritual or a medical emphasis, is also surprisingly well assimilated, and my general suggestion that Aristotle perhaps understood drama as a healthy control on the emotional demands of a rhetorical democracy has at least the merit of prompting thought.

This proposal can be elaborated by pointing out that the role of the *ios*, or 'person similar to' ourselves, permits in Aristotle's *Rhetoric* the pity or fear that the audience may feel to register on their own self-interest.[12] This may help to explain some of the confusions Aristotle creates for himself in the *Poetics*, in his discussion of the appropriate leading figure for tragedy, which provided Freud with his starting point.[13] Aristotle lays great emphasis on the need for a person who is 'similar to' or 'like' ourselves to engage the appropriate emotional mix of fear and pity, in a resumé of the rhetorical theory, and then passes on to name Oedipus and Thyestes. 'We', apparently, are not 'outstanding for our manly achievements or sense of justice', and yet are more likely to commit error (*hamartia*) than be corrupt or cowardly. This is the profile given in this section of the *Poetics* to Oedipus or Thyestes, because the rhetorical theory demands that it has to be: an *ios* has to be found as the typical figure of tragedy, or the tenets of Aristotle's theory of reception will not hold. For Freud, this curious construction was the invitation to explain why such an explicitly 'unlikely' figure as Oedipus might be alarmingly 'like' us. In my brief commentaries I tend to point out that Oedipus acts on a stringent sense of justice to the bitter end, despite many warnings and obstructions; and that what might be described as part of his problem (the award of the queen as his wife) came about because he was also considered 'outstanding in manly achievements', as the saviour of Thebes from the sphinx. If that leaves Freud as a necessary explicator of Aristotle, then who am I to argue? But it may well be that the weak link in the theoretical chain is the requirement for the *ios* (the 'person similar to' ourselves). I doubt if sympathy is confined to such a narrow band, or if a band of that kind can effectively be shared by a mass audience. What matters initially is that the concept mattered to Aristotle, and is a crucial part of a relatively democratic and social theory of reception.

An appropriate research

It might seem apparent that the chosen subject of this chapter would occasion an accompanying programme of research. Whether or not 'research' is an appropriate term for written activity in the arts is another matter and one which rarely receives any attention. I must admit that I was for a few years almost completely confused about what I should write. My first engagements were pragmatic, turning an interest in verse towards translation and adaptation for studio performances. If you are to translate well, you should probably not just translate from one culture or era, and so I translated diversely, determining a contemporary style that I might apply with rather more confidence to ancient texts. Apart from that activity, my energy was spent on reading as widely as I could to develop the kind of understanding of the material I wished to pass to the students. I had at one stage to justify going to Greece to obtain the photographs I needed (of the city walls, of the *agora*, of angles in the theatres) to teach effectively. I recall that, because this was not a conference in Birmingham (Alabama or Britain), at which I would deliver a 'paper' to well fed colleagues, 'research' funding was denied. I went anyway and scrambled across the topographical obscurities of ancient Athens, Piraeus, Eleusis, Lavrion (the silver mines of Athens, dug by slaves) hoping for effective slides. I also had maps prepared, by a friendly colleague employed by the institution as a cartographer, who made them when he was not busy. His view was that he was paid to draw maps and might as well do them for another department. All this, as you will conclude, is historical, even quaint in its sense of vocation; but it happened in the early 1980s.

I recall that it was from about that time that written research became an absolute requirement. As it transpired, I began to work on issues to do with performance, largely, I feel, because this component of my initial assumptions about teaching theatre studies had remained partly unrealised. I suppose it is fair to say that the leading problem for me was one of acting areas, because it was one inevitably faced by my students. It did seem then, as it still seems to me now, to be impossible to develop the subject in theatre studies without a firm decision about the conditions of performance. Writing about or discussing the *theatre* of antiquity meant having a view of the theatre which did not fade in and out according to critical priorities. One might discuss an entrance or an exit, or a tableau, or the use of properties, but I had to discuss whole plays. These had to be performed somewhere and the equivocation I found in the school of writing that was dominant, and which followed the lead of Taplin, was not helpful. Fortunately, I came into contact with another con-temporary scholar who felt as I did and we decided to advocate our convictions about the performance of plays in the *orchestra* (Ewans and Ley, 1985). On my own account, I wrote a series of studies of selected tragedies by Sophocles and Euripides, which aimed to follow the indications in the texts in tracing a pattern of performance for what might be called a convention (Ley, 1988, 1991, 1994). Over the last ten years something of a consensus has gathered about per-formance in the *orchestra*, with a notable contribution coming from Rush Rehm on the performance of suppliant plays, which require a tomb or an altar in the playing space, at which refuge can be found (Rehm, 1988). Since this is a single-issue argument, affecting many plays, it may be more effective than my own concordant conclusions, which draw on a greater diversity of evidence. I sincerely hope so. Altars are not found on the doorsteps of temples, still less tombs on the doorsteps of palaces or private houses, and temples and private houses form the backdrop of the *skene* or 'scene-building' to the relevant plays.

While I mention the *skene*, it seems worthwhile reiterating that what we happily term an 'entrance' or an 'exit' in our traditional vocabulary of production is an abuse of what confronts the spectator in the ancient Greek theatre. The triumphant, ceremonial, defeated, climactic, or even incidental 'entrance' of a character into a defined scene building should not, perversely, be called an 'exit'. Laterally, if characters come into the playing space from one of the side entrances they cannot 'enter' anything, and certainly not in a chariot, but they do 'arrive', often slowly; they also 'leave', either quickly or slowly. When they 'appear' from the scene building, they do just that, and often do so suddenly: when someone conspicuously comes *out* of a building, it is stretching credibility to call that an 'entrance'. The Greek theatre is, of course, an open space and so public by definition; our theatrical vocabulary accommodates an interior space.

The chorus: aggression, apprehension and reassurance

One of the most fascinating and frustrating aspects of the ancient Greek theatre is the chorus, and perhaps the chorus as a theatrical resource is best taught or introduced through comedy. I have not written of comedy much in this chapter, because the social qualities of Aristophanes are more evident to any reader or student than those of tragedy. Even if the political jokes fall flat, and the political issues addressed by the comic chorus in the *parabasis* are obscure, comedy has the merit of seeming overtly political, intricately concerned with the contemporary public sphere. Rituals of the public assembly, the procedure of the law courts and the secrecies of festivals – although parodied and distorted – at least indicate their undoubted social referent, even if they do not declare its certain details. Almost every character has a plain social definition, although the characters with aristocratic strains are perhaps more puzzling to those who feel that a democracy abolishes all its archaic features.

The metaphorical quality of Aristophanic choruses is relatively easy to communicate. So, for example, because charcoal is prepared in the woods near Acharnai, the fierce *Acharnians* are charcoal-burners, just as the old jurors sting defendants almost indiscriminately, like so many *Wasps*. Nor is it difficult to provide a little more. The passages in Thucydides that mention that the Acharnians formed the backbone of the Athenian hoplite army, and were enraged at the burning of their land and homes by the invading Spartan army, are relatively easy to read without drama students feeling that they have been drawn, screaming or yawning, into too much military history. The fantastic aspirations of an individualistic comic figure are readily understood, since selfishness seems so 'human' in contrast, for example, to the altruistic or ideological self-devotion of characters in tragedy. Explicit violence is also a great deal easier for a modern readership than concealed, remote, or symbolic violence, even if it is not regarded as being particularly funny. That the comic chorus is often, perhaps usually, violent in feeling and intention is something that occasionally needs to be emphasised, because the individual or the pair regularly commands attention.

The thematic antagonism between leading figures and the chorus in comedy has provided me with the best approach I have found to encompass the chorus of tragedy. The spectre of the 'ideal spectator' still haunts undergraduate essays, though quite where they read of it now I find hard to detect, and introductions to formal responsion, imagery, dramatic function, and even song type (prayer or hymn are generally recognised) do not instil a dynamic understanding. In fact, how could they? This is a cultural gap of immense magnitude and no amount of emphasis on performance modes in the workshop or in production will do much to close it, because it is just as immediately found again in any audience. But if attention is turned to Aeschylus, it is not difficult to begin to speak of a tension between choral group and a leading figure or figures which works through terror, aggression, apprehension and revulsion. The alternative to this is, of course, profound loyalty or, more mildly, dutiful compliance, variations of which tend to define the chorus regularly in its less active but still dynamic forms that we find in the tragedies of Sophocles and Euripides. One can also comment here that in Euripides' *Bacchae* the chorus sings of an aggression which is finally acted out by characters, who constitute a thematic chorus out of sight, and return to become individuals (notably Agave). It is not difficult to establish a development, or a loss, if you prefer, between the *Eumenides* of Aeschylus and the chorus of Euripides' *Bacchae*.

My suspicion in relation to this whole problem depends on an acceptance of the remarkable reduplication of choral performances at Athens in the early fifth century and is one I have expressed in writing rather than teaching (Ley, 1993). It is hypothetical in the extreme. In my teaching, I might declare my suspicion that later fifth-century comedy, as we find it in Aristophanes, is traditional: namely, that it preserves without much alteration some of its original features, one of which was aggression in the chorus. I also suspect that tragedy, even in the composing hands of Aeschylus, accepts a similar aggression in its chorus, but redirects it towards the portrayal of apprehension and uncertainty, and a desire for reassurance.[14] In this respect, I would find tragedy to be the art form for a rhetorical democracy, because it requires decisions made by spoken argument, and I would reconcile that with a democratic willingness, despite all sympathy, to dispense with the dynasts from whom those decisions are required. It is a moderate thesis, with little appeal to the profound aggression of a repressed modernity; but there again few of us know what it is like to survive continually by means of our own decisions and arguments. The tensions involved, dramatically, in the resolution of apprehension can be followed in the choral songs of most tragedies. If that is only a basis for understanding, then I confess that in my teaching I am often and largely concerned with basics.

Changes of emphasis

Throughout a decade and a half I have generally found support from, and been encouraged by, publications. The social history of Greece and the ideology of Athens have received almost constant attention and the resultant propositions have at times been inspiring. One obvious example is provided by Winkler's suggestion – it should, perhaps, be a contention – that tragic choruses were performed by *ephebes*, the young men passing from adolescence to recognised maturity in Athens (Winkler, 1990). The value of this is twofold: first, it explains why chorus members on Athenian vase paintings of the era are of that age, and secondly it re-opens a critical approach that had never quite closed. In his rather wordy and dilatory study of the Greek male, the psychologist Slater had proposed that many Greek myths reveal a desperate cultural urge to remove the perceived dominance of the mother from the young Greek boy: in this respect he argued that the myth of Orestes was typical.[15]

If the performance of tragedy was a transitional rite (of passage) for young Athenian males, then this would help to explain a considerable emphasis in the dramaturgy on the instability of the lives of young men, on situations which demand that they determine their cultural maturity through decision and action, or are seen to fail. For Slater's particular thesis, the case of Hyllos in *Women of Trachis* would also be exemplary, as would that of Pentheus; for the more general view, Neoptolemos in Sophocles' *Philoctetes* provides a pattern of ethical success, whereas Haimon in Sophocles' *Antigone* offers a vision of failure, with *eros* proving more powerful over his youthful affections than duty to his father. Under Slater's scheme, Oedipus will once again be the type of trauma, since he does the opposite of what is meant to happen and does it very thoroughly indeed. Euripides will then be understood as providing remarkable variations and sub-versions of a common narrative pattern for tragedy, with trauma almost as a state of being for the young man in *Orestes*, with Alcestis confirming the value of the mother to the *oikos* at large, and with Medea actually killing offspring, rather than posing a perceived threat to them.

The ideological role of tragedy, and of the festivals of Dionysos, came into prominence with the work of Goldhill, who drew attention to the rituals and ceremonies that preceded performance, which included the parade of war orphans and of the tribute taken as a tax from Athenian 'allies' (Goldhill, 1987).[16] Goldhill concluded para-doxically that tragedy was granted the licence – or took it – to submit Athenian values to question and his ideological interests made him doubtful of the value of what he termed 'performance criticism'. The brief debate between Goldhill and Wiles on this subject was in-conclusive.[17] For my own part, I find it odd that an explicitly cultural analysis such as that advocated by Goldhill can afford to ignore what a culture took so seriously, namely performance. The nuances of space and spatial relationships are quite precisely what performance offers to the view and reconstituting them and – or, as I would prefer it, *before* – interpreting them does not seem to me the act of a critical philistine. In my own work, I find differences in scenes that others regard as comparable because they fail to see their precise differences, and I am fascinated by the use of space to express degrees of support, sympathy, or rejection. The 'third dimension', to express it crudely, is exactly what is lacking in almost any other evidence from antiquity and to disregard it seems extraordinary. We have indications of physical movement in the Greek theatre and we have hardly started to examine them. But an excessive textuality has always been, if nothing else, a sign of impatience.[18]

Ideological research has been productive, within certain limits. So Loraux (1986) has made the values of one kind of Athenian rhetoric – the funeral speech for the dead in war – into a useful scheme for understanding Athenian 'identity' and Hall (1989) has given some bearings on how drama helped the Athenians define themselves by 'inventing the barbarian'. But the tendency to regard tragedy as a ideological 'discourse' has also resulted in a reductive criticism, in which, for example, Euripides' *Women of Troy* can be seriously and conclusively described as a 'lecture on war' (Croally, 1994). I remain unconvinced that a lyrical tragedy can be a lecture of any kind, at least until I go to a lecture which has men dressed as women singing and dancing, others dressed as gods, another man dressed as a woman arriving in a chariot, and allusions to two other lectures of a related kind which immediately preceded this one. In which case, I should be more inclined to call it a play, and pay a little attention to the lost plays which came before it, and which revealed the Greeks as vindictive and prejudiced against intellectuals, and the Trojans as dynastic snobs whose tendency to violence was only matched by their catastrophic stupidity.[19] A 'poster' or a triptych on war might just capture it; but not a 'lecture'. There is some value to theatre studies and perhaps even to performance studies. I doubt very much if a lecture could reproduce the extraordinary effects of Hecuba's tending of the body of her grandson in the pathetic compass of the shield of his father and her son; but a performance might. I shall try to be patient, and work towards that end.

Notes

1. The second edition of *Dithyramb, Tragedy, and Comedy*, revised by Webster (1962), did offer translations from the Greek; but the second edition of *The Dramatic Festivals of Athens*, revised by J. Gould and D. M. Lewis (1968, and with a further supplement in 1988) did not.
2. I am not attempting to offer a full or contemporary bibliography here or elsewhere in this chapter, but am simply noting points of reference to formative works.
3. The list here could be very long: I worked largely from Kurtz and Boardman (1971) and Humphreys (1983); but Garland (1985) is also useful.
4. For these rituals see Kurtz and Boardman (1971, ch. 7, 'Funeral Rites', pp. 142–61).
5. On this general subject see Rehm (1994).
6. On the *epikleros* or orphaned 'heiress' in Greek culture see Schaps (1979, pp. 25–47).
7. For a comparable framework of understanding in relation to Renaissance England see Jardine (1983, ch. 3 '"I am Duchess of Malfi still": Wealth, Inheritance, and the Spectre of Strong Women', pp. 68–102).
8. I tend to use Paolucci and Paolucci (1975) for translated references to Hegel.
9. On this subject Burkert (1966) can be linked with Foley (1985) and

Loraux (1987). Van Hooff (1990) refers to ancient evidence from two sources, one of them medical, in connection with the suicides of young women, at p. 5 and pp. 22–3.

10. Russell (1946, p. 196) was patronising about both the metaphysics – 'Plato diluted by common sense' – and the ethics – 'Aristotle's opinions on moral questions are always such as were conventional in his day' (p. 196). Russell himself showed a particularly English common sense in excluding all poetics from his history.

11. I refer here to Aristotle's *Rhetoric*, and the opening chapters of Book II.

12. Aristotle, *Rhetoric*, Book II, 5.15.

13. Aristotle, *Poetics*, ch. 13.

14. I cannot here write 'early tragedy', because the surviving tragedies of Aeschylus date from the last 15 years of his life, from 472 BC forwards. If there is evidence about earlier tragic dramaturgy, it must be drawn from what is known of the fragments of Aeschylus, many of which have now been translated by Ewans (1996). Those suggestions I have made in writing (Ley, 1993) correspondingly refer, beyond the surviving plays, to some of the fragmentary plays and trilogies of Aeschylus.

15. Slater (1992), a study that was originally published in 1968.

16. The essay also appears, in a later version, in Winkler and Zeitlin (1990).

17. Wiles (1987), in response to Goldhill (1986), was answered by Goldhill (1989).

18. The existence of a substantial tradition of critical appreciation of the practice of the Elizabethan theatres and companies, running from Bradbrook (1935) to Dessen (1984), and continuing, seems to be largely ignored by classicists.

19. For the details of this trilogy see Scodel (1980) and Coles (1974).

Works cited

Bradbrook, M. (1935) *Themes and Conventions of Elizabethan Tragedy*. Cambridge University Press, Cambridge.

Burkert, W. (1966) 'Greek Tragedy and Sacrificial Ritual'. *Greek, Roman, and Byzantine Studies*, vol. 7, pp. 87–121.

Coles, R. A. (1974) *A New Oxyrhynchus Papyrus: The Hypothesis of Euripides' Alexandros*. Institute of Classical Studies, London.

Croally, N. T. (1994) *Euripidean Polemic: The Trojan Women and the Function of Tragedy*. Cambridge University Press, Cambridge.

Dessen, A. C. (1984) *Elizabethan Stage Conventions and Modern Interpreters*. Cambridge University Press, Cambridge.

Ewans, M. (1996) *Aeschylus: Suppliants and Other Dramas*. J. M. Dent, London.

Ewans, M. and Ley, G. K. H. (1985) 'The Orchestra as Acting Area in Greek Tragedy'. *Ramus*, vol. 14, pp. 75–84.

Foley, H. P. (1985) *Ritual Irony: Poetry and Sacrifice in Euripides.* Cornell University Press, Ithaca.

Garland, R. (1985) *The Greek Way of Death.* Duckworth, London.

Goldhill, S. (1986) *Reading Greek Tragedy.* Cambridge University Press, Cambridge.

Goldhill, S. (1987) 'The Great Dionysia and Civic Ideology'. *Journal of Hellenic Studies*, vol. 107, pp. 58–76.

Goldhill, S. (1989) 'Reading Performance Criticism'. *Greece and Rome*, vol. 36, pp. 172–82.

Hall, E. (1989) *Inventing the Barbarian: Greek Self-definition Through Tragedy.* Clarendon Press, Oxford.

Halleran, M. (1985) *Stagecraft in Euripides.* Croom Helm, Beckenham.

Hourmouziades, N. C. (1965) *Production and Imagination in Euripides.* Greek Society for Humanistic Studies, Athens.

Humphreys, S. C. (1983) *The Family, Women and Death.* Routledge and Kegan Paul, London.

Jardine, L. (1983) *Still Harping on Daughters: Women and Drama in the Age of Shakespeare.* Harvester Press, Brighton.

Kitto, H. D. F. (1939) *Greek Tragedy: A Literary Study.* Methuen, London.

Kitto, H. D. F. (1956) *Form and Meaning in Drama.* Methuen, London.

Kurtz, D. C. and Boardman, J. (1971) *Greek Burial Customs.* Thames and Hudson, London.

Lacey, W. K. (1968) *The Family in Classical Greece.* Thames and Hudson, London.

Lefkowitz, M. R. and Fant, M. B. (eds) (1981) *Women's Life in Greece and Rome.* Duckworth, London (2nd edn, 1992).

Ley, G. K. H. (1988) 'A Scenic Plot of Sophocles's *Ajax* and *Philoctetes*'. *Eranos*, vol. 86, pp. 85–115.

Ley, G. K. H. (1991) 'Scenic Notes on Euripides's *Helen*'. *Eranos*, vol. 89, pp. 25–34.

Ley, G. K. H. (1993) 'Monody, Choral Song, and Athenian Festival Performance'. *Maia*, vol. 45, pp. 105–24.

Ley, G. K. H. (1994) 'Performance Studies and Greek Tragedy'. *Eranos*, vol. 92, pp. 29–45.

Loraux, N. (1986) *The Invention of Athens*, trans. A. Sheridan. Harvard University Press, Cambridge, Mass.

Loraux, N. (1987) *Tragic Ways of Killing a Woman*, trans. P. Forster. Harvard University Press, Cambridge, Mass.

Paolucci, A. and Paolucci, H. (eds) (1975) *Hegel on Tragedy.* Harper and Row, New York.

Pickard-Cambridge, A. W. (1927) *Dithyramb, Tragedy, and Comedy*, 2nd edn, revised by B. L. Webster. Clarendon Press, Oxford (1962).

Pickard-Cambridge, A. W. (1953) *The Dramatic Festivals of Athens*, 2nd edn, revised by J. Gould and D. M. Lewis. Clarendon Press, Oxford (1968).

Pomeroy, S. B. (1976) *Goddesses, Whores, Wives and Slaves: Women in Classical Antiquity.* Schocken Books, New York.

Rehm, R. (1988) 'The Staging of Suppliant Plays'. *Greek, Roman, and Byzantine Studies*, vol. 29, pp. 263–307.

Rehm, R. (1994) *Marriage to Death: The Conflation of Wedding and Funeral Rituals in Greek Tragedy.* Princeton University Press, Princeton.

Russell, B. (1946) *A History of Western Philosophy.* George Allen and Unwin, London.

Schaps, D. M. (1979) *The Economic Rights of Women in Ancient Greece.* Edinburgh University Press, Edinburgh.

Scodel, R. (1980) *The Trojan Trilogy of Euripides.* Vandenhoeck and Ruprecht, Göttingen.

Slater, P. (1992) *The Glory of Hera.* Princeton University Press, Princeton.

Taplin, O. (1977) *The Stagecraft of Aeschylus.* Clarendon Press, Oxford.

Taplin, O. (1978) *Greek Tragedy in Action.* Methuen, London.

Van Hooff, A. J. L. (1990) *From Euthanasia to Suicide: Self-killing in Classical Antiquity.* Routledge, London.

Wiles, D. (1987) 'Reading Greek Performance'. *Greece and Rome*, vol. 34, pp. 136–51.

Winkler, J. J. (1990) 'The Ephebes' Song: *Tragoidia* and *Polis*', in J. J. Winkler and F. I. Zeitlin (eds), *Nothing to Do with Dionysos? Athenian Drama in Its Social Context.* Princeton University Press, Princeton, pp. 20–62.

Winkler, J. J. and Zeitlin, F. I. (eds) (1990) *Nothing to Do with Dionysos? Athenian Drama in Its Social Context.* Princeton University Press, Princeton.

6

Adaptation and
the Drama Student

James MacDonald

In our postmodernist culture, where narrative structures are fragmented, theatre substitutes for 'the marketplace' and its various
contributors become subsumed in the whole. In this context, the
author is not so much 'dead' (Barthes, 1977) as indivisible from the
totality, her/his personal strategy – the text – becoming one strand,
merely, among many.

At the same time, the nature of theatre has altered from being
primarily an interpretation of a distillation of experience to being a
further manifestation of it. Curtailing its mimetic function, it begins,
instead, to represent *itself* as an experiential 'entity', offering engagement on the basis of familiarity, attractiveness, even bipartisan
dialogue with the audience.

In this context, 'adaptation' may be taken to be the process by
which individuals come together to interact. Individuals 'adapt'
themselves into an audience; they 'adapt' themselves into performers.
'Adaptation' may signify codes of behaviour, but it does not replace
personal interaction; it merely provides a convenient channel for that
interaction. Every member of an audience will bring a different
meaning to the event, will extract a different meaning from it, and
each is deemed 'valid', so long as the code of collective behaviour –
'the adaptation' – is observed. We come together as an audience or as
performers. Once we have observed the rules of this 'adaptation', we
are free to participate as we wish, through our understanding. No

restrictions of meaning have been imposed. An individual is at liberty to understand for her/himself. No single meaning is omnipresent to police that understanding; it is based almost entirely on personality and on personal understanding. Continued presence at the event denotes personal involvement and individual contribution. Collective enjoyment denotes the overall success of the 'adaptation'.

The postmodern 'adaptation' of meaning may place theatre in the foreground of experience, but it does not distinguish it qualitatively from other forms of communication. All those who enter a theatre building as performers or audience participate in the creation of theatre experientially. The French for 'attend' (*assister à*) may originally have meant no more than 'take a seat', but, as 'assister' has been assimilated into English, it aptly illustrates the postmodern theatrical experience. Everyone 'adapting themselves' to the theatrical mode contributes to its existence. We all *assist* in that experience. Through our enjoyment, we may all take personal pride in its factual presence. Our creative 'adaptation' has given life to something that was not there before and will not exist again once we have ceased to participate. Fragmentation has rendered meaning transitory but its significance was undeniable. We draw inspiration from it in our continued desire to adapt ourselves into theatrical mode – desire replacing moral function in Friedrich Nietzsche's anticipation of postmodern thinking (Nietzsche, 1971, p. 36). Theatre continues to *mean something* to us, however subjective that meaning may be.

The author who formally adapts a piece of written work for dissemination among a group of drama students will engage with such notions of general adaptation continually as s/he seeks to lend that contribution to the whole. Such an author will be familiar with the various shifts from author-led, text-based theatre to the present notion of theatre as a predominantly interactive medium. If an author has worked with a group in workshop, s/he will know already that his/her contribution is an adaptation, that the text that emerges is merely a formal record of the event. Perhaps it is going too far yet to call the author a play's amanuensis. But, increasingly, the term 'playwright' is seen as a mere remnant of a former age. To the extent that 'author' has greatest significance in the bookshop or library (far removed from the theatre building and even further from the theatrical event), authorial significance to theatre may cease to be even a legacy. The script exists, individuals have set down its words on paper, but, in a postmodern sense, its relation to the event may be little closer than that of a fairly resonant souvenir. This is particularly true of adaptations or of translations, which in many cases have been commissioned to *assist* the specific event. Very rarely do producers and directors look for translations 'off the peg', as it were. They will either employ a new author to conform to their own notions or they will further adapt an existing text. Since most printed texts are protected by copyright from liberal alteration, new translations for production tend to be commissioned. Their subsequent publication (if it happens) stands as a written testament of the production. The recent founding of Absolute Classics (by Nick Hern Publishers), creating its list from successful new revivals, certifies this practice. But so does the currency of several new versions of Chekhov, for example. The contemporary adapter has been there to assist the recent revival, which has 're-invented' the Chekhov text.

Pedagogically, then, an adaptation serves the drama students' early experience of theatre in several ways. It is there as a link between interpretative creativity and initiative creativity, to facilitate the progression from informal improvisation to the often daunting first acquaintance with text. In some instances, for students, the adaptation is precisely the written inscription of group improvisation. If its source is a text in another literary form, then the adaptation will inscribe the most successful portions of that improvisation, and the group will seek to refer to it as a means of retaining for themselves what was most meaningful. They will use the text as a resource and, in so using it, will come to rely on it and to trust what it says. The progression from this to existing dramatic text is clear and although the transition may still daunt, its mystification may be removed. The student group will have engaged in its own form of adaptation already, once they have sought to express a concept in theatrical form. The person who expresses this work in written form is helping to make the resource more accessible. If students create and present a 20-minute piece of theatre as the practical part of their final examination, they will have seen for themselves the correlation between actor/idea/director/author. They will have made their own adaptations. Work with the teachers along the way has been designed to enhance an understanding of the process.

My own experience as an author employed to enable the process of adaptation has engaged with a variety of forms of adaptation. With the sanction of the project leader, I have scripted improvisations into dramatic scenes, augmented an existing text with additional scenes based on a group's need for adequate parts, rendered a new translation according to a particular group's dynamics and adapted a classic novel as a production text, once again according to the needs and dynamics of a specific group. These projects constitute my working knowledge of adaptation as a pedagogical tool, and each project has been undertaken to provide a range of challenges for the student.

Back to basics

The first example is from a five-week project with drama students at the beginning of their second year of an honours degree course. The project was designed to prepare them for formal production work and they needed to approach text in as relaxed a manner as possible.

Gabriel García Márquez's *One Hundred Years of Solitude* was chosen as the project text. Purportedly a family saga spanning seven generations of internecine conflict, its narrative structure is kaleidoscopic rather than linear. Events tumble after one another, often beyond immediate comprehension. As a picture of Central American life, however, it has the chiaroscuro quality of the daguerreotype which features in the opening chapters. Márquez makes explicit reference to the dawn of creation and to the primitive lifestyles of Third and Fourth World cultures. The family of gypsies arrives at the village of Macondo 'to discover and to invest the world'. In the process, of course, they will discover and will invent, perforce, the seeds of their own destruction: material greed, sibling rivalry, sexual jealousy. But they are destined to survive, in legend and in reality, and the story of that survival has the ingenuous quality of creation itself.

Its appeal to drama students at this stage in their course was palpable. Like the characters, they too were embarked on a journey of discovery and of invention. The loose structure invited an improvisational approach initially and in the opening sessions they were assigned the task of relocating the protean literary imagery in appropriate dramatic form. As the characters in the novel discover the new world, so the students became empowered by their discoveries of the text. Indeed, they sought to make their dramatic discoveries by looking in detail at the discovery of objects in the novel. These they found inherently theatrical, as the novel's opening makes clear:

> Many years later, as he faced the firing squad, Colonel Aureliano Buendia was to remember that distant afternoon when his father took him to discover ice. (Márquez, 1967, p. 9)

The main problem at this early stage was to find an effective way of linking these images into a coherent narrative. Like Thomas Pynchon's, Márquez's method is resistant to traditional storytelling and the delineation of character (Bigsby, 1986, pp. 95–107). In groups of two and three, the students worked with caution on the images, initially using the family's arrival in Macondo as their narrative. In effect, the new arrivals carry human experience from the creation of the world to the development of 'civilisation'. One character, Melquiades, is a scientist who works in rapid succession on a series of commonplace implements which bring about major advances in science and medicine, while his protégé, José Arcadio Buendia, seeks to emulate his mentor in astrological research. To attempt to simulate even one of these achievements, the students risked being caught up in a degree of literalism that was the antithesis of the kind of freewheeling truth that the novel aims to capture. In response to this dilemma, the project leader introduced a theoretical text which corresponded to the core text and which would serve to underpin the whole project. This was Jerzy Grotowski's *Towards a Poor Theatre* (1969).

Grotowski's method was central to the aims of the project and these, in turn, serve an understanding of this example of adaptation. A key element to this part of the technique is simplicity. As Grotowski summed up in a radio broadcast in 1979:

> Let us say that there exist actions, led by a group of prepared people, who present a certain situation to people from the outside. The simplest such situation may for example be whatever is obvious in a given moment: do not dance, unless that really takes you, don't pretend what you don't feel. In this case we have a situation in which one is not looking for how to play, but only for how not to play. (Quoted in Kumiega, 1987, p. 235)

The instruction 'not to play' was not a cryptic shorthand for method acting. It was intended to be taken quite literally, to remind the students that this was a 'project showing' and not a production, and to advise them that the best way to present the material was without a sense that an audience was present and therefore that they were not, in a formal sense, acting. Grotowski had aimed these words at adolescents and the students working on Márquez were at a similar stage in their development.

The instruction was a watershed, freeing the students of the necessity to do more than what was required of them initially. That is to say, provided they focused clearly on a given image, they could forego the necessity of making it mean something else. The student working on José Arcadio's experiments, for example, could confine her/his attention to one experiment, approaching it very much as a demonstration rather than as a piece of performance. Providing s/he was clear enough, the suspension of disbelief would compensate for the fact that s/he was not using actual instruments.

My work of 'adaptation', duly, was to re-introduce elements of the novel which would follow the students' work on image. Other students sought to locate characteristic attitudes for other characters in the novel, also concentrating on physical actions they could effectively 'demonstrate'. José Arcadio's long-suffering wife, for example, might be represented in the act of doing laundry and the student who simulated this activity would try to locate the simplest gestures for conveying this. Once she had succeeded in this, it was but a short step to adding an accompanying phrase from the novel which, orchestrating the action, would also sum up their whole marital relationship.

Appropriate words and actions were sought for the range of characters and events, and the students were given the freedom to choose. The job of adaptation, then, became one of ordering the images into a pattern that would convey to an audience what the students had discovered about the novel. One obvious device came directly from the early pages in the novel, when the village of Macondo presents itself to the world at a carnival. This is, in fact, the central event of the opening section and the students adapted it to present their crucial discoveries about the material. This carnival or trade fair became the first part of the eventual project showing, presented with thrust staging as a theatrical happening. Dramatic 'scenes' assumed the characteristics of experiments, as the physical activities of the novel became demonstrations of performing technique, the best of them as absorbing as were the scientific demonstrations in the novel, especially since they originated from the common source of native discovery.

It was essential that my adaptation work should follow the students' lead. With the 'dramatisation' of the opening section, they came to feel that the novel had become their own and my intervention with scripted text was not to undermine this sense in any way. My presence throughout the project enabled me to function as a resource. In those opening sessions, I had made myself available to students as an audience for their improvisations. When they moved on to subsequent sections of the novel, which deal with more concrete events, they looked on me as a member of the group and my script work followed their improvisations as far as possible.

As it happened, the most scripted part of the project was the second section, which, in the novel, covers a hundred pages of warfare. The tone is altogether different from the celebratory tone of the opening section and a certain loss of momentum would have ensued had the students been charged with the responsibility of presenting war on their own. They were actually grateful at this point to work from a script and, as I had tried to base my script as much on their improvisations as on the text itself, the students were already familiar with the material I gave them. This, I imagined, was similar to the process Caryl Churchill had gone through with Joint Stock, Monstrous Regiment and other companies for whom she wrote (Churchill, 1986). It seemed a logical way for a writer to work with a group in a context which stressed collective participation.

Effectively, the project showing shadowed the form of a four-movement piece of music – the scripted sections corresponding to the *adagio* and *coda*. The other improvised section was a choral piece following the war and involving the women who stay behind. This was as much the students' commentary on their characters as it was a summation of what happens to the women in the novel. Inasmuch as it was the third section in the showing, it benefited both from the freedom of the first section in its musical form and from the scripted section in its focus on narrative events. The breakthrough, however, had been achieved in the vital first section, which established the direction of the project and governed the response of the audience to the showing overall. It enabled the students to trust their abilities and, with that trust, to make the creative links between personal involvement and general communication.

Process over product

My work on Lorca's *Blood Wedding* was, in an important way, a development of the Márquez project, as it would have been for the group had they been the ones who had mounted the production. It was a full production rather than a project showing and this particular group was working from the start with a text. The text, it is true, was prepared specifically for them and they were at a similar stage of development to the Márquez group. They were being directed, too, by the project leader of *One Hundred Years of Solitude*. But the differences were more illuminating than the similarities, which underpins a significant point about student drama. Each group is distinct, with its own dynamics, its own problems, its own rate of development. In recognising this distinctiveness, a teacher soon becomes acutely aware that his/her role must first be in direct response to that distinctiveness. While the aim always is to minimise problems within the group, it would be wrong to identify distinctiveness, *per se*, as a problem to be eradicated. Often, a group's own awareness of its distinctiveness is the single most important element in the success of its working together.

The group who worked on *Blood Wedding* were unfamiliar with the demands of public performance, both as individuals and together. They were shy, though generous, and they were unsure of their abilities. In these circumstances, it seemed entirely appropriate that the director should employ similar techniques to the ones he employed with the Márquez group. Indeed, I believe he chose the Lorca play on similar grounds to those on which he chose the novel for the other group. Novel and play share a similar Hispanic origin, a similar emphasis on an agrarian background and much the same emphasis on elemental passions. Importantly, the material and group dynamics would seem to benefit from Grotowski's method of concentrating on basic physical action. The play is a peasant tragedy, involving jealousies in a close-knit, self-contained community. Actions are direct, motivation clear, almost classic, involving betrayal, revenge and bereavement. There seemed little need to locate the action in complex theories of motivation.

It is important, as well, to bear in mind the function of production work in this learning context. While the standard may approximate professional theatre, expectations are inevitably lower and the notion of achievement is measured against pedagogical rather than professional criteria. The students are not employed, and texts are chosen in order to challenge groups in a manner appropriate to their development, both as individuals and collectively.

These factors need to be borne in mind in relation to my work on *Blood Wedding*, because the project was illustrative of key issues in student work and the script engaged with these issues integrally. More than with a professional production, where a script would conform to the director's notion of a play, the script for this production of *Blood Wedding* aimed to take full account of the group's needs in relation to their development within the course framework. For this reason, the process of the production was far more important than the product that resulted. I say this not in *apologia* for my script, but because the project would have to be deemed a failure if viewed as a finished production whereas, as a pedagogical model, it revealed a considerable amount about student work in drama. The project, in this sense, successfully raised serious issues and the script was an integral part of the process.

The size of the group fairly matched the size of the cast, with a reasonable distribution of male and female parts. In one instance, I was asked to augment a speech towards the end of the play in order to give the student an adequate challenge. This was her first big moment before any audience and the speech, involving an expression of native grief, was designed to offer her a real challenge within limited parameters. The larger roles were designed to challenge the other students similarly, according to their development (in more cases, this meant their level of personal confidence). Grotowski's techniques were applicable here, too. Lorca's language, in any translation, is direct, even in his use of verse. It is also physical, referring to primary emotions and to decisive physical action. The language, as Raymond Williams says, does not so much embody the action as it *is* the action (Williams, 1973, p. 186). This would make it an ideal text for students, fresh from working on movement in their first year, who were being set the task of communicating straightforward actions as clearly and as cleanly as possible.

My task, in revising a literary translation for a specific production, was to make the language even more a coordinate of the action. Thus, the opening of the play read:

BRIDEGROOM: I'm off again, Mother.
MOTHER: Off? Where?
BRIDEGROOM: Vineyard.
MOTHER: Wait.
BRIDEGROOM: What for?
MOTHER: Have some food first.

The practice of providing actors with generous space round the dialogue was extended beyond professional courtesy. In this case, it was intended to complement their movements, almost as directly as if the words were verbal captions. Everything could be brought to the surface directly, immediately discovering intention and establishing the actors' relationship with their physical surroundings. If not precisely Brechtian in dramaturgy, it contained the element of clarity that would allow the actors to concentrate on physical action. Lorca's text invites it, inasmuch as the scenes are often structured round specific physical actions with functional props – the kneading of bread, mending of clothes, brushing of hair. These are tasks that involve repetitive movement, ideal for an actor to focus on and to perfect.

My task, again, was to simplify the dialogue so that it would accompany the physical action. So when the servant was brushing the bride's hair, the speech she uttered would accompany the movement she made.

SERVANT: I can't get this wave to move.
BRIDE: Persevere.
SERVANT: You're so lucky to put your arms round a man, to feel his weight. And then when you wake in the morning, there he is, next to you, his breath like a feather.
BRIDE: Ouch! Don't yank so.

The student could time her movements to the rhythm of her speech without needing to worry that her voice was conveying sufficient emotion. Provided she had developed the action, after Grotowski's technique, the words would orchestrate it.

To give the students the maximum degree of confidence, as well, the director took pains to work with each individually before the formal rehearsals, and I would often revise scenes based on the progress the students were making. This was crucially true of the wedding scene, the most problematic for us all. To begin with, the scene is inordinately short, as written. It is no more than ten pages long and yet it incorporates the vital transition from festival to incipient tragedy. The emotional action is largely unscripted, but it has to be performed, or at least implied. An eating scene was devised, but this provided little scope for the build-up of tension, because that occurs off-stage, with the disappearance of the bride and the lover. A ballet of the play, current at the time of our production, dealt better than we did with the scene, because dance (festivity) is its primary movement. Our students had only reached the stage where they could perform honest actions. To introduce the element of dance would have been wholly gratuitous.

A second, related difficulty had to do with the decision to mount the production in black and white. We were working in an unfamiliar space and we had no practical experience of its dimensions. Faced with such uncertainty, the director decided to revert to neutral white and placed the action against a white cyclorama to help focus the audience's attention. It became a matter of course to costume the actors in black, but this seemed associationally to restrict their ability to move spontaneously. In the event, the production's stark appearance all but intimidated the group. The dialogue, instead of facilitating movement, more often left frightened actors with nowhere to hide. They tended to deliver the lines in desultory fashion, often more anxious to get off in panic than to say the lines naturally.

Play translation is a relatively humble form of playwriting. Little is ever made of it, in publication or in production. In production, indeed, it is more commonly thought of as a literal rendering of the foreign original or as a transcription of the director's concept of the play. This may be why a large number of productions employ newly commissioned translations, albeit by notable dramatists in their own right. I was pleased that my work on *Blood Wedding* so nearly matched what the director was trying to achieve with the students, even though the result was less than a satisfying evening's viewing. For me, as an adapter of another man's language, it raised vital issues about the cultural transactions involved in translation.

The Shakespearean model

Vassa Zheleznova, Maxim Gorky's final play, exists in two versions, the first, written in 1910, a second, from 1936. A Russian film version, from 1984–5, extends the picture of bourgeois decadence by making Vassa's brother bisexual. A radio version, broadcast by the BBC in 1987, differs again from translations of the two stage versions and from the film. As such, I am more diffident now than I was when asked to 'augment' the text for production, in February 1986. I was reluctant to set myself up in competition with the author of *The Lower Depths* and might not have done so had the 'contract' been less determinate. The director said my additional scenes would need to be ready for the first day of rehearsal, at the beginning of January. I decided to undertake the project as an act of homage to both Gorky and Lillian Hellman, whose work it resembles and who has a lasting influence on my own plays. There are distinct similarities, in fact, between *Vassa* and Hellman's *The Little Foxes*. Each play is piloted by a strong woman who engineers her husband's death in order to gain control of a lucrative business. Zheleznov, it is true, is a paedophile on the point of exposure, while Hellman's Horace is thoroughly benign. But the focus in both plays is the destructively greedy character of the bourgeoisie. ('Zhelezn' in Russian means iron.) The plays rely on capitalist history.

This latter quality made *Vassa* attractive for students to do and it was central to the challenges I set them. The task, essentially, was Shakespearean (Thomson, 1984, pp. 56–83) – to rework an existing text to accommodate the needs of the particular company. Allowing for one woman playing two maids, the play has substantial parts for six women. There is an equal number of men's roles, but they are thinly written. Only Prokhor, the protagonist's brother, is given a substantial part, but his mutation in the film indicates the potential for development even here. The others (Zheleznov and various servants and

employees) have a greater presence off-stag
be the key to expanding them for the gr
improvisation, except that the scenes were to t
outside the immediate company, and I was c
possible to avoid extraneous 'character-building'.
In the event, the result turned into something r
of Stanislavsky and Brecht (not forgetting the elem
perceived earlier). The mode remained realistic, but .   ыi went
beyond the strictly personal to the social and political.   ɪe characters
were to be defined in terms of their social functions and behaviour
would be explained (counter Stanislavsky) mainly in terms of its
political consequences. These exist in the text as it is. Zheleznov's
debauchery is explained in terms of his social standing and ne'er-do-
well lethargy. Vassa's rivalry with her daughter-in-law for custody of
her grandson is accounted for by the mother's insecure status as a
Jewess and a revolutionary; no deeper reasons obtain. In giving the
male students more to do, I was giving the whole play a more resonant
social context, which would be useful, in any case, to British students
of a foreign and historical play. This, I hoped, would be a variation on
Brechtian drama; it might even qualify as 'socialist realism', whose
charter Gorky originally signed (MacNeal, 1988, p. 154).

It was not difficult to locate the social dimensions in Krotkikh, the
first character I chose to expand. He appears almost immediately as
Vassa's foreman, receiving her orders. After he leaves, she tells her
secretary, Anna, 'Socialism to him is what God is to Prokhor'. Thus,
he is 'notionally' a socialist. It seemed natural to confirm or to
challenge this assumption in a scene between Anna and Krotkikh and
so, in our newly augmented version, she challenges him straight out
about his commitment to better pay and conditions for the men. He
defends himself but flirts with her, giving his character the rounded
appearance of a double standard. 'Oh, you'll increase trade,' Anna
says, 'That I believe. But as for the workers receiving the benefit.' To
determine Krotkikh's character too clearly, perhaps by writing in a
confrontation with Vassa, would affect the outcome of Gorky's play.
What was entirely possible was the delineation of character through
interaction. In this way, too, the complex network of class divisions, in
a framework of acute social tensions, would be made available to the
students.

Melnikov, the next man to face Vassa, is even more ambiguous. He
is a tenant, also receiving her orders, but he is nonetheless of a
different stamp from Krotkikh. To begin with, he has to gainsay her:
she asks him to use his influence to bribe the jury in the impending case

...t her husband. This makes him more than a messenger – and much more could be examined in scenes with the other male characters. There was an initial ambiguity in the fact that Krotkikh and Melnikov do not behave strictly according to type. As a mere employee, Krotkikh might be expected to be subservient to Vassa. Yet he refuses to humble himself after the dressing down. His response to being dismissed is to say, rather proudly, 'We finished up well, you know. Quite a tidy profit.' Melnikov, who is higher in the social scale, begins to panic when Vassa entreats him 'to offer them more money'. There was room here for an examination of the difference in demeanour. Krotkikh, although an overseer, is still of the *muzhiki* or underling class. Melnikov, as a district court official and with a son in the military, is of the *muzhi* or superior class (Pipes, 1977, pp. 87–8). If they behave against type, the anomaly suggests either a shift in the social balance or a covert weakness in Krotkikh's character. Both possibilities would give the students ample room for investigation. With this in mind, I provided the following socially searching scene between Krotkikh and Melnikov, with Melnikov's son Yevgeny as a catalyst:

MELNIKOV: Yevgeny. Please come home with me.

YEVGENY: I'm due at the barracks in half an hour.

MELNIKOV: There's something I've got to ask you....

Enter KROTKIKH

KROTKIKH: It's very busy today for 11.00 in the morning. You'd think it was Sunday, wouldn't you? (*To Yevgeny.*) Do you sit at Nata's feet reciting your verses? You're out of luck, my boy. That's no way to woo her. She's more of a liking for Pyatyorkin's guitar. He can't have been much of a soldier, but I doubt he reneged on his gambling debts.

YEVGENY: I don't know what you're talking about.

MELNIKOV: Don't think we don't know what *your* game is.

KROTKIKH: I only repeat what you'll know for yourself in due time. They say he's the prize cheat.

MELNIKOV: That's slander.

KROTKIKH: Then have him deny it to you.

MELNIKOV: What is the truth, Yevgeny? Did you offend an officer's son?

YEVGENY: I don't want to be a soldier. That's the truth.

KROTKIKH laughs.

MELNIKOV: Oh, Yevgeny. What will we do? How bad is it? You'd best tell me everything.

YEVGENY: Oh, you bore me, Father. I really don't care what I do, so long as I don't end up the town's boot-black. (*Turns to leave.*)

MELNIKOV: Son.

KROTKIKH (*calling after him*): Your father dignifies every room he enters. An honourable son would realise that.

MELNIKOV: He lacks a mother's care.

KROTKIKH (*derisively*): Is that what it is?

With this scene, I hoped to offer the students the chance to work on dramatic status within the context of historical research. The place of the military and of the civil service in Russian society is both crucial and well documented, as is Krotkikh's rise to power with the growing politicisation of the *muzhiki*. The play is set during the watershed year 1905–6, at the time of the First Revolution. I wanted this to explain Krotkikh's behaviour as much as anything does; for, clearly, he is party to political knowledge more significant than Yevgeny's misdemeanour.

The dénouement of this tension between Krotkikh and Melnikov would be presented in Act II, with the appearance of Rachel, Vassa's daughter-in-law, providing the trigger. Vassa accommodates it with her references to a disturbance in the hallway and by alluding to Melnikov's membership of the League of Russian People, a nationalist group which organised programs (Gorky, 1979, p. 861). It was even possible to resume the action from where it is left in Act I:

MELNIKOV and KROTKIKH appear.

KROTKIKH: You're wasting your time shaking that rug out of my window. What should it matter how bad a socialist I am? Vassa Borisnova hardly complains – we're growing rich together. If I am, as you claim, a Slavophile renegade....

MELNIKOV: You mistake me.

KROTKIKH: ... wouldn't that make us closer allies? We're both monarchists.

MELNIKOV: But why spread these rumours about my son...? He failed to get his commission.

KROTKIKH: But I'm truly sorry. Life seems to have dealt you some severely low blows.... Foreigners look at us and see progress, cohesion, national pride. They've no idea of cracks beneath the tidy surface.

MELNIKOV: Poor Zheleznov.

KROTKIKH: Among the living, too. In this house even.

MELNIKOV: Something about Vassa Borinova?
KROTKIKH: As if I would. But her daughter-in-law is a Jewess.
MELNIKOV: You're mistaken, surely.
KROTKIKH: Ah, who's to say whose blood is tainted.
MELNIKOV: My ancestors drove out the Tartars.
KROTKIKH: So did mine!

This almost comic resumption of status-playing develops the play's main crisis while further explaining the men. What I hoped was that as much of the nation's turmoil as possible would be reflected in this domestic crisis. Moments later, then, Prokhor returns drunk from a *duma* meeting and begins to pick a fight with Melnikov. It comes to nothing, principally because Vassa dies in Act III, on the point of informing on Rachel. But this additional scene leaves an attentive audience with the clear impression that Melnikov still could inform on Rachel if pushed. If anything, he is a right-wing radical, a zealot, while Krotkikh, one feels, would not hesitate to proclaim his socialist credentials, if pushed.

The dynamic that developed between these two was the main subplot in these additional scenes. Students admitted that the political context of their relationship was important. In this respect, my work on the script attempted to address the wide pedagogical issue of the extent to which higher education courses can be inter-disciplinary. Clearly, the production project was intended to encourage work on the text in a wider framework than that defined as drama. My work was a conscious nod in recognition of the fact that contemporary study of the arts needs to be inter-cultural, indeed multi-cultural, which makes it, in practice, another form of adaptation.

Commenting on the text

Adapting *A Tale of Two Cities* is the most ambitious project I have undertaken with drama students. The text, also, comes closest to being a 'response' to an original piece. Intended to coincide with the bicentennial of the French Revolution, the production, in February 1989, involved a large group of varying ages and abilities; it was nearly double the size of the group who did *Vassa*. Again, I was asked to augment parts, this time mainly for the women. Again, the students would be required to investigate the political context of the material. The fresh challenge was to work from a text created entirely for this occasion. The students would be involved in the process. The director, who had also directed our *Vassa*, gave me a specific brief that included the directives to tell the story from the French point of view as far as possible, to reduce the romantic intrigue as far as possible and to give each of the suggested 12 scenes a Brechtian *Gestus* (Needle and Thomson, 1981, pp. 124–5), if we could decide between us what Brecht meant by *Gestus.*

In the writing, I understood him to mean each scene having at its core a social issue, as in the discrete episodes that make up *Mother Courage and Her Children.* I did not know that I could replicate anything similar, for I am more naturally drawn to character delineation, albeit with political reference points. But I tried, in the early scenes at least, to frame each scene round a social issue with a visible image. For instance, in a scene in the Bastille where Lucie Manette meets her father, the emphasis given to his shoe-mending is a conscious attempt at *Gestus.* He does not acknowledge her as his daughter, denies by word and by deed that he has ever been a doctor and sets about mending the shoe with surgical focus and diligence – the point being that his role in life now is of greater social moment than are either his family history or his role as a doctor. (Although casting was outside my brief, the cross-gender casting of Dr Manette made it easier for the actor to comment on her role, in Brechtian fashion, and particularly in this early scene.)

Elsewhere I sought to replace the emphasis by transposing Dickens' mysterious dénouement (the secret of the birth of Darnay/Evremond) to the beginning as a prologue, and then proceeding with events leading up to the fall of the Bastille, before shifting to England. I also sought to contextualise the English scenes by placing them in the midst of the Gordon riots. So Darnay's arrest off the boat is orchestrated by rioters, on the one hand, and by a crowd who have assembled to hear Mary Wollestonecraft speak. She would have been active at the time Dickens is writing about; she *was* in Paris in 1792, and it seemed advantageous to include her, among other historical figures, in our politically aware response to Dickens.

Cross-casting commentary inspired the idea of having two actors in the role of Lucie. Both were women, but one would comment on the other by representing her unconscious self. If Dickens created the character with a marked degree of Victorian high-mindedness, it seemed legitimate to present the Victorian underbelly through her double. Lucie II appears for the first time during Lucie's testimony at the Old Bailey. As Lucie I tries her utmost to speak up for Darnay, Lucie II catches sight of Sydney Carton and is immediately attracted to him. Halting testimony in the one becomes sexual excitement in the other. And, with each appearance of Carton, Lucie II emerges in a frenzy. There is even the suggestion that he is syphilitic and that she may be too, having succumbed to his allure. Finally, when Carton takes Darnay's place in the Bastille, Lucie II is seen persuading him with her sexuality. The development of the second Lucie was intended as a commentary on Dickens' escapist use of the love intrigue, challenging the Victorian values underpinning the original narrative.

There was similar counter-pointing in the introduction of historical figures and the redefinition of existing characters. Madame de Stael is shown attempting to secure funds for her flight from the chaos of the Paris streets. As the daughter of the discredited parliamentarian Necker, her actual role in revolutionary France was decidedly pre-carious. She would have had to flee Paris under cover simply in order to avoid the guillotine. By having her appear in disguise at Jarvis Laurie's Paris headquarters, then by having him mistake her for Miss Pross's sister, I hoped to offer a commentary on the socio-political perspective of both the asexual Madame Defarge and the equally asexual Miss Pross, who tries to secure funds for her escape with Lucie and Darnay. Further commentary would be provided through an additional piece of cross-casting. In the novel, Jean Barsad emerges as a spy for the republic. So he does in the play. But by having him emerge as Miss Pross's cross-dressed sister, I hoped to provide a commentary on the 'happy ending', whereby Miss Pross successfully outfights Madame Defarge. The ending remains as Dickens has written it, but now Miss Pross cannot escape without entering into conspiracy with her sister and with Mary Wollestonecraft, both of whom accompany her, Lucie and Darnay on the journey. In Dickens, the latter trio retreat across the English Channel with nothing more inflammatory than an empty shibboleth. Now, as proof that more than their individual safety was at risk, they were emissaries in a radical cause, carrying secret funds to support women's suffrage. This would also serve as a talisman for what the English took from the French Revolution.

For an overall statement of the response to Dickens, I found useful this line from Edward Bond's play, *Summer:* 'You can do without kindness, but you can't do without justice' (Bond, 1982, p. 25). This seemed an apt description of the opposing forces in Dickens' novel and I used it to delineate the play's central conflict. The struggle for justice, indeed, would sanction Madame Defarge's behaviour. So would ingenuous kindness redefine English behaviour. Kindness, in Bond's morality, is insufficient. So it is in our politicised version of

Dickens. At every turn, I sought to redefine that kindness with a sharp appeal for justice. Lucie Manette's attraction to Darnay is doll-like alongside the reality of sexual longing. Laurie's honest brokerage is childishly foolhardy alongside the amoral pursuit of money. In nurse-maiding Lucie, Miss Pross seems but barely to have escaped the nursery herself. These adaptations may be broadly comic in style, but their intention was clear when placed alongside the brutal necessities of the French struggle. In Dickens, the emphasis is on the brutality; I wished to emphasise the cause. For this reason, the French section occupies two-thirds of the play and the third that remains to the English section is given a political dimension which the novel avoids altogether. I make no boast for the quality of the result other than to say it became the students' text, replete with political commentary. I leave it to the reader, familiar with Dickens, to decide whether or not this adaptation sounds credible. I have tried here to give an accurate summation of what was attempted in the script.

One final element deserves comment. Although the text does not specify staging, my writing contributed significantly to how the production was mounted. As I embarked on the second act, I approached the director with the request for a crowd. 'What do you mean by "crowd"?', he asked. I explained that Dickens characterises the Revolution as a black mass of humanity. As such, I said, it would be advantageous to our purpose if at least a sense of that teeming throng could inform what else we did. Since the crowd does seem to be the author's most resonant commentary on what we were intending to give significant weight, we would be as well to incorporate it into the production. The result was a promenade production, with the action shifting from location to location in the large performance space. Performers moved with the audience to create the crowd I had asked for. They emerged when it was time to assume their specific roles. It is not for me to comment on the effectiveness of this production mode. But this did enable us to contextualise the English scenes with the Gordon riots and to present the incidents of the Revolution with sprawling vivacity. No one could say that it was not about the French Revolution, and it removed the novel from the sedate drawing rooms of both London and Paris.

Conclusions

Adaptation, finally, is a matter of being able to occupy someone else's space. William Boyd (1995) has likened the process to the difference between the sea and one's bath. I am not altogether certain that the metaphor aptly characterises the function of adaptation in work with students, if swimming is the operative part of the metaphor. Students, after all, are fully equipped to engage with the 'sea' of the novel and there is something tacitly diminishing in the suggestion that dramatic representation can be no more invigorating that 'a thorough soak'. David Edgar has consistently refuted the suggestion that his adaptations stand apart from his original plays as inferior examples of his overall achievement (Edgar, 1988, pp. 143–59).

With the four adaptations discussed in this chapter, I would like to argue for the role of the adapter for drama students as a specialised function, if it is done proficiently; it needs specialisation to be done proficiently. For the student, in any case, adaptation provides challenges that do not exist either in improvisational work or in the formal production of even a new play. At best, perhaps, it is able to demonstrate to the participants (actors and audience) how the text becomes indivisible from the presentation of the text. This is certainly the most significant lesson for the students working on these texts. If the teaching has tended towards a comprehensive engagement with theatre, practical as well as theoretical, creative no less than interpretative, I would like to believe that adaptation has taken its place in this dynamic approach to theatre-making, and that these adaptations were at least consistent with that approach.

Works cited

Barthes, R. (1977) 'The Death of the Author', in *Image–Music–Text*, trans. S. Heath. Fontana, London, pp. 143–8.
Bigsby, C. (1986) *Joe Orton*. Methuen, London.
Bond, E. (1982) *Summer.* Methuen, London.
Boyd, W. (1995) *Daily Telegraph,* 11 June 1995, p. 32.
Churchill, C. (1986) *Plays One*. Methuen, London.
Edgar, D. (1988) *The Second Time as Farce*. Lawrence and Wishart, London.
Gorky, M. (1979) *Plays*. Progress, Moscow.
Grotowski, J. (1969) *Towards a Poor Theatre*. Methuen, London.
Kumiega, J. (1987) *The Theatre of Grotowski*. Methuen, London.
Lodge, D. (ed.) (1988) *Modern Criticism and Theory*. Longman, London.
MacNeal, R. (1988) *Stalin: Ruler and Man*. MacMillan, London.
Márquez, G. G. (1967) *One Hundred Years of Solitude*. Picador, London
Needle, J. and Thomson, P. (1981) *Brecht*. Methuen, London.
Nietzsche, F. (1971) *Beyond Good and Evil*. Penguin, London.
Pipes, R. (1977) *Russia Under the Old Regime*. Penguin, London.

Thomson, P. (1984) *Shakespeare's Theatre*. Routledge, London.
Williams, R. (1973) *Drama From Ibsen to Brecht*. Pelican, London.

Not referred to in the text but useful background reading is:
Page, A. (ed.) (1992) *The Death of the Playwright?* Macmillan, London.

All play quotations are from the manuscripts of my adaptations of *Blood Wedding* and *Vassa Zhelesnova*.

Part III

Case Studies in Researched Performance

The final section of this book is, we hope, self-evident. While all the preceding chapters have drawn on a range of practices as points of reference, none of them quote examples of complete projects under-taken in the recent past. 'Timor Mortis Conturbuit Nos: Improvising Tragedy and Epic', 'Melodrama and Methodism' and 'Teaching the Politics of Theatricality' aim to do just that. All three case studies employ a wide range of information, both personal and documentary, as their source material. By doing this they afford themselves the opportunities to compare differing perspectives and methods of recording experience. In the final analysis, the burden of thought and the impetus of progression are the responsibility of the students involved in each project.

There are no detailed and conclusive thoughts to be derived from these 'case studies'. They are not intended as definitive examples of how one *should* work. What they aim to express is a synthesis of thought and action through clearly defined processes integral to the practices of drama and theatre.

7

Timor Mortis Conturbuit Nos: Improvising Tragedy and Epic[1]

Anthony Frost

The starting point for this chapter lay in two productions mounted by the Drama Sector of the University of East Anglia in the early 1980s: *The Epic of Gilgamesh* (1982) and *The 1984 Game* (1983).[2] My intention in writing up this work has been to exemplify and describe a kind of original improvisational drama not dealt with anywhere else and to suggest that improvisation can be used in the teaching of drama for much more than just the acquisition of 'impro' skills, linking practice to theory in a variety of ways.

The two plays differed greatly in style and content, but shared a number of common characteristics. It seems important to stress that these were not simply 'devised' pieces. Both were created from improvisation in rehearsal; but both plays were also improvised *in performance* – using scenarios created by the rehearsal process. Both were 'serious' plays, in the sense that they were based on works of literature and intended to convey as much as possible of the richness of their originals to their audiences (plus some riches of their own) and, while they frequently used humour, they were deliberately not intended as comic pieces, as many devised or improvised plays tend to be.

Casting for the plays was both *aleatoric* and *ungendered* (that is, the casting was randomised and any performer, male or female, was prepared to play any role at any time). Both men and women could and did play Gilgamesh. For example, on one occasion in *The 1984 Game*, we were presented with a powerful love scene between a female 'Winston' and a male 'Julia'; the previous night the same roles had been played by two women. Both plays were crucially about acting and the nature of performance itself, performance-testing the principle that notions of 'role' and 'gender' are arbitrary and artificial constructs, adopted for convenience but subject to alteration at the whim of the production.

Both plays were highly verbal; yet there was no written script. Both were peopled by specific and detailed characters; yet no actor was assigned a specific role. Both told complex stories; yet there was no fixed, unalterable narrative which had to be transmitted. There was only the scenario which could, and did, alter in response to the actors' creativity.

Producing them, watching them develop from the initial workshops and rehearsals into the final performances, and gauging the performers' and audience's responses to the plays provided much material for the book *Improvisation in Drama* (Frost and Yarrow, 1990) and for my teaching practice. I do not pretend that both plays were totally or equally successful and many of my own discoveries were made in reflecting upon failures of various kinds.

In *The 1984 Game*, for example, I found myself taking many of the processes worked out in *Gilgamesh* for granted, rushing things, wanting to hurry past the simple to the complex, to engage with theories of fictionality before I had established what story we should tell. I therefore ceased to be *disponsible*, and then wondered why the actors were reluctant to commit themselves in rehearsal. In a serious improvisation piece, without the immediate feedback of audience laughter, the performer needs constant reassurance and encouragement, and a sense that the director (at least) knows where the work is heading. If the time is not taken to establish that trust, and if the director has not made it absolutely clear that thinking you know where you are going sometimes stops you getting there, then it becomes increasingly difficult for the actor to act and the director to direct. The actor holds back, or cannot find anything (cannot risk anything). And both the director and the actor set about rationalising the problem in destructive ways.

I had never worked in this way before *Gilgamesh*. I was really only aware of applied improvisation, a rehearsal device used in the development of certain types of role. This production certainly altered and clarified the way I saw improvisation and it seems appropriate, therefore, to concentrate this account on that play, making occasional cross-reference to the later piece if it provides clearer illustration of a particular idea.

Background and aims

I had some experience of partially randomised role distribution from a 1975 production of the Wilde/Douglas *Salome* at the University of Birmingham (directed by the late David Hirst). In this, five women shared the role of Salome and were selected each evening by a form of 'spin-the-bottle' involving the revolve unit and the actor playing Jokanaan! After the first few nights the selection was no longer truly random (though it still appeared so to the spectators). In 1981, my colleague Julian Hilton successfully produced with first-year students a devised piece based upon his translation of a German *Verlorene Sohn* ('prodigal son') play. Part of the success of this production stemmed from its use of improvised material in the performances as well as in rehearsal; and its use of partially randomised casting (though again, towards the end of the run, the cast knew who was almost certain to be given the remaining roles). In both these examples, randomness had no narrative implications; it was merely a way of keeping the cast fresh and alert.

The following year, in spring 1982, I agreed to direct a *wholly* improvised play which would extend some of the ideas generated by the prodigal son play. I chose to base the project, originally a form of 'research in action' into the aims and methods of improvised theatre, on *The Epic of Gilgamesh*, a text which I had first studied as part of a course on the epic at Birmingham. And it was from epic – in its largest sense – that the work derived.

But the central platform on which my productions rested was not, as might be supposed, a theory of randomness. The use of chance mechanisms was less philosophical or aesthetic than pragmatic. It was not the operation of randomness itself (as in early surrealist experiments, the music of Cage, the painting of Pollock, the more recent descriptions of 'quantum' or 'chaotic' theatre by David George and others[3]) that interested me. The use of the aleatoric was principally a matter of pragmatics rather than praxis – though it was not un-informed by theory – ensuring the attainment of certain clear learning objectives for the students and avoiding certain traps in the casting. As a teaching stratagem, randomness was a mechanism for ensuring parity of opportunity, for constantly denying students the chance to settle into fixed, mechanical roles, for continually demonstrating the

principle that any actor can play any role: and it was the principal
mechanism for degendering the casting and disrupting assumptions
about whose subjectivities could be explored on stage (see Case,
1989).

The principle at the centre of these experiments, however, was a
narratalogical one, which linked to the study of epic forms. It was a
dissection of the storytelling process. The practical method enlisted
the aid of the students in defining the crucial narrative constituents
and asked them to cooperate in their translation (here, because of the
improvisatory method, their simultaneous translation) into performance.

Recent theatre historiography[4] delineates a polarisation of opinion
regarding theatre and drama's European origins. The opposed approaches can be defined as primarily anthropological versus classical/
philological. The former approach, stressing origins in either religious
ritual (e.g. Harrison, Murray, Cornford) or shamanic healing (e.g.
Kirby, Schechner), has tended to dominate thinking and teaching in
drama departments (its appeal is romantic, practical rather than
literary, and does not require much classical Greek!). This approach
began to give ground in the 1980s to a revitalised classicism centred
upon theatre's re-investigation of its relations to other literary and
performative modes. So, for example, as well as Taplin's (1978, p. 23)
robust rejection of all speculative origin theories, we have Lesky's
(1983, p. 23) review of the classical source material which reminds us
that the ancients themselves clearly saw Homer as the father of
tragedy, and Herington's (1985, pp. ix–xii and p. 51) identification of
the earliest actors with the class of *rhapsodoi*, the singers and reciters
of the Homeric *epos*.

There is some comparative evidence from the epic traditions of
later western Europe for a similar relation of tale-telling to early
drama,[5] however literary the epic form later becomes. Modern
anthropology is beginning to close the gap between the disciplines by
exploring the importance of narrative forms in pre- or proto-literate
cultures (Gillison, 1983, 1993), or descriptions of Aboriginal *milpinti*
storytelling.[6]

We must not mistake stories for trivial things. Northrop Frye's
archetypal notion of a 'self-contained literary universe'[7] seems ultimately solipsistic. Story is always grounded in experience and returns
to experience in use. Stories are utile, explaining the world in some
way.[8] Stories can be told for entertainment, of course, and often are:
but the matrix of story is never trivial. The materials out of which story
is woven can be described variously as natural, cosmological or

imaginary/exemplary: historical, mythological or legendary; real, super-real or fictional. The tale may be woven with separate or simultaneous intent to edify and entertain. It may function as instructive parable or as amusing anecdote, but its telling always has a binding, bonding social efficacy. It creates a community, however temporary, between the teller and his/her listeners, and among the listeners, the group for whom *this* story has a meaning and a significance. There are many cultures without drama: there are no cultures (because there is no culture) without story.

The renewed emphasis on theatre's debt to poetry and to the poetic *agones mousikoi* (poetic contests) of pre-Peisistratean Athens therefore relocates performed narrative at the heart of the theatrical encounter. The rhapsode both personates and impersonates the characters he evokes. His work is to tell these important, culture-defining stories in verse, improvising within the rhythms of the oral formulae he operates.

Epic, says Aristotle, predates tragedy. It is drawn from the same well as tragedy, but given different form. 'Tragedy,' says Herington (1985, p. 51), 'is poetry, but poetry enlarged by a dimension.' We could not pretend to inhabit even temporarily the cultural matrix which shaped the tales of the ancient Greek *rhapsodós*, Anglo-Saxon *scop* or medieval Irish *sgélaige* (the latter evidencing a remarkable fusion of the oral, literary and performative traditions: trainee bards being set themes by their professors, and given a night and a day in a darkened room to compose them before being given light by which to write them down, and then having immediately to perform them for their masters[9]). But although our context was radically different, and recon-struction of ancient forms and methods not our aim, the literatised record of the epic tradition was available to us and became crucial in our search for appropriate materials.

Our experiments had, therefore, both a theoretical/historical and a pedagogic basis. We were concerned to replicate the processes of dramatic evolution – starting with the single actor, improvising a tale in front of an audience using a shared or imparted mythopoesis – and also to develop a teaching style that would enable us to work practically on a variety of tale-telling forms, while opening up key theoretical issues for discussion. For these reasons, improvised and partly improvised storytelling was the centre of the approach.

The aims of the research programme can be listed thus:

(1) to explore ways in which epic or literary narrative could be transformed into dramatic action,

(2) to examine the processes of play-writing and to discover what steps are necessary in the creation of a dramatic text (here, extended scenarios),

(3) to experiment with concepts of the aleatoric in drama by randomised casting,

(4) to investigate the effects of totally ungendered casting,

(5) to explore the advantages and limitations of improvisation as a formal method of rehearsal *and* performance,

(6) to create a 'serious' piece of work using improvisatory means,

(7) to discover how well first-year students could cope with the difficult and unfamiliar form of work and to challenge their received notions of what constitutes a 'play',

(8) to investigate the method as a way of introducing aspects of dramatic theory,

(9) to examine practical techniques of narration and tale-telling, but also

(10) to explore *ideas* through improvisation, rather than merely to recount narrative.[10]

After much comparison, I chose *The Epic of Gilgamesh* as the raw material of our investigations.

The Epic of Gilgamesh

The ancient Sumerian story of Gilgamesh and his desperate search for immortality was orally composed in the third millennium BC. It existed in written form – 'engraved on tablets of clay', as the story tells us – as early as 2000 BC and was popular throughout the Middle East until the death of the Assyrian Emperor Assurbanipal in the seventh century before Christ. It was in his buried library at Nineveh that the tablets containing the Gilgamesh story were rediscovered in the nineteenth century AD. Thus, it is the oldest complete piece of literature in the world. Its poetic beauty, strong narrative, episodic structure and its naturally dramatic incidents translate superbly into theatrical terms, easily by-passing the difficulties of audience unfamiliarity with the material.

The story itself is simple and very beautiful. Although preserved in the form of an epic poem, it is inherently dramatic (according to one line of scholarship, it originally was dramatic in form[11]), telling the story of man's tragic struggle against the remorseless enemy, death. N. K. Sanders, the translator of the text used, writes:

The story is divided into episodes: a meeting of friends, a forest journey, the flouting of a fickle goddess, the death of the companion, and the search for ancestral wisdom and immortality: and through them all runs a single idea, like the refrain of the mediaeval poet, *'Timor mortis conturbat me'*. (Sanders, 1972, p. 22)

The theme of death and its meaning became central in our personal explorations, too. I shall return to this subject later.

The episodic structure not only proved very amenable to dramatisation, it also made the task of analysing the source work very much easier. The themes of male friendship (with its implicit homo-erotic component), sexual jealousy, loss, the struggle against death and the final submission to, and acceptance of, human frailty by the semidivine Gilgamesh were clearly delineated and frequently suggested analogues in the students' actual or vicarious experience which could be drawn upon later in the process.

Rehearsal and workshop

The project lasted eight weeks. The cast were asked to keep log-books of the production (as part of their assessment). The logs helped the actor to remember and use the workshop experiences, to record decisions and discoveries made, and to jot down ideas to present to the group. They were an invaluable objective record of research and a way of recording very subjectively the effects that the process was having on oneself. (This production was also carefully logged by the director and that log forms the basis of both the present article and the book.)

The first-year students also had to complete their more traditional seminars during this period, which placed limitations on rehearsal time. This kind of production demands ensemble work and so we had to rehearse mainly in the evenings, weekends and in odd blocks of time during the week. The first four weeks were, nonetheless, largely given over to workshops on improvisation rather than direct work on creating the play, which was put together in the second half of the project.

This was important. It was well worth risking the possibility that the 'finished' play would not emerge in time, in order to ensure that the methods of work used to create it were properly understood and authentically experienced. It was also essential – as it is in any kind of acting, but critically so in improvisation – to establish group unity, and a sense of trust.

The early workshops were concerned with just this. When an improvising actor gets into difficulties, s/he has to know that somebody will come to the rescue and that somebody will take what s/he is offering and develop it. In the earliest sessions there was a tendency to hang back, to watch a fellow actor flounder. This is wholly impermissible. Every member of the group is responsible for every other. The most frequent direction given at this time was, 'Go on, help him somebody!', until the sense of personal responsibility was instilled.

Another way of developing this was the use of the many 'trust games' which actors employ – all of which found their way directly into the final performances – such as the 'trust circle', 'fish dives', falls, blindfold-leading, and carrying-aloft. 'Fish-diving' is a game which develops impulses and self-trust. The actor has to suppress the fear of being dropped, has to believe that the human 'net' cares about her/him and has to commit her/himself fully to the leap. Falls are basically the same exercise, one stage on. The 'fish' becomes a 'bird', climbing on to a tabletop and swallow-diving down into the catchers' arms, first facing forwards and then, as confidence grows, backwards. Blindfold-leading stresses cooperation, one partner being totally responsible for the other and silently (or very quietly) leading the blind one safely through a complicated maze – often stopping to invite the partner to explore strange and wonderful tactile experiences (letting them feel the curtains, the furniture, other people). This develops not only trust but also the actor's tactile awareness and pleasure in objects.[12] Carrying-aloft, first at shoulder height, then on the extended arms of the whole group, demands that the person being carried is wholly relaxed, wholly surrendered – more difficult than it sounds because the feeling of motion conflicts with the sense of relaxed submission needed.

We also played related games to develop reflexes, touching, listening, speaking, rhythmic sense. Two group favourites were 'The Fight in the Dark' (which we called 'The Pauper and the Eunuch') and 'The Court of the Holy Dido'. The first develops attention, balance and 'body-think'; the second develops strong discipline and demands verbal improvisation within a very strict set of codes (which the actors learn how to break as well as obey). A version of 'The Fight in the Dark' became a very powerful scene in the final play. Both these games (and many of the other exercises we used) were derived from Clive Barker's *Theatre Games* (Barker, 1977, p. 57).

Keith Johnstone's *Impro* (Johnstone, 1981, pp. 33–74) had just emerged in paperback. I had not fully assimilated Johnstone's work on 'status' at that time, although I had a second-hand version of it from various workshops at the University of East Anglia and elsewhere, particularly those of Jon Oram. We made more use of Viola Spolin's *Improvisation for the Theatre* (Spolin, 1973, p. 89) and especially the 'who/where/what' exercises. Johnstone finds this technique unhelpful (Johnstone, 1981, p. 27) but this is because his aims are different. We found this approach most useful in the creation of a consistent piece. It concentrates the attention and removes distractions, without limiting creativity. It gives the actor something to start with and to build upon. Given a 'who', a 'where' or a 'what', the actor can create the other two. Given nothing, the actor can still choose one of these and generate a consistent and coherent piece of improvisation. For example, the 'who' might be 'a farmer'; this suggests the 'where' (for example in a field) and the 'what' follows quite naturally (for example planting potatoes). But the 'who' might just as easily be 'yourself', in the same field doing the same thing – or some other 'where' doing something else. The exercise asks that the imagination remains constant to the 'set'[13] chosen or specified. If the 'who' is a king, the actor has a constant imaginative focus to return to; he must behave consistently like a king (and that, of course, implicitly involves status work too) or he must consciously choose to alter the set (which is permissible, although not as often required in this type of work). The advantage of Spolin's work for us lay in the fact that we had a source text, the poem: this invariably gave us at least one of her parameters and that made the exercise of improvised dramatisation relatively straightforward.

We also concentrated on the difference between 'showing' and 'telling' ('Don't tell us, show us!'). 'Telling' avoids the full physical involvement of the body. It substitutes codified signs (words, pantomimic gestures) for full bodily response. An actor can 'tell' the audience s/he is 'walking through a doorway' by miming reaching out and turning a door handle and stepping forward (or by saying 'Oh look, here's a door. I wonder what's through here...'). The audience will understand what is happening, but they will not believe it. The actor 'shows' us the doorway by first imagining the door (creating its reality in her/his mind) and then changing her/his whole posture as s/he steps from one visualised space into another (creating its reality in her/his body). When a person steps from a small room into the open air, the spine lifts, the head rises, the eyes change focus. This happens naturally in life. As long as the actor imaginatively recreates the circumstances and obeys them (that is creates the mental 'set' and conforms to it imaginatively), s/he will 'show' the audience where s/he is. If, through haste, s/he just wishes to signify the change, s/he will 'tell' the audience. The result is significantly different. Showing was shown to be more telling than telling. These explorations are treated at greater length in the resultant book.

During the workshops, the students organically discovered some of the major theories of acting for themselves. Sometimes an improvisation can be too easy. Everybody cooperates. The actions of the narrative are related, but the scene appears to have no point. The students themselves discovered that a good scene usually incorporates a resistance to be overcome, a difficulty to be surmounted. It was relatively easy to introduce at that stage the Stanislavskian idea (and terminology) of the 'want' or 'intention' and how to play it against the conflicting wants of other characters. We called this (with no great originality) 'objectives and resistances'. It can work in some very strange ways and not only ways connected with Stanislavskian theatre. For example, Gilgamesh simply wanted to pass through a doorway – but the doorway chose to resist him! We gave the role of 'doorway' to an actor – making the inanimate animate and thereby creating the possibility for it to act. Gilgamesh had to talk his way through or fight his way through. We extended this idea by creating an animate forest, whose task was to confuse or frustrate Gilgamesh on his journey. Whenever a scene was flagging, or lacking in impact, we would devise or strengthen the resistance, often personify it, and challenge the actors to overcome it, invariably producing new improvisations.

They discovered for themselves the Brechtian idea of the 'tenses of acting', which Clive Barker also describes (Barker, 1977, p. 156). They had no trouble with changing person from first to third, or tense from present to past. 'But how,' asked one, 'do you act in the future?' The answer came from within the group: 'Dreams, prophecies, visions take you forward into the future – just as memory takes you back into the past.' A character lost in a vision of his/her own future death behaves differently from one reminiscing about the past. This was to prove vital for *Gilgamesh*, which is crucially concerned with both futurity and memory.

While the workshops were developing, we were also starting slowly to work on the source material and starting to make technical decisions regarding the set, costumes, publicity and other matters. We broke the text up into units (which the episodic structure easily suggested) and created a dramatic narrative from it, which we then sought to animate in various ways.

The scenario was evolved by the whole group. They were asked to write down the incidents that they felt were the most important. The primary objective was to create a coherent narrative. We wanted the story to be understood and easily followed. Discussion of narrative priorities was very lively and very instructive.

Alison Oddey's book on devising has led to consideration of what might be called 'the patriarchy of narrative' (Oddey, 1994). We were governed and disciplined by the source text, adhering to its linear form. More recent devised forms lay greater stress upon free association and less upon dramatising an original. I accept this as a valid and important method. Indeed, *The 1984 Game* proceeded from the idea that Orwell's novel was merely the raw material for our own creativity. During *Gilgamesh*, too, we constantly debated the validity of altering the source, or inventing new material within a traditional framework. But for that play, and using that method, it seemed essential to base the devising process on the linear structure of the received narrative – simply so that the improvisers could rapidly orientate themselves. Eventually, from the many incidents in the original, the following basic scenario emerged and formed the basis of the later rehearsals:

Part 1

- Prologue/the creation of Gilgamesh, the semi-divine King of Uruk/the creation of Enkidu, the wild man/the taming of Enkidu by a harlot/the meeting of friends, in which Gilgamesh and Enkidu meet, fight and come to love one another.
- The hunger for fame, and the hero's need to do immortal deeds/a forest journey/the fight with Humbaba, a demon whose glance can kill.
- The seduction of Gilgamesh by the goddess Ishtar/Ishtar's vengeance: the bull of heaven/the tribunal of the gods/the death of friend for friend.

Part 2

- The quest, Gilgamesh's decision to search for immortality/the journey, fighting the blind revenant of Enkidu/meetings with Siduri and with the boatman, Urshanabi/an ocean voyage/ meeting with Utnapishtim, the only mortal to have obtained immortal life/the flood.
- The test/the end of the quest/finding and losing the answer/ return/death and immortality.

Using these basic incidents as a skeletal framework, we set to work to dramatise each unit. Decisions followed rapidly. The actors were encouraged to be inventive and they invented magnificently. The one firm stylistic rule was that everything, every idea and every image, had to be related to and through the *body* of the performer. So the sounds of animals gathering at a nocturnal watering hole – where the harlot encounters the half-animal Enkidu for the first time – were vocalised by the cast. The sound of raindrops in a gathering flood (an Assyrian variant of Noah's flood) were made by the actors drumming their fingers on the floor as they looked wildly around them – becoming both the water and its victims. Images were kept simple and powerful; for example, as Gilgamesh travelled across the floor of the drama studio, the mats over which he walked were turned upside down by the other actors to symbolise the changing landscape, the floor surface changing from red to black as he passed. The mats themselves were gymnastic fall mats and their use gave the actors physical confidence about the acrobatic elements of the performance.

Often we broke into small groups to concentrate on finding dramatic ideas for particular incidents. This worked extremely well (and dispersed the creative focus among the group rather than allowing it to become a directorial prerogative). One member of the cast took some of the poems in the text and set them to beautifully elegiac music. Others worked like Trojans on designing and constructing the set, or on lighting. We worked as a plenary group on other elements, such as mask-making.

It was decided that: the gods should be masked, the mortal characters should not be, and demons and mythical beings should be portrayed by combinations of actors (for example, the 'bull of heaven' sent to destroy Uruk by the jealous goddess Ishtar was played by two actors – actor A bent down and put his head between actor B's legs and lifted him so that B's outstretched legs became long, vicious horns with which to charge the citizens; the 'man-scorpion' that guarded a way Gilgamesh had to traverse was even more complex, the feet of one actor becoming the 'sting' while the other actor spoke, then suddenly reversing positions, rather like the classic image of the fool's banner[14]).

It was the actors' choice that we should incorporate the rehearsal games into the play wherever they seemed appropriate (and this was also a choice made in creating *The 1984 Game*, to weave game structures into the very fabric of the piece). I welcomed the decision at the time. Reflecting on this choice later, I wondered whether we had fallen back on something we thought we knew, instead of thinking more imaginatively. I decided that it was a positive choice: the actors were calling upon a physical vocabulary that they had just acquired together and which bonded us. It re-incorporated into the performed work reference to the processes which had shaped it and it also introduced an external discipline. Liz LeCompte has used much the same approach (for example in *Brace Up!*, her version of *The Three Sisters* for the Wooster Group[15] and in other shows). Game structures give the actor a shape within which to work and a set of exterior, non-psychological objectives. They focus the performer's attention (s/he is listening or watching for specific cues) and they generate dramatic creativity in their own right.

An example of this was provided by a scene (not in the original text) devised during rehearsals. Gilgamesh, on his quest, re-encountered the beloved Enkidu. But death had changed Enkidu (if indeed it was he, and not some demon inhabiting his costume). The revenant claimed to be blind and goaded Gilgamesh into fighting him again, as they had fought at their first meeting. Slowly, the 'blind' Enkidu took off his belt and flicked it towards Gilgamesh, taunting him until the king agreed reluctantly to the contest. But Gilgamesh scorned the advantage of sight and bound his eyes.

In the original game, the fight in the darkened room takes place in a ring of chairs and the 'weapons' are rolled newspapers. The other actors, enthralled by the scene, were nonetheless worried that the fighting pair might step beyond the bounds of the space and lash out at the audience with their weapons (their belts in the public performance). The action took place in the sunken well of the drama studio floor (16' × 16', with a 2'-wide step around it). The audience were on three sides of the acting space and very close to it. So the remaining members of the cast – who were all present on stage throughout the play – sat on the surrounding step and hissed softly as the fighting figures approached them too closely. The blindfolded actors had to listen for each other's steps, for the tiniest rustle of clothing in the stillness, to know where they were. The sinister hissing from the sidelines as the actors slowly circled one another charged the already powerful scene with tension.

During these rehearsals we got used to the idea of switching characters around. A scene would begin between two actors; then two more would play it – using the discoveries of the first pair, but trying to develop them or to do it completely differently. It became clear that there were certain moments in the story when Gilgamesh *changed* – usually at the end of a group of incidents in the first part of the play (the second part seemed much more consistently to do with one person). We decided, therefore, to select different players for each unit in the first half, but to let a single actor – randomly chosen by the processes of Part One – play Gilgamesh in Part Two.

Remembering the prodigal son play, we wanted to create a format in which (during performance) none of the actors could know in advance which character they would be playing in which scene. So we devised ways of changing the roles on stage. At the death of giant Humbaba, for example, the entire cast danced in celebration (except for our two musicians who, for technical reasons, were only able to play Gilgamesh in certain scenes). A cloth that had formed part of the giant was thrown into the air. It was never allowed to touch the ground, so actors had to rush to catch it and fling it up again. Whoever was holding it when the music stopped – at the discretion of the musicians – was 'it', was Gilgamesh for the next unit. S/he chose the next Enkidu and Ishtar, and the selection concluded with a formalised exchange of the emblems of the roles. It was a form of musical chairs, but very effective – ensuring that nobody could prepare in advance what they were going to do when their turn came.

Most of the smaller roles were left entirely to volunteers in the performances. The actors knew that a trapper or a harlot was needed in this unit; they were responsible personally for the success of the piece, so they got up and did it. They had learned that the one unforgivable sin is to leave a fellow performer stranded. They took those responsibilities very seriously. (Sometimes people did sidle into position a little early in order to make sure they were in the right place to volunteer to do a favourite small role. This did not matter, as they were never able to play it in the same way, or with the same person twice.)

The initial selection of the actors who would start the play was made by the director in the Green Room a few minutes before the play began. It became an important ritual in itself – part of the event, though the audience never saw it. After the group warm-up, the cast stood in a circle, eyes closed, facing outwards, with the director in the centre. Saying 'Choosing a Gilgamesh…' I would touch somebody on the back; then '…choosing an Enkidu…' touch somebody else; and so on until the necessary initial roles had been assigned. A few seconds later, I would leave the Green Room and the play would begin. Occasionally an actor was chosen because s/he did not appear to have had one of the big roles yet, but for the most part I found myself totally unable to remember which actor had been chosen for which part – until the play began and the characters appeared. And from then on randomness took over.

This approach ensured spontaneity. The actor or actress who was chosen to play Gilgamesh in the second half had to begin (according to the scenario) with a powerful solo speech on his/her fear of death and the reasons for the immortality quest. We agreed that for the performer to have written and rehearsed that speech, important though the ideas in it were, would change the style of the production too much. The speech had to be improvised – and had to be made personal to the performer playing it. In a way, it was the actor's fear (both of the idea of death and of the challenge facing him/her in the scenes to come) that made that scene so charged.

Death

On the minor matter of death.... The chosen epic's *raison d'être* is mankind's struggle against, and necessary reconciliation with, mortality. To perform this seriously must, at least to some extent, involve the students in imaginatively turning to face that encounter themselves. Death is not a taboo subject: but it is one which requires delicate approaches. Death as a theme perhaps means more to us as teachers now than it did 10 or 15 years ago; given added poignancy by the loss of our own teachers, students and friends during the last decade, and the shadow that hangs over so many more. But, even then, it was a subject requiring careful handling.

We deliberately did not work too directly on this. After all, death is by definition unimaginable. It is blankness and non-being. It is unplayable. It cannot be played through, just as it cannot be lived through. All the actor can do directly is explore the psychological and physiological mechanics of *dying* and the emotional processes of surviving someone else's death. We did not, therefore, choose to work on the various stages of coming to terms with one's own death (for example the critical phases of 'denial', 'anger', 'bargaining', 'grief' and 'acceptance' seminally described by Elisabeth Kubler-Ross[16]). But these were discussed in outline and were clearly discernible in Gilgamesh's second-half scenes, never far below the surface, imparting to the work both a desperate urgency and a strange, elegiac sadness. We were, in a curious way, mourning for someone long dead – and each of us, when summoned or chosen, being fitted for his clothes.

Death and the personal confession

The second half began, as indicated, with Gilgamesh's speech about his personal fear of death. Whoever played Gilgamesh for that scene was given the interval to prepare – though not to write down – the speech. Preparation was essential: the speech had to tackle difficult subjects and the performer needed time to work out and sink inside him/herself a consciousness of Gilgamesh's crisis of mortality. The actor needed time alone to do this during the interval. But it was important to discourage the memorisation of a pre-composed script. Not being able to write, or polish, the 'fear of death' speech not only stayed true to the oral tradition, it also ensured that improvisation continued into the performance itself.

But every actor naturally imagined him/herself playing Gilgamesh in that scene – whether or not they were actually chosen to play it during the run. Every actor, therefore, underwent a personal improvisatory process on the theme (analogous to the *sgélaige*'s night and day of darkness). To some degree, each performer mentally composed this speech and privately rehearsed the process of their own future death. When, however, they were chosen – death's finger, as it were, pointing to them – they went straight into performance. The pre-composed script could only partly be remembered and they also had to respond to whatever had just happened in Part One that night. The actor had to continue creating as s/he spoke and felt the response of the audience. The result was a powerful series of very different treatments of the issue and a remarkable sense that the speaker owned the speech.

Performances

The public performances of *The Epic of Gilgamesh* took place in March 1982. With the two dress rehearsals, this made six major performances, which was enough to guarantee that everybody in the group got to play most of the major roles.

In performance, the lessons learned were very important. The play succeeded extremely well in terms of its narrative. No one who saw it felt that the story was in any way unclear. Nor was anyone ever confused by the switching of roles, or by the sudden switches of gender: we often had male and female performers playing Gilgamesh in successive scenes. The act of designation or, more correctly, of nomination – assisted by simple and clear costume semiotics – was all that was required by an audience not only to understand, but also to respond emotionally to the character. The poem's ideas, too, were clearly transmitted. The themes of male friendship, animality in opposition to divinity, nature seduced by civilisation, and the fear of death were all clearly represented. What was more variable, though, was the emotional mood of the piece, which was very difficult to gauge and sustain given this style of acting. The actors learned most of all about the fragility of mood. The actors had to learn to sensitise themselves to the mood they were creating. The first half was reasonably jolly and rumbustuous – until the death of Enkidu shattered its jollity. Ishtar's vengeance demands the death of both Gilgamesh, who has rejected her blandishments, and Enkidu. The gods convene a tribunal and vote to condemn one of the pair to death. Enkidu dies for his friend. (Once, when the voting somehow went against the Gilgamesh, the Enkidu impulsively rushed forward and committed suicide to save both his friend – and the plot.) The grieving for Enkidu, by candlelight, set to haunting music, ended Part 1.

Part 2, as already mentioned, began with Gilgamesh's soliloquy on death. It was the only time an actor was alone on the stage. But the others were present, listening from behind the set, because the whole of the second half would develop from the tone set by that speech. The performers had to judge what they had created and try to develop or sustain it. (Once, when the mood had become terribly sombre, the woman playing Utnapishtim, the immortal, felt that this had gone much too far – the play had become too morose – so she very sensibly changed it: Utnapishtim mocked Gilgamesh and lightened the heavy gloom that lay on the performance.)

One thing was not really tried which, perhaps, more experienced and confident players might have been able to do. The scenario was never completely abandoned in performance to create wholly new scenes. On the very last night of Gilgamesh, one actress inserted a completely new and spontaneous scene, which the other actors used well. Although it changed the developing mood of the play entirely, and perhaps prevented the outcome from being truly tragic on that occasion, the play lived anew in that moment. And it taught the director something about accepting the process rather than trying to steer the piece towards a predicted result.

Language

One layer of the play which I felt was never fully realised was its language. *Gilgamesh* (in translation) is not a particularly beautiful poem; it has few memorable lines. Its power resides in the surge of narrative and in the formality of its diction. The oral formulaic structures are familiar to storytellers everywhere (for example it uses a

great deal of formal repetition, especially during Gilgamesh' s quest).
The actors began to learn about those structures but were never fluent
in them. The young actors were able to quote the text easily enough
during formal scenes or moments, but found it much harder to
improvise dialogue between those moments or when they were
exposed in difficult key scenes. Sometimes phrases jarred; equally,
though, the modern and personal language created its own very
powerful stylistics. If we had chosen to script the play from the early
improvisations there would have been no problem. But since the
actors were improvising, the script was being composed as they
uttered it – which raises questions as to the limitations of the
improvised method for developing young actors.

F. R. Benson's actors could convincingly 'pong' and 'fribble'
(improvise in blank verse or prose respectively[17]) when they forgot
their lines because they were steeped in Shakespearean language.
Vocabulary, word order and rhythm were internalised over years of
reading the classic repertoire, speaking it in rehearsal and on stage
and, no doubt, by playful imitation of it away from the stage. Student
actors cannot yet call on that experience and a devised piece may not
present them with direct linguistic paradigms to copy. They have to
get that from separate research. They can be encouraged to read, but
the process is a slow, cumulative one. And on stage, the improviser's
imaginative flow can be interrupted by referencing – by 'looking up'
the 'right' words in the head. A good *solo* improviser like John
Sessions (who is not a good group improviser, since he never listens to
and always competes with his partners) is steeped in literature. His
head is full of the vocabularies of Shakespeare, Hemingway, Kerouac,
and he can improvise tirelessly 'in the style of'.[18] Student actors have
yet to develop that ear for language. Few are born with it and English
secondary education may very well have inhibited it.

So, with hindsight, what could we have done? We could have
borrowed or invented a stock of archaic or poetic phrases specifically
for the play and worked to get these fixed early on in rehearsal. To
some extent, this happened naturally. But I am glad we did not
formalise this. A pseudo-elevated, pseudo-archaic style would have
been false to the spirit of the piece. Archaism would have jarred with
the presentness of the actors and the play was as much about them
and their telling of it as it was a redaction of the original. Yet the piece
also had to belong to the original, to take over its language and
internalise it.

How could we have achieved that? We could have read more and
read aloud to each other (a key exercise in Copeau's training); our

work on 'set' (on staying within the agreed parameters of the role) could have been more explicitly extended to language, until the play found a voice that was formal, but not necessarily archaic; and we could have told more stories in rehearsal and used them to extend our imaginative as well as verbal range.[19] Storytelling was, after all, our key task and we were exploring various storytelling techniques in the performances. There was, for example, one planned moment when the cast turned outwards to the surrounding audience and simultaneously began to tell those nearest to them the story. Each had to find eye contact with a small number of people and tell the story directly to them in their own words. We tried other storytelling methods, too, including moments of choric narration and personal third-person narration. One of the successes of *The 1984 Game* was in tackling this problem and in internalising and learning to improvise 'Newspeak'.

Does the language matter? The production demonstrated that the piece worked well enough within its own mixed conventions. But, in practice, the mood is thrown by a sudden or inadvertent clash of linguistic registers, nearly always a comic effect. The audience are dumped unceremoniously out of the past and back into the present. There are deliberate, ironic effects to be used here, but to be used with care. Sometimes, trans-temporal expressions had an unsettling, eerie effect that was exactly right. When once the blind Enkidu deliberately teased Gilgamesh into fighting with 'Come on Gilgamesh, don't be such a party-pooper!' we were allowed to play with levels of time. When an actor inadvertently said 'OK, Gilgamesh', we were not.

Finding the voice of the play matters because the young actor's own language can be as much masking as self-expression. One's diction ties one's imagination to one's own experience and it is essential to check the natural tendency of improvisers to bend the character to their own language rather than extending themselves into the characters.

Conclusions

Each project took a group of new students through their first joint public performances. It deliberately challenged their conception of what a 'play' is: although it is noticeable in recent years how many more incoming students have been involved in devised shows at school, youth club, or drama group. It allowed them to learn about play creation, action, narration, physical skills, spontaneity, textual criticism (of literature as well as drama), stage technique, voice, movement and a host of related practical subjects. It also introduced them – experientially rather than academically – to a large body of dramatic theory (from Stanislavsky to Brecht and Grotowski). The projects allowed all these things to happen and gave them a focus and an experiential meaning, allowing them to be validated by a critical audience.

Both *Gilgamesh* and *The 1984 Game* were successful pieces of research – as well as being (in differing degrees) theatrically and pedagogically successful. Both managed the act of translation very well, illuminating their narrative sources as well as exploring genre boundaries, demonstrating that the techniques of improvised creativity can be applied to plays of complex ideas as easily as to Theatre Machine-style freely associative humour.

Both used the aleatoric principle successfully. It was fascinating to study the ways in which meaning shifted as each major role was played in turn in a unique and personal way by each member of the cast. One knows that every performance is different from every other; here one was able to demonstrate it graphically and to examine the differences.

We had established a nominative form which made gender- and role-switching perfectly acceptable to the audience as well as the cast. Place and person could be nominated by the simplest means, by assuming a garment, a posture, a name. Scenes in which actors had willingly to accept and sustain roles of the opposite gender and, improvising, make them credible to the spectators were the perfect demonstration of all the processes we had been studying.

Finally, both pieces were about living with, and living through, larger existential fears of which the stresses of performance are simply analogues (*timor mortis conturbuit nos* – as *conturbare* implies being not just disturbed, but collectively and individually turned inside out) and about using drama to reconnoitre that hidden territory. That fundamental seriousness of purpose dictated the choice of *Gilgamesh*, the stylistic approach and a return to praxis – not only in the modern sense of a practice informed by ideology, but in Aristotle's original sense of action as the substance or soul, the essential meaning, of tragedy.

For 'as Aristotle saith, it is not *gnosis*, but *praxis* must be the fruit'.[20] What it implies is the transmutation of painfully uncovered private knowledge into public action and revelation. We take our authority as storytellers, and our essence as performers, from the confrontation with death. Walter Benjamin knew that the darkness of myth is fundamentally a coming to terms with death: 'Death is the sanction of everything that the storyteller can tell. He has borrowed his authority from death' (Benjamin, 1970, p. 94). The ultimate task of the storyteller, for Benjamin (1970, p. 102) (and of the improviser, for me) is to show how the human spirit can confront mortality with *Mut*, *Untermut* and *Übermut*; that is to say, with courage, cunning and high spirits.

Notes

1. An earlier version of this chapter appeared in 1990 in *Studies in Theatre Production* (published by the Standing Committee of University Drama Departments, SCUDD). I am grateful to the editors for this opportunity to revisit and revise that work.
2. The same two productions inspired the author of this chapter's contribution to Frost and Yarrow (1990).
3. For example articles by George (1989); Vanden Heuvel (1993); Demastes (1994). I am indebted to Jonathan Pitches of Nene College for these examples.
4. For example Vince (1984, p. 4). These ideas are discussed in more detail in my forthcoming work for Routledge, *Theatre Histories*.
5. For example Philpotts (1920) and Andersson (1978).
6. *Milpinti*, a girl's storytelling game in which the narrator draws and erases images in the dust with a wire, is described in Booth (1991).
7. Frye (1957) and cf. Cuddon (1992, pp. 570–1).
8. Cf. Benjamin (1936), 'The Storyteller: Reflections on the Work Nikolai Leskov', posthumously published in Benjamin (1970).
9. Cf. *Memoirs of the Marquis of Clonrickarde* (1722), in Ó Coileáin (1978, p. 175).
10. For *The 1984 Game* I added to these objectives an examination of the notion of fictionality in drama by devising a meta-theatrical framework in which the events of Orwell's novel could coincide with the real acts of the performance, allowing the actual to comment on the virtual.
11. Cf. Cook (1974, p. ii). Cook argues that *Gilgamesh* was originally a ritual drama, predating Greek drama by 1500 years. Theodore Gaster's *Thespis* (1961) does not support this contention. Whatever the truth, the text was orally transmitted for over a millennium before being committed to clay tablets. In a sense, therefore, *Gilgamesh* has always been amenable to improvisation.
12. Isaac Pocock's 1813 melodrama *The Miller and His Men* (Act I, Scene 4), performed in Covent Garden, contains a surprisingly analogous scene of blindfold leading, with the villainous characters creating for both the blindfolded hero and the audience the confusions of a forest journey by placing obstacles in his path. The villains 'take each a hand, and lead Lothair round the stage, interposing their swords to cause him to raise his feet and stoop his head, so that he may have no idea of their path' (see Pocock, 1964, pp. 43–87).

172 TheatreTheatre Praxis

13. Natadze (1962, pp. 421ff.).
14. The fool's banner of the *Infanterie Dijonnoise*, from the fifteenth century to 1630 (in the 1742 etching by M. du Tilliot) is reproduced in Gascoigne (1968, p. 111, fig. 91).
15. Described by Suzie Mee and Euridice Arratia in separate articles in *The Drama Review*, vol. 36, no. 4, winter 1992.
16. Kubler-Ross (1973, 1982) and more recently Glassock and Gressor (1995).
17. I am indebted to Peter Thomson for the reminder about these ancient and honourable practices (cf. Thomson and Salgado, 1987, pp. 380, 399).
18. Sessions' best game on *Whose Line is it Anyway* was always 'Authors' (a prepared game, the actor providing the author, the audience the subject matter). His one-man shows are, similarly, full of literary and cinematic references.
19. I am thinking here of projects on storytelling undertaken at the University of East Anglia by my colleague Tony Gash, with help from professional storyteller Hugh Lupton, for example 'The Man With No Story To Tell' (1989). The process of turning the actor into a man or woman *with* a story to tell is crucially developmental. Hearing and retelling stories, from as many cultures as possible, and exploring the myriad ways in which they can be told or enacted are vital training. Mike Alfreds' early work with Shared Experience is also very instructive.
20. Sir Philip Sidney, *An Apology for Poetry*. Written *c.* 1580, published 1595, line 669.

The courageous, cunning and high-spirited group who created *Gilgamesh* were: Sarah Britt, Diana Brotherton, Sarah-Gay Cornell, Vivien French, Stephen Gray, Nadia MacKay, Olwen May, Robert Palmer, Duncan Reekie, Andrew-John Rogers, David Whelpton and Helen Wright. Music was by Stephen Gray and Olwen May. We were assisted by Gregor McElvogue, Pamela Heywood, Lisa Morgan and Kevin Piper, with technical help from the Sector staff, especially Julian Hilton and John Landymore.

Works cited

Andersson, T. M. (1978) 'The Icelandic Sagas', in *Heroic Epic and Saga: An Introduction to the World's Great Folk Epics*, ed. F. J. Oinas. Indiana University Press, Bloomington, pp. 144–71.
Arratia, E. (1992) *The Drama Review*, vol. 36, no. 4.
Barker, C. (1977) *Theatre Games*. Methuen, London.
Benjamin, W. (1970) *Illuminations*, trans. H. Zohn. Jonathan Cape, London.
Booth C. (1991) 'Elements of Theatre in the Culture of the Australian Aborigines', unpublished research paper, University of East Anglia.
Case, S. E. (1989) *Feminism and Theatre*. Macmillan, London.

Cook, C. W. (1974) *Gilgamesh: The World's Oldest Drama*. Meriwether, Colorado.

Cuddon, J. A. (1992) *Dictionary of Literary Terms and Literary Theory*. Penguin, London.

Demastes, W. (1994) In *New Theatre Quarterly* 39, vol. X.

Frost, A. and Yarrow, R. (1990) *Improvisation in Drama*. Macmillan, London.

Frye, N. (1957) *Anatomy of Criticism*. Penguin, London.

Gascoigne, B. (1968) *World Theatre*. Ebury Press, London.

Gaster, T. M. (1961) *Thespis: Ritual, Myth and Drama in the Ancient Near East*. Doubleday, Garden City, New York.

George, D. (1989) In *New Theatre Quarterly* 18, vol. V.

Gillison, G. (1983) 'Living Theater in New Guinea's Highlands'. *National Geographic Magazine*, vol. 164, August.

Gillison, G. (1993) *Between Culture and Fantasy: A New Guinea Highlands Mythology*. University of Chicago Press, Chicago.

Glassock, G. and Gressor, M. (1995) *Coping With Loss and Grief*. Robinson, London.

Herington, J. (1985) *Poetry Into Drama: Early Tragedy and the Greek Poetic Tradition*. University of California Press, Berkeley.

Johnstone, K. (1981) *Impro*. Methuen, London.

Kubler-Ross, E. (1973) *On Death and Dying*. Tavistock Publications, London.

Kubler-Ross, E. (1982) *Living with Death and Dying*. Souvenir, London.

Lesky, A. (1983) *Greek Tragic Poetry*, trans. M Dillon. Yale University Press, New Haven.

Mee, S. (1992) *The Drama Review*, vol. 36, no. 4.

Natadze, R. (1962) 'On the Psychological Nature of Stage Impersonation'. *British Journal of Psychology*, vol. 53, pp. 421–9.

Ó Coileáin, S. (1978). 'Irish Saga Literature', in *Heroic Epic and Saga: An Introduction to the World's Great Folk Epics*, ed. F. J. Oinas. Indiana University Press, Bloomington, pp. 172–92.

Oddey, A. (1994) *Devising Theatre: A Practical and Theoretical Handbook*. Routledge, London.

Philpotts, B. (1920) *The Elder Edda and Scandinavian Drama*. Cambridge University Press, Cambridge.

Pocock, I. (1964) 'The Miller and His Men', in *Hiss the Villain: Six English and American Melodramas*, ed. M. Booth. Methuen, London, pp. 43–87.

Sanders, N. K. (1972) *The Epic of Gilgamesh*. Penguin, London.

Spolin, V. (1973) *Improvisation for the Theatre*. Pitman, London.

Taplin, O. (1978) *Greek Tragedy in Action*. Methuen, London.

Thomson, P. and Salgado, G. (1987) *Companion to the Theatre*. Dent, London.

Vanden Heuvel, M. (1993) In *New Theatre Quarterly* 35, vol. IX.

Vince, R. W. (1984). *Ancient and Mediaeval Drama: A Historiographical Handbook*. Greenwood Press, Westport.

8

Melodrama and Methodism: An Approach Through Practice

Peter Thomson

The relationship between academic research and workshop sessions is not a relaxed one, but there are occasions when it may be uniquely dynamic. The project I will be describing in this chapter was, for me, one such occasion. What had begun in my head as the inkling of a perception was tested and, to a measurable extent, validated through the skills and experience of a group of students. The association of melodrama and Methodism that I shall be proposing is based on two claims, neither of which I have room to argue fully. The first is that the study of drama invites from its teachers an investment in a visceral pedagogy whose outcome for the student is by no means always predictable. The second, more contentious perhaps, is that the popularity of melodrama in nineteenth-century Britain was culturally aligned with the mingled guilt and hopefulness of salvationary Nonconformism. My immediate purpose is to describe a drama project which attempted to explore the propriety of the second claim in such a way as to advance the first. At the time, it had some of the anxiety-creating uncertainties of a genuine melodrama.

Some initial problems were caused by the subject itself. It is easy enough to demonstrate the widespread popularity of melodrama in Victorian London by itemising repertoires, from the comparatively highbrow Lyceum to the determinedly lowbrow trans-pontine theatres. Easy, too, to persuade students of the continuing currency of melo-dramatic modes in the cinema and on television. But it is altogether

174

more difficult to recover an appreciation of the original impact of plays whose characters and plot mechanisms seem so rudimentary and whose language generally carries a moral freight that it is too weak to sustain. Even those few students who express admiration for the narrative energy of selected melodramas tend to find their outcome too predictable and their conduct unthreatening. As a result, the student view of the original audience and its cultural predisposition is likely to be an unwittingly patronising one.

Such an absence of historical perspective ought to be tackled. This group of 16 students was neither inert nor complacent, but Victorian melodrama was not ruffling them. Although most of the plays we looked at in the first week were entirely new to them, their natural response was one of familiarity on the way to contempt. To borrow a Brechtian line, they could not be surprised by material they so readily took for granted. By the afternoon of the first Friday, I felt a pressing need to destabilise the reading of the texts. I had in mind, at this stage, an approach to Leopold Lewis's version of *Le juif polonais* (*The Bells*) that would receive an initial impetus from Edward Gordon Craig's long description of Irving's first entrance as Mathias (Craig, 1930, pp. 55–61). There might be enough there to set small sub-groups to work on a re-creation of that first impression. But then, Irving, as Shaw pointed out, 'could give importance and a noble melancholy to any sort of drivel that was put into his mouth' (St. John, 1931, p. xx). It was Mathias's self-lacerating guilt and the genuineness of his terror of the mesmerist that I needed to contextualise.

Irving continued to play Mathias for 35 years, from 1871 to 1905, and there was more to that longevity than a single actor's brilliance. While Charcot's use of hypnosis in the treatment of neurosis at the Salpêtrière hospital in Paris was earning medical respect as the nineteenth century ended, there was widespread public suspicion, only increased by ignorance and surreptitious experiment. Ambrose Bierce's definition of mesmerism in *The Devil's Dictionary* catches the word on the hop: 'MESMERISM, *n*. Hypnotism before it wore good clothes, kept a carriage and asked Incredulity to dinner' (Bierce, 1993, p. 81). The mesmerist was assumed to have unprecedented access to carefully concealed truths, so that, when Irving embodied Mathias's consciousness of secret guilt and terror over its imminent exposure, there must have been members of the audience with uneasily stirring consciences. The appeal of *The Bells* was contingent on a sense of sin and the fearful temptation to confess. If the student group was to get 'inside' melodrama, some such visceral anxiety might be a necessary learning aid.

Hypnosis seemed to me a promising avenue. It still produces in audiences a curious over-excitement, a present-tense awareness that, although the on-stage action may appear to be under control, it may suddenly get out of hand. The act of hypnotism places participants and onlookers in a circle of transgression and it was a feeling for the original transgressiveness of melodrama that I was seeking to engender in the students. But I knew no hypnotists. I opened the Yellow Pages and telephoned the first named in a short list of hypnotherapists. The man who answered was cautious, but keen to advertise his mystery. He agreed to hypnotise a student or two, provided that he could begin with a serious medical account of hypnotism.

At the beginning of the second week of the project, then, the students found themselves unfamiliarly seated in a lecture room, though an unusual one. There were three rows of reclining armchairs, facing a table, and a generously windowed wall. The hypnotherapist himself was disconcertingly nervous. He began apologetically, admitting that some of his listeners might fall asleep while he was talking; *but* – and here he paused for long enough to make the point – one of them would not, in fact, be asleep. S/he would be in a deep trance. For the next 80 minutes, he delivered one of the dullest lectures I have ever heard and *everyone was riveted*. They were as terrified as I of drifting off and we spent the time alternatively attentive to the lecturer and to ourselves. As the hypnotherapist dwindled to his end, I caught the eye of other people looking round the room. Was there anyone in a trance? The lecturer stepped forward, placed the palm of his hand on the head of a student in the front row, Nick, a notably stable member of the group, and told him that, although he had just come out of his trance, he was now about to go back into it. A bit of pressure and the student's head dropped slackly on to his left shoulder. There was an audible intake of breath in the room. Because the bell had tolled for someone as familiar as Nick, it was tolling for them, too. The hypnotherapist's treatment of the entranced Nick was entirely benign, but it was clear that it need not have been. The tension of that first moment of recognition was not dissipated. From this session on, the project was never without a sense of danger.

To the Victorian, in an age of compulsive concealment, the figure of the mesmerist could evoke an eschatological terror. He might pronounce the last judgement on the secret sinner, as he does in the dream of the respected burgomaster Mathias; or he might, like Svengali, approach from the Devil's side. He fed the Victorian appetite for the unspeakable. The peculiar excitability of the Victorian public, their erethism, was shared and exploited by painters, poets and novelists, and it was the psychological playground of melodramatists. They knew that the allure of the perverse drew to the playhouses people whose public commitment to virtue was unfailing. The threatened heroines and lustful villains of melodrama transported these people as far into soft pornography as their reputations licensed them to go. Those who felt a little guilty about being at the play may also have been dimly aware that they were at the play because they felt a little guilty. The Nonconformist conscience has always been responsive to such contradictory impulses. In acclimatising the Alsatian burgomaster to London, Leopold Lewis provides him with a recognisably British (perhaps more Scottish than English) middle-class family; one that has recently risen, through industry and thrift in the approved Methodist/Presbyterian manner, from humbler origins.

Coming to *The Bells* after the hypnotic session, the students were not inclined to under-rate the mesmerist's threat to Mathias's respectable domesticity. But they had still no reason to accept my view that popular religion and popular melodrama occupied the same cultural territory in Victorian Britain. I left well alone for the rest of the second week. It is an error, to which I am prone, to advance too quickly from point to point in a project. If recognitions are to be bodily as well as intellectually absorbed, they require time and opportunities for testing. We worked on scenarios of the divided self in Victorian literature – Poe's *William Wilson*, Hood's *Eugene Aram*, *Dr Jekyll and Mr Hyde*, such characteristic melodramas as *The Lyons Mail* and *The Corsican Brothers* and at the diptych of Sydney Carton and Charles Darnay in *A Tale of Two Cities*. The students ended the second week with their eyes open to the melodramatic tug on behaviour of the buried life.

This is a point, in a five-week project, when you can no longer delay wondering about how to end it. If the goal is set too early, students can sometimes neglect the learning opportunities in the approach work. I had started without a conclusion and I was still uncertain. But the mood of the group was uncommonly open. The work on the divided self had been not so much a historical discovery as a discovery about history. They were beginning, without dictation from me, to embody an apprehension of Victorian values during the period when the high confidence of the establishment was under threat from post-Darwinian uncertainty. I had already set each student a biographical research exercise, to culminate in a ten-minute individual presentation. The subjects had been selected in order to challenge any mind set that the Victorians were a dull bunch: Swinburne, Ellen Terry, Lillie Langtry,

Edward Lear, 'Skittles' Walters, Laurence Oliphant, Lewis Carroll, John Addington Symonds, Dante Gabriel Rossetti, Florence Nightingale and so on. There was plenty of Victorian guilt on display in the two sessions occupied by these presentations. It seemed to me important to develop this further.

Melodrama eases the access of its audiences to the moral shortcomings of its invented characters, thereby preparing the battlefield for a *psychomachia* in the minds of the real individuals in the auditorium. Those most inclined to self-laceration would have castigated themselves for being in a theatre in the first place. T. De Witt Talmage, one of a number of American evangelists who toured Britain in the second half of the nineteenth century, has a warning for them:

> One went forth from a bright Christian home. There was no reason why she should forsake it; but induced by unclean novelette literature and by theatre-going, she started off, and sat down at the banquet of devils. Every few weeks she would come back to her father's house, and hang up her hat and shawl in the old place, as though she expected to stay; but in a few hours, as though hounded by an inexorable fate, she would take down again the hat and the shawl, and start out. When they called her back she slammed the door in their faces, and cried, 'Oh mother! it's too late!' (Talmage, n.d., pp. 182–3)

Even when attacking theatre, Talmage selects a parable that itself belongs to melodrama. That is how the Nonconformist imagination worked. And melodramas, even comparatively highbrow ones like Tennyson's *The Promise of May* and Pinero's *The Second Mrs Tanqueray*, are peppered with moral exhortations, addressed to the impressionable, in terms no less sombre and ominous. One foot on the slippery slope and the chances are that your momentum will carry you all the way down. It is not far from the Methodist magazines that haunted the childhood of the Bronte children to the crime and temperance melodramas that shared a moral mission with them. That is to say that the language of moral correction, heard first in the nursery, was drummed into the ears of the Victorian public even in Satan's pleasure-house. For many melodramatists, the narrative models were provided by Christian parables.

Beyond knowing my own, perhaps autobiographical, need to expose this partial paradox to the group, I was not much closer to determining the goal of the project. For the moment, I proposed that we consider the impact of the charlatan on a vulnerable society. I had in mind D. D. Home and the Davenport brothers. Home's extraordinary career began in 1851 and continued, with occasional scandalous interruptions, until his death in 1886. In his presence, heavy tables rose from the ground, objects moved without being touched, phantom white-gloved hands, detached from visible arms, rested on the shoulders of members of the seance, accordions spontaneously played tunes. There were cases of levitation. In 1868, at Lord Dunraven's house in Ashley Place, Home floated out of one window and in at another (there were three high-society witnesses). At a notorious 1855 seance in Ealing, Elizabeth Barrett Browning had a wreath mysteriously placed on her head and her husband harboured the first intimations of the festering hatred of Home that would culminate in the composition of *Mr Sludge, 'The Medium'*. E. J. Dingwall, in what is still the most balanced account of Home's erratic progress (Dingwall, 1947, pp. 91–128), ascribed the extremity of Browning's loathing as much to his suspicions about Home's sexuality as to his confidence in Home's fraudulence. Society was split over both issues. Home's wife provided respectable cover for his homosexuality and the genuineness of his psychic powers was upheld by the monumentally respectable Mrs Milner Gibson, wife of the President of the Board of Trade. If Home was entirely a charlatan, he was an unusually gifted one. His cachet, like that of Lord Byron earlier in the century, was enhanced by what Mrs Browning called a 'mystery of iniquity, which everybody raved about and nobody distinctly specified' (Dingwall, 1947, p. 105); and he was certainly a shrewd exploiter of the contemporary mania for the supernatural.

Iniquity and the supernatural, as Henry Irving knew well, were fertile soil for melodrama. For all its cultural aspirations, his Lyceum was always hospitable to both. Herbert Swears has a suggestive description of the physical aura of the building:

> It was not then so much a theatre as a temple to be entered with bated breath. There was a sacerdotal air about the entire building. The entrance hall was covered with sombre hangings. The lighting was dim. Small boys like acolytes distributed the programmes. When you entered the precincts you at once absorbed this rarefied atmosphere. A high priest in the shape of Mr Joseph Hurst, sat remotely in a box office. If he smiled when rendering your change, it was a thing to be remembered. (Swears, 1939, pp. 195–6)

Home, too, set the scene for his performances with an eye to detail: the sitters gathered at a round table on which they rested their hands;

the room was dimly lit by gas or candles and a tense silence was maintained. As at the Lyceum, the audience contributed to the creation of an atmosphere in which anything might happen. There was more than a streak of charlatanism in the staging of most successful melodramas. To hold a seance during an evening session – much though students tend to relish such encounters with the numinous – would have been an inappropriate forcing of the point. I turned attention, instead, to the historical encounter between Irving and the Davenport brothers.

Surprisingly perhaps, some people believe still that some of Home's claims were genuine; but no one doubts that the Davenports were utterly bogus and Irving's personal contribution to their exposure was an inventive one. The story could be fairly easily researched and the idea was that we should start the fourth week of the project with a full-scale re-enactment of it. We had ended the previous week with a session in which the students, either singly or in groups, had performed a sequence of extended turns as conjurors or illusionists. Some of these had displayed a degree of melodramatic menace which I hoped could be recaptured. William and Ira Davenport were Americans, who made their money by carrying the taste for parlour seances into theatres. Their act, which involved the recalling of departed spirits, was introduced and provided with a soupy commentary by the 'Reverend Doctor' Ferguson, whose function was to instil in the audience the kind of devotional humility which imparts an urge to believe. Before the eyes of the audience, the Davenports were roped into chairs set inside separate wooden frames. Musical instruments were then placed just out of their reach, and the stage-lights were dimmed. In the darkness and holy silence, the chosen spirits of the dead would play the instruments for the entertainment of their living relatives, the oh-so-sincere clergyman keeping the audience informed the while. When the lights came up, the Davenport brothers were still trussed in their chairs and the audience was assured of an afterlife and God's interest in each and every one of them.

In early 1865, these religious charlatans were performing in Manchester, when Irving was in the company of that city's Theatre Royal. According to his grandson, 'Irving's lingering Methodism was outraged by what he regarded as vulgar blasphemy' (Irving, 1951, p. 119). One of his friends was an amateur magician and together with another actor colleague they devised a facsimile of the Davenports' spiritual show. On the eve of his twenty-seventh birthday, Irving stood before a bemused invited audience at the Manchester Athenaeum and described the bogus 'seance' that had offended him: 'they wished people to understand that they were in some way connected with spiritualism – that, in their own words, they were producing a new hope to all mankind'. Having further explained that his aim was to expose 'the blasphemous pretensions of the unlicensed spirit-dealers' (Irving, 1951, p. 121), Irving left the stage, completed a quick change and returned as the unctuous Dr Ferguson, to provide a commentary on his friends' entirely explicable reproduction of the inexplicable antics of the Davenports. Although the willingly deceived elsewhere in England remained Davenport devotees, their chicanery was effectively revealed.

As for Irving, there was a lesson in the event that he never forgot. What he considered legitimate deceit was never shunned at the Lyceum during Irving's years of glory. The thunderous applause that always greeted his first entry was secretly augmented and prolonged by kettle drums in the orchestra pit. The mysterious effects of limelight were used to enhance the impact of his own strange presence. If the spectators could be overwhelmed by scenic tricks, that was all to the good. Melodrama thrives on them. It seems to me certain that the childhood experience of guilt and gloom in the sternly Methodist home of his Cornish aunt, Sarah Penberthy, found its adult expression in the repertoire of the Lyceum. Irving could combine pathos and malignity in his public brooding in a way that would have been recognisable by anyone similarly assailed in childhood by sticks of sin and carrots of virtue. The Irving who created Mathias had not lost touch with the ten-year-old boy who had announced his conversion to Christ as he emerged from an ecstatic fit in a Cornish chapel. It was through Irving that I now planned to move the project forward from charlatanism to the pieties of salvationary Nonconformism.

I do not remember when, or even whether, I introduced the students to the fact of my own (eccentrically liberal) Methodist upbringing. There was, then at least, a great deal of frozen Victorianism in the average Methodist congregation and it may be that the combination of prurience and puritanism which my memory evokes does not reflect, as accurately as I have persuaded myself that it does, the typical audience of nineteenth-century melodrama. The remainder of the project served as a (necessarily inconclusive) test of my belief in the comparability of the emotional tactics of melodrama and the strategies devised by the Methodist Home Mission Department. There is, for example, the matter of money. The great majority of melodramas boil down to wrangles about money, charting the eventual passage of wealth out of the wrong hands, over or through hideous obstructions, into the right hands.

Early in my religious education, I was confronted with the vexing paradox that, although money was the root of all evil, the possession of it by Methodists was considered 'a good thing' and thrift a quality liable to be rewarded by appointment as a chapel steward. There were only two moments in a Methodist service when the congregation acted in religious unison – one when we recited the Lord's Prayer and when we all stood for the blessing of the collection. There were no hassocks for communal kneeling, no responses; and hymn-singing, although often hearty, was decidedly individual. But the clumsy, mid-service ritual of the collection had a palpable solemnity. As the wooden plates were passed from hand to hand along the pews, there were furtive glances at the deposits of neighbours. Regulars were spared the risk of revelation by being allowed to conceal their weekly offerings in small, square envelopes (obtainable from the chapel stewards). And when all the pews had been finished and the plates collected, the stewards would process up the aisle and deliver them to the minister with a reverence that would have befitted gold, frankincense and myrrh. The minister had only to mutter, 'Let us all pray', for the coughing to stop and everyone to stand. Why did we stand for that prayer and not for the others? When I asked my father, who was a minister, he said it was just a custom. It was, I think, a custom that owed less to the Bible than to Samuel Smiles, whose *Self Help* (1859) had the status almost of an alternative Bible in late-Victorian Methodism. The idea of a collection figured later in the project.

The recreation of Irving and the Davenports had given a few of the students a pretext for practising some of the tricks of the melo-dramatic trade. In order to involve all of them, I distributed role cards at the beginning of the fourth week. A typical one is shown in box 1.

The card was typical in a number of ways. It gave a fairly detailed background but no indication of 'character': it left Ethel Slade in desperate straits, and it referred to a missing brother and a lost lover. Unknown to this student, the holder of another card *was* the missing brother and a third student had been Arthur Seaton's co-plotter in a bank fraud, for which Arthur had been imprisoned. There was a role card for the preacher, a man with a reeking past and a holy present, for a pianist, who nursed a hidden passion for the preacher, and one for a policeman, the only 'actor' in a group of sinners, who would be meeting in the 'chapel' for the last session of the fourth week. He was there in response to a tip-off that Arthur Seaton's accomplice might be among the congregation. What he did not know was that the preacher was the father who had abandoned him and his mother in Cornwall, many years ago. Each of the cards set the holder a series of

Box 1: *Ethel Slade*

Born in Frinton (Essex) to elderly parents. (Your mother was over 40 and your father over 50 at the time.) Brought up in the boarding-house they owned. You can dimly remember a brother, much older than you, who ran away to sea to escape the oppressive atmosphere of your ultra-religious home. Your parents were Congregationalists and your childhood seemed to be full of Sundays – services morning and evening and Sunday school in the afternoon. Your father died when you were ten, and your mother went into a decline. You nursed her for six years, running the boarding-house alone for the last two. When she died, she left you the house on condition that you signed a Rechabite pledge – not difficult, since you had never touched alcohol anyway. But you were lonely, and Arthur Seaton was so charming. Quite rich too; his father was a bank manager and a pillar of the Congregational chapel. You let Arthur lead you into bad ways – dancing, visiting the fairground and even (once) a music hall, where he bought you a gin. And then another.... That night, he made you pregnant. When his father found out, he sent Arthur away. You were scared. You needed him. Where was he? London? The solicitor who sold the boarding-house for you cheated you out of most of the money, but you took the rest to London, where you rented a room in a small hotel in Tottenham. You looked everywhere for Arthur. By the time your baby was born, funds were running low. You had the baby in your hotel room, with a grubby midwife attending. She told you it was born dead and took the corpse away with her. You were very ill, but the woman who owned the hotel was kind. She made you drink a lot of stout to nurse you back to health. After a while, she brought a man to see you. Then another.... What are you now? A prostitute and a drunkard? So they say.

small research tasks. Ethel Slade would need to find out something about Victorian Frinton, Congregationalism (George Eliot's *Silas Marner* was a Congregationalist) and the Rechabites, for example. The students were given a free session to carry out these investigations. They were not allowed to show their cards to anyone else.

There was something solemn about this secrecy, which contributed to the atmosphere of the climactic Friday 'service'. That session proceeded as follows.

The date was 1880. All the students knew that, and they knew also that the place was a Nonconformist chapel in a grimy back street of London's East End. They were to arrive, in costumes they had selected and in role, between 10 and 10.30 a.m., when the service would start. During that half hour, tea and biscuits would be available in the 'vestry'. My role was that of chapel steward. As people arrived, I gave them an order of service and a hymn sheet (one or two, of course, were illiterate). They arrived at intervals, mostly shamefaced and down-at-heel, to be welcomed by preacher and pianist. Conversation was sticky, although there were brazen sinners as well as shoddy ones, so that the preacher's task was not impossible. Even so, more rested on him alone than was ideal in a mass role-play session. He had to take his cue from the order of service I had prepared, controlling the pace and sequence of events. The inspiration for the form of 'worship' I had outlined dated from my National Service. On church parade, we were customarily divided into RC (Roman Catholic), C of E (Church of England) and OD (other denominations). One of the people I had got to know in the OD group during my eight weeks of square-bashing was subsequently sent to the same Joint Services camp in Scotland. He was from Widnes and, I think, a Baptist. It was certainly to a Baptist chapel in Anstruther that he took me one Sunday in late November 1956. Anstruther in summer is a pleasant little fishing town on the coast of Fife. Anstruther in winter, when the east wind blows, is a polar hell. The old minister of the chapel had recently died of pneumonia, contracted while baptising (total immersion, of course) a clutch of Anstruther youths in the harbour and the new minister was an enthusiast for salvation. The service to which I had been guided consisted of rousing hymns, interspersed with testimonies from members of the congregation. They positively jostled for the chance to say their piece. I particularly remember a woman, in her forties I would guess, but prematurely aged and heavily powdered to cover facial cracks. She stood at the front, with tears burrowing through the powder, recalling the days before Christ came into her life, when she used to indulge in 'the drinkin', the smokin' and the dancin', day after day and night after night'. But now she had seen the wounds of her saviour. 'Hallelujah!', everyone said. So the order of service in our back-street chapel read as follows (the directions in italic being on the preacher's copy only):

Say a few words of welcome, especially if any first-timers are looking nervous.

(1) Hymn 1 on the hymn sheet.

Read the whole first verse before asking the pianist to play: let her play through a whole verse before starting the singing yourself.

(2) Prayer.

Let yourself go on this. Extempore prayer is a Nonconformist preacher's beatific soliloquy. Concentrate on yourself and others as sinners.

(3) Testimonies.

Encourage people to come forward. If no one does, ask the pianist to set things off.

(4) Hymn 2.

When you're sure no one's ready to 'bear witness' yet.

(5) Prayer.

Try asking someone who's already spoken to speak this prayer. If not, you'll have to. You could try some lyricism about the beauty of the natural word – God's handiwork.

(6) Testimonies.

Urge people to lighten their burden by confessing and testifying. Jesus hears.

(7) Hymn 3.

(8) Reading.

The passage is marked in the Bible on the lectern. It's the parable of the prodigal son. Try getting one of them to read it.

(9) Testimonies.

Remind them that the prodigal son was forgiven. You should make your own testimony this time; that will put real pressure on the laggards.

(10) Hymn 4.

(11) Collection.

There's a collection plate on the piano. The pianist will take it round. Tell them that the money goes towards the saving of souls.

(12) Blessing of the collection.

A reverent prayer, talking about using people's gifts of money for God's holy work.

(13) Hymn 5.

(14) Final testimonies.

Really press them!

(15) Hymn 6.

(16) Blessing.

*Something to send them happy on their way. Then get to the door to
talk before they leave. You'll have a word for everyone.*

I had begun with very little idea how the session would go. I had
certainly not expected it to last so long (three hours), nor to rise to
such levels of intensity. The group was predominantly agnostic and
there were no 'born-agains' in it, nor any hard-line Nonconformists,
but they entered into it with such spirit that you might have thought,
as an onlooker, that the spirit had entered them. Every confession,
and all the students confessed in the end, was a melodrama waiting to
be written. The six hymns were Ira Sankey's contribution to the
splendidly eclectic *Methodist Hymn Book*. Sankey was an altogether
gentler, more encouraging American evangelist than De Witt Talmage.
He and Dwight Moody made their first visit to England in 1873,
bringing with them a new, homely style. Moody's pietistic preaching
employed the language of the people and Sankey's simple tunes
(figure 1), played by himself on the harmonium, slipped easily into the
popular repertoire, above all that of the Salvation Army.

It was during the 1870s that the Salvation Army established its
popular practices, importing into religion the stirring military images
and rituals that had been mediated to the masses during the Indian
'mutiny' and the Crimean War. It is a short distance from Tennyson's
The Charge of the Light Brigade to the Salvation Army, and what
happened in our improvised chapel on that Friday morning persuaded
me that I had rightly gauged the proximity of Methodism and melodrama.

Ever since the hypnotism, the students had gifted themselves to the
project with a commitment that slightly unnerved me. I was certainly
unnerved by the Baptist totality of immersion in their roles that some
of them displayed. The example of the policeman was particularly
startling, although necessarily untypical. To camouflage his real
purposes, he volunteered a confession when the service reached item
6. It was an entire invention, nothing to do with his actual role card.
Although I was the only person in the room able to recognise it, his
was a meta-theatrical presence in an essentially Stanislavskian game.
But a change came over him when, under item 9, the preacher made
his own confession. The secret policeman rose from his seat at the
back, edging his way down the aisle until, as the preacher came to an
end, he could step forward to greet him as 'Father!'. If the preacher
had had space in his crowded agenda to acknowledge the possibility
that this was, indeed, his abandoned son, there might have been a
flood of similar recognitions. As it was, he brushed the policeman

Figure 1. 'The Christian Life', from a Methodist hymn book.

aside to announce the hymn and there was no re-uniting of separated siblings, childhood friends or mothers and daughters. There was, however, a tremendous warmth in the welcome extended to fellow-sinners and by the time the service ended (it was approaching 2 p.m.), a sentimental community of the nearly damned had been established. The policeman did not arrest Arthur Seaton's accomplice. He had his own reasons for that change of plan.

The group did not meet again until the Monday of the project's final week. They had left the service, and the building, in role and I have no idea how long they sustained those roles. We had now to determine what of the work we should show to the rest of the department on the final Friday. There was no way of reviving in public what had been an intensely private event and it might have been a mistake – it was certainly an invitation to anti-climax – to decide, as we did, to retain the form of a religious service. There were, however, significant changes. The students chose to greet the audience with a freak show. With some help from lighting and more from inventiveness, they created a two-headed woman, an elephant man, a hermaphrodite, a dwarf with arms where her legs should have been and legs for arms. There was a particularly hideous exhibit of a deformed fetus (culled from the nightmare shape in many of Beardsley's prints) in a tank of water. The intention was to release a certain prurience in the audience, a link to Victorian erethism, before leading them into a cleansing service of salvation. We retained the outward form of the earlier session, although much abbreviated, selecting confessions that would lead into excerpts from various nineteenth-century melodramas, summarily rehearsed during this last week. The then Professor of English, who had sung the hymns with some abandon, asked me afterwards, 'What was all that about?', and then added 'a bit near the knuckle, I thought'. The session on the previous Friday had got near to my solar plexus, but the knuckle was probably as far as the public performance reached. What I knew then was that the students had learned far more, emotionally as well as historically, than I had been able to teach them. I do not recall the substance of the post-project seminar, but I shall conclude this essay with some points about Methodism and melodrama that I might have made.

I have so far presented a one-sided view of Nonconformism. If Methodism tended to darken the greyness of my own adolescence, it lightened the lives of thousands during the nineteenth century. The main branch ('the old connection') of the Methodist church, which began the century with 825 recorded chapels in Britain, had 11,007 by 1851; and that figure disregards the various splinter groups. The most notable of these, the so-called Primitive Methodists, had broken away in 1810 in order to pursue its peculiarly fervent mission among rural and urban workers, out of sight of the expanding middle classes. To join the old connection, as many people discovered in the years before and after the Reform Bill of 1832, was one way of accelerating progress into the middle class. What is more, the evangelical revival, which had lost impetus by the mid-century, received a second wind in

1859 from the blast of Charles Darwin's *Origin of Species*. For two decades after 1859, the increased activity of the established Church was overmatched by the proselytising of Nonconformist orators. When the Municipal Reform Act of 1835 lifted the bar to the holding of civic office by Dissenters, Leicester, Leeds, Manchester, Birmingham, Liverpool and Derby were quick to elect Unitarian mayors. There was political significance in this. Nonconformists traditionally, and often passionately, supported the Liberal party, so that their ceaseless conflict with the Church of England shaded into antagonism towards Conservative policies. Later in the century, it was predominantly Methodists who guided the formal establishing of a Labour party. Many of the articulate artisans who voiced the views of the underclass had gained the confidence to speak in public as local preachers in Methodist chapels. Arthur Henderson, who began his political career as a Liberal agent before rising to a position of leadership in the new Labour party, was only the most prominent of them. What is of great significance is that Methodism, more systematically than the other Nonconformist denominations, endorsed sentiment and intuition as a passage to faith. To many of the underprivileged, it offered a first encounter with music and literature, not least through the imaginative provocation of hymns.

With the publication, in 1860, of *Hymns Ancient and Modern*, the Church of England was catching up with the long-established choral sound of religious dissent. Hymns, often melodramatic in the extremity of their expression, were the common stock of nineteenth-century poets. They offered a personal encounter with mysterious powers. I have a private memory of belting out Walter Smith's 'Immortal, invisible, God only wise, / In light inaccessible hid from our eyes' to that rousing Welsh melody 'St Denio', and feeling that, if I could manage unknown words with so many syllables, I could surely reach God. It is only now, when I look at the fustian of Smith's second stanza, that I realise how I could be manipulated: 'Thy justice like mountains high soaring above, / Thy clouds which are fountains of goodness and love'. There was more aspiration than accuracy in the language of Nonconformism. Had he been so inclined, Walter Smith (1824–1908) could probably have written a melodrama.

While it is broadly true that churchgoing Methodists would not have visited theatres, we cannot assume that their theatregoing neighbours knew nothing of Methodism. No middle-class neighbourhood in Victorian Britain was untouched by Nonconformist values; and fingers of Methodism reached further into the slums than even the most evangelical Anglicans, whose practices were anyway indistinguishable from those of the Methodist Home Missions. Chapel and playhouse may have looked askance at each other, but they had much in common: a direct appeal to strong feeling, a dependence on exemplary, moral narratives, an unsuppressable response to the lubricious tug of evil. It was an alignment memorably signalled in 1856. In the previous year, Lord Shaftesbury had guided through Parliament a Bill rescinding the ban on meetings of more than 20 people for religious worship except in churches or licensed chapels. The Bishop of London encouraged the subsequent holding of mass services in Exeter Hall, but the high-church vicar of the parish in which the Hall was situated, considering the activity demeaning, imposed an inhibition of his own. As a result, the Anglican missionaries were forced to hold their services in 'seven low theatres rented in the poorest parts of London' (Clark, 1962, p. 187).

It was important that the students should understand the contribution of Methodism to beneficial social change in the nineteenth century. But it was important also that they should recognise its less attractive features. Matthew Arnold's squeamish reaction to the vulgarity and self-righteousness of Nonconformism, which informs every chapter of *Culture and Anarchy* (1869), arose from much more than his own adherence to the high abstractions of 'sweetness and light'. The 'Nonconformist conscience' was first mentioned during the malodorous campaign to oust Parnell from leadership of the Irish party of the House of Commons because of his relationship with a married woman. The moral smugness of the godly Methodist made him as inflexible over Parnell as was the Irish Catholic. Parnell and the prospect of Home Rule perished together in October 1891. Such are the wages of sin.

We ought, as audiences of melodrama, to be pleased when the villain is defeated, but not to lose sight of the fact that improved financial status is frequently the best evidence of heroic victory. In melodramatic fiction, the spoils go to the deserving, thus reinforcing bourgeois prejudice. Arnold is magisterially scornful of the industrialist Sir Daniel Gooch, who quoted to factory workers in Swindon his mother's golden rule: 'Ever remember, my dear Dan, that you should look forward to being some day manager of that concern' (Arnold, 1935, p. 80). Gooch was a minor luminary among Nonconformist Victorian industrialists. W. H. Lever was a Congregationalist, Samuel Courtauld a Unitarian, Thomas Cook a Baptist, George Cadbury a Quaker and Jesse Boot a Methodist. When the collection was taken at our improvised service, the largest sum was donated by the least repentant of the penitents. Her role dictated it. Sir George

Kenning, who was a member of my father's Sheffield congregation from 1946 to 1953, and Tom Hardy, who was a steel magnate, used to contribute £5 per week. When Hardy discovered that Kenning had upped his weekly payment to £10, he matched it. It was not for Sheffield steel to lose to the motor industry.

Methodism, like melodrama, is Janus-faced. It sides with the dispossessed while privileging the wealthy. It was Aneurin Bevan's view that the Sunday schools of South Wales moulded the characters of future miners and at the same time cultivated their expressive gifts (Francis and Smith, 1980, p. 10) and it has been argued that Ernest Bevin owed his political principles and some of his parliamentary dexterity to his early experience in Nonconformist debating societies (Obelkevich, 1990, p. 345). Trades unions owed much, in their early years, to the egalitarianism and organising skills of Methodists and that is a tradition that continues. But something meaner and more vindictive is inherent, too. Alongside Ernest Bevin might be set Alfred Roberts, son of a Northamptonshire shoemaker, and Methodist to the core. Roberts left school at 13 to work for a grocer. Before the outbreak of the First World War, he had saved enough to buy his own shop, to which he added another on the other side of town after the armistice. Then came the depression:

> Careful husbandry was necessary to ensure that a business survived. This Alfred had little difficulty in providing. He was by nature a cautious, thrifty fellow, who had inherited an unquestioning admiration for certain Victorian values: hard work, self-help, rigorous budgeting and a firm belief in the immorality of extravagance. (Young, 1989, p. 5)

Roberts was a Methodist local preacher and both his daughters attended Sunday services at Finkin Street Methodist Church, Grantham. One of them later trained as a physiotherapist. The other emerged from her Methodist chrysalis as the butterfly Margaret Thatcher. When she spoke to the people on television, her manner was as unctuous and patronising as my Sunday school teacher's but she turned centres of government into stages for melodrama.

Works cited

Arnold, M. (1935) *Culture and Anarchy*. Cambridge University Press, Cambridge.

Bierce, A. (1993) *The Devil's Dictionary*. Dover Publications, New York.

Clark, G. K. (1962) *The Making of Victorian England*. Methuen, London.

Craig, E. G. (1930) *Henry Irving*. J. M. Dent and Sons, London.

Dingwall, E. J. (1947) *Some Human Oddities*. Home & Van Thal, London.

Francis, H. and Smith, D. (1980) *The Fed*. Lawrence and Wishart, London.

Irving, L. (1951) *Henry Irving: The Actor and His World*. Faber and Faber, London.

Obelkevich, J. (1990) 'Religion', in *The Cambridge Social History of Britain 1750–1950*, ed. F. M. L. Thompson. Cambridge University Press, Cambridge, vol. 3, pp. 311–56.

St. John, C. (ed.) (1931) *Ellen Terry and Bernard Shaw: A Correspondence*. Constable & Co., London.

Swears, H. (1939) 'Irving as Synorix', in *We Saw Him Act: A Symposium on the Art of Sir Henry Irving*, eds H. A. Saintsbury and C. Palmer. Hurst & Blackett, London, pp. 191–6.

Talmage, T. De Witt (n.d.) *Sports that Kill*. James Blackwood & Co., London.

Young, H. (1989) *One of Us*. Macmillan, London.

9

Teaching the Politics of Theatricality: Case Study, Meyerhold

Christopher McCullough

Training! Training! Training! But if it's the kind of training which exercises only the body and not the mind, then no thank you! I have no use for actors who know how to move but cannot think.

(Vsevolod Meyerhold, 1934)

This chapter argues the case for a materialist understanding of the value of an engagement in practical theatre as a method of learning. The model is based on Meyerhold's sense of 'theatricality' as a mode of political theatre and will argue the case for 'praxis' in learning, as opposed to the concept of a transcendent ideological neutrality through 'practice'. Employing Meyerhold's work as the vehicle, the chapter examines the potentiality of both a material and a materialist argument for 'doing'. An engagement with the context and meaning of the politics of theatricality should offer an opportunity to challenge those forms of theatricality that rest upon a sense that 'doing' is innocent of ideology.

Most drama students will have had their first encounter with radically progressive theatre through a selective reading of the work of Bertolt Brecht. But, not the least because Brecht's theory and practice are often misrepresented, this encounter will not have provided them with easy access to the dialectics of theatre as proposed and practised by Vsevolod Meyerhold. Until his tentative return to East Berlin in 1949, Brecht was working and writing in and for pre-revolutionary societies and was thus pre-occupied with the business of alerting the potential audience's consciousness to the contradictions inherent in capitalism. What is more, few people would argue that post-war East Germany provided a model of a post-revolutionary society. By contrast, Meyerhold's work, developed amid pre-revolutionary cultural tensions, was continued through the immediate aftermath of revolution and snuffed out only when Stalinism closed its fist on art. To a degree, then, Brecht is pre-revolutionary and Meyerhold (post-)revolutionary.

This distinction is, however, over-simple. Like Brecht, Meyerhold developed his own practice out of the urge to contradict the practices of others. His 'praxis' was born out of a reaction against the pre-revolutionary aesthetics of naturalism and pictorial realism. But he came quickly to the conclusion that Stanislavsky's way was no less repressive than the style he sought to replace:

> The naturalism of the Art Theatre is the naturalism adopted from the Meiningen Players; its fundamental principle is the *exact representation of life* ... the naturalistic theatre denies not only the spectator's ability to imagine for himself, but even his ability to understand clever conversations. (Braun, 1969, pp. 23, 27)

Meyerhold observed that this obsession with the detail of veracity, at every level of theatrical production, created what we may term a social totality: a stage picture where not only every detail of that world is represented, but that complexity of detail prevents, by its insistence, any possible alternative view of that world. We may say, 'This is how the world is, nothing can be done to alter this state of affairs; this is reality.' However, Meyerhold observed the radical potentiality of a theatre that did not attempt to represent that sense of a social totality:

> In the theatre the spectator's imagination is able to supply that which is left unsaid. It is this mystery and the desire to solve it that draws so many people to the theatre.... The stylised theatre produces a play in such a way that the spectator is compelled to employ his imagination *creatively* in order to *fill* in the details intimated by the action on stage. (Quoted in Braun, 1995, p. 71)

If a theatrical practice declares that its aim is to create an *exact representation of life*, we may infer that reality, in that ideological structure, is determined as an absolute concept. Reality is human nature is a transcendent state and the 'laws of life' aₗ immutable. For the spectator in the theatre of illusion nothing is left to the imagination, the narrative unfolds both dramatically and visually in front of her/him in a process not unlike that required by the act of reading a novel. S/he consumes the art as a product, a cultural commodity that provides little or no space for active participation in the production of meaning. What Meyerhold (like Brecht and Piscator in Germany) sought was to make the spectator an active participant in an open-ended cultural activity. With the actors, the spectator was to become an active participant in the production of meaning, a meaning that could and would change. Obviously, this is an issue that must be confronted if we are to understand the agenda of the experiments of Meyerhold and other radical theatre practitioners.

A materialist analysis must challenge fixed concepts of reality. Focusing a project on Meyerhold and the politics of theatricality demands that the pedagogic methodology must be responsive to Meyerhold's challenge to an 'exact representation of life'. There would be little value in presenting this material by a method that did not allow for a discourse between the student and the teacher. It is through such a discourse that the material may be best understood. A system that prosecutes a conventional relationship whereby the lecture is the starting point for group discussion in the seminar, which in turn may lead to 'trying out some of the ideas' in practice, does not offer the necessary avenues for the students (in collaborative and individual exercises) to pursue an heuristic investigation. It seems to me that the purpose in attempting to understand the radical experiments in early socialist theatre is invalidated if the pedagogy denies the student's potential voice in the theatre praxis. It is worth reminding ourselves of the dangers of making the efforts of the early twentieth-century experimenters in theatre into just another stimulating subject to be included in the university curriculum. Some of them (Meyerhold was not alone) were employing a 'scientific' theory of human society in order to advance the means by which to transform that society. This does not mean quite the same thing as the heightened spiritual awareness that may be derived from the modern appropriations of ancient tragic forms, but is more directly related to the voice that generations may discover in order that women and men may free themselves from certain forms of exploitation and oppression. To lose our sense of this material relevance in theatre is to negate the struggles of the individuals who form the focus of our work. The task is not to recreate Meyerhold (or anyone else for that matter), but to

sense of history to inform our own practices, so
he potential to become praxis.
the outline of, and commentary on, a project that
d's theory and practice. Some (but not all) of it will
al project based on daily three-hour sessions and
la꜖ꜗ ꜄s. The pedagogy incorporates extra-mural research,
which then ⸝ ⸝ be expressed in intra-mural seminars, but the main
emphasis is on a methodology of teaching through practice whose aim
is/was to explore the potentially radical concept of self-reflexive
theatricality or *stylised theatre*. It is to facilitate presentation and
reception that I describe the project under three headings: 'Physical
skills', 'Contextual research' and 'Textual explorations'. Such divisions
inevitably risk misrepresenting the student experience.

Physical skills

> For us the art of manufacture is more important than any tediously
> pretty patterns and colours. What do we want with pleasing
> pictorial effects? What the *modern* spectator wants is the placard,
> the juxtaposing of the surfaces and shapes of *tangible materials*! (On
> the staging of Verhaeren's *The Dawn*, Braun, 1969, p. 173)

Stylisation and physical action

The phrase 'physical skills' is often treated conceptually in much the
same way as the more general term 'practice'. An all-too-ready
assumption that physical skills, as a constituent part of practice, are
simultaneously (and in a contradictory fashion) both radical and free
from ideological conditioning hampers much of the work needed to
develop the pedagogic skills that enable practical theatre work to
operate as an intrinsic part of the university syllabus.

The work of Meyerhold helps us to see how we may be able to
understand that a physical action on stage, and the skill needed to
communicate that action, is a self-conscious gesture. It is not innocent
in the way that is implied by the attempt to depict 'reality' that was the
central concern of naturalism. The illusion of everyday action is no
more 'natural' than the concept of 'nature' itself. Between 1905 and
1917 Meyerhold was developing the studied discipline of gesture
and motion. Whereas Stanislavsky (in the earlier phases of his
work) concentrated on training the actor to study the psychological

motivation for gestures, Meyerhold encouraged the actor to study the conventions of gesture throughout the history of older theatre traditions. In particular, the skills that had been developed by gymnasts and circus performers became the focus of interest. It may be argued that naturalism, in its many manifestations, has always carried the seeds of its own contradictions. In the efforts to depict 'an exact representation of life' there is also the denial of art. An action that on the stage declares itself to be a representation of reality is, itself, a contradiction of the fact that it is 'pretence'. Ultimately we must accept the logic of the argument that perceives all actions or representations on the stage as conventions of one kind or another: ideologically rooted cultural formations. The forms of the circus and of *commedia dell'arte* created clearly defined signs and gestures that are manifestly not life as we perceive it in our day-to-day existence, but certainly were related to the actions of life, framed as consciously determined gestures with an ideological point to them.[1]

Meyerhold was, in many ways, anticipating Brecht's concept of *Gestus*. The meaning of *Gestus* is complex and difficult to understand in any direct translation into English. However, it is possible to separate the *Gestisches Material*, or social meaning of a play, from the individual *Gesten*. Emphasis on such *Material* will encourage a fragmentary, episodic and contradictory style of acting that reveals human beings in their constantly changing roles: the human character as a material cultural construct capable of change.

So, what possibilities exist for a springboard into physical theatre work that may lead to an understanding of Meyerhold's socialist theatricality? In 1926, Leon Trotsky gave a number of lectures under the broad title of 'Culture and Socialism'.[2] Central to Trotsky's argument is the problem that must be confronted by a revolutionary culture: the exact nature of the relationship between work and art. While the essay analyses the problematic nature of the relationship between an emergent revolutionary materialist culture and the residual bourgeois 'spiritual' culture, an interesting feature emerges in his statement that 'we now can say: it is good when poets sing of the revolution and the proletariat, but a powerful turbine sings even better' (see Pearce, 1962, p. 90) This is not an argument against poetry or philosophy, but, in the context of the essay, a call for the need to understand that a revolution needs a revolution in all aspects of social relations. 'The decisive instrument in the cultural revolution must be a revolution in technique' (Pearce, 1962, p. 90). If a revolution calls for new ways of thinking derived from new conditions of social relations, for instance a new relationship between the individual, work and the product of work, then in the making of art it is necessary not only to construct new imagery (content) but also necessary to understand the potentiality of new relationships between the individual and the techniques of production in art. If the singing of heroic songs for the revolution (or the dancing of heroic dances) is no longer entirely appropriate, then what is? In the sense of material well-being we may observe that there is a more immediate need for tractors than there is for songs. However, Trotsky was never so crude. There is a need for the means of production of songs to be re-assessed as well as what the song is about.

The new industrial society of the emergent Soviet Russia required new art forms and necessarily new techniques by which to express those forms. Art was to relate to what was important and significant in people's lives, namely the industrial process required in order to transform a feudal state into a modern socialist state. Out of this 'new' social relationship was born Meyerhold's concept of biomechanics. Although biomechanics, as a system for training actors, predates the revolution by about four years – it was used by Meyerhold in his studio in St Petersburg in 1914 – Meyerhold claimed that the system was based on F. W. Taylor's scientific studies of the organisation of labour. Taylorism, as it has become known, is popularly understood as 'time and motion study', or more recently the 'science' of ergonomics, whereby the movements and shape of the human body may be related to the machine or environment in the most efficient and appropriate way. Of course, this study of machine–human relationships may be appropriated by any ideology and the efficient action of the worker may be for the profit of the shareholder as much as it may be for the collective good of the worker's community. Taylorism was itself a product of capitalism, as Mel Gordon points out:

> In 1918, Lenin, himself, held up Taylor's principles of scientific management, or Taylorism, as a primary example of those achievements of capitalism, which, however brutal and exploitative in intent – the augmentation of work output and resulting profits – represented a grand and revolutionary approach to the entire work process worthy of Soviet emulation. (Gordon, 1974, p. 74)

This preliminary skirmish into the origins and purpose of Taylorism would mean very little to a group of undergraduates who may well have only the vaguest sense of Meyerhold's theatrical practices. The problem is to discover a way by which a five-week project may find its starting point. Working on the principle that an heuristic approach to education still retains some virtue (if not cost-effective in the view of administrators), an interesting problem-solving situation may be presented to students who are about to commence work in the first class of the five-week project (occurring, that is, before any preliminary contextualising research).

Working on the premise that the initial problem to be addressed was the fact that theatre action (movement) is not intrinsically different from 'work' movement and that we may observe physical movement more in terms of bodily mechanics than in terms of an often vague sense of idealistic aesthetics, I proposed to the group of 20 students that we consider undertaking a series of problem-solving tasks in physical movement. There was to be no hint of making art, simply the idea of setting ourselves problems and helping each other to solve them. It is important to emphasise that this work was preceded by a physical warm-up that served the dual purpose of enabling the students to prepare for physical work (for all the obvious reasons of personal safety and the more socially orientated purpose of creating a passage into the mode of the group work with which we were about to engage). The challenge posed was that, in pairs, the students were to locate a movement with which they found difficulties (such as a cartwheel or handstand) and help each other towards the successful completion of that movement. The element of personal choice was important at this stage in order to avoid imposing physical actions that could be 'better' performed by either women or men, or that relied too much on a certain type of body.

There is an important principle of pedagogy to be confronted here. The issue of power structures in the 'classroom', and the questions that may surround the teacher as the site of power, are particularly urgent in the evolution of a teaching methodology for overtly political theatre. As teachers, we (often, but not always) instigate the area of learning, but this privileged status does not mean that we should also determine the outcome of a pedagogy that claims its provenance in an heuristic ideal and its process in research through practice. To have the teacher at the centre of the interaction, the site of power, is not always the most appropriate way by which to proceed. When setting a problem-solving physical exercise, account must be taken of the demands of the activity, particularly if the suggestion is read as an instruction. To attempt an action based on gymnastics created in a number of students a degree of inhibition, and even antagonism for a few. However, a strategy that involved the removal of the teacher from the centre of power in this context meant that the students were free to devise the mechanics of their own physical actions as the exercise developed. In the event, many of the exercises focused on the mechanics of weight distribution related to balance. Similar problems are the basis of elementary gymnastics, but here they were eventually confronted in the students' own terms, rather than imposed by a centralised pedagogy.

These early experiments with the mechanics of action allowed the students to develop confidence in their own bodies. As this was not primarily a training context, it was important to allow time for discussion of the outcome – in terms of body perceptions as well as mechanical problem-solving.

Biomechanics

Before practical sessions on the exercises (*études*) incorporated in Meyerhold's biomechanical training could be instituted, a period of information-gathering had to be undertaken, in order that the exercises could be understood in some kind of context. Biomechanics is a broad generic term that has no single authority or meaning. Meyerhold did not invent the term; rather it evolved from the many sources that informed Meyerhold's early experiments. Braun (1995, p. 172) quotes from Meyerhold on the subject.

> In the past the actor has always conformed to the society for which his art was intended. In the future the actor must go even further in relating his technique to the industrial situation. For he will be working in a society where labour is no longer regarded as a curse but as a joyful, vital necessity. In these conditions of ideal labour art clearly requires a new foundation.

This 'new foundation' was the claim to be scientific about the making of art. Constructivism, the movement arising in the early years of the revolution, had, according to Meyerhold, 'forced the artist to become artist and engineer. Art should be based on scientific principles; the entire creative act should be a conscious process' (Braun, 1995, p. 173). Quite what we may understand by the idea of being scientific about art requires some thought. Often, the claim is made in university drama/theatre departments that the time given over to practical work is commensurate with laboratory time in the science and engineering faculties. This claim is both valid and invalid. It is valid in the sense that theatre, like the sciences, possesses a material nature. The movement of action from the literary form to performance involves a confrontation with the material business of 'putting theatre on'. However, unlike science, the task of verifying the results of a material experiment in theatre is problematic in terms of objectivity. Science may have its own problems, but there is a common acceptance of the form of empiricism involved in a scientific experiment. Can the same be argued in the case of the theatre laboratory, when an attempt is made to subsume the subjectivity of human experience into the objectivity of scientific tradition? Of course, there are substantial arguments by which to challenge both this 'subjectivity' and this 'objectivity' and, while not directly addressing the matter, this chapter will draw on aspects of the debate.

It is necessary to examine closely what is meant by being scientific in the arts if we are to gain from our exercise in pedagogy. Meyerhold expressed a formula for acting, thus: $N = A1 + A2$. N = the actor; $A1$ = the artist who conceives the idea and issues the instructions necessary for its execution; $A2$ = the executant who executes the conception of $A1$. There is nothing remarkable in producing such a formula but it does gives us clear guidelines as to how Meyerhold analysed a part of his theatrical method. In the same sense Meyerhold analysed what he described as the acting cycle as: (1) intention; (2) realisation; (3) reaction.

(1) *The intention* is the intellectual assimilation of a task prescribed externally by the dramatist, the director or the initiative of the performer.

(2) *The realisation* is the cycle of volitional, mimetic and vocal reflexes.

(3) *The reaction* is the attenuation of the volitional reflex after its realisation mimetically and vocally, preparatory to the reception of a new intention (the transition to a new acting cycle).

(Quoted in Braun, 1995, pp. 173–4)

If what is meant by being scientific requires artists to analyse the mechanics of expression in a materialist sense, then the term would seem to possess a degree of validity. It is possible, for example, to combine a precise analysis of movement with an application of Brechtian *Gestus* in a manner analogous to the scientific method. However, problems surely arise in the analysis of *meaning* in the outcome of an experiment. The scientist or engineer, when dealing with commonly accepted phenomenal 'facts', represents the tested result in terms of physical laws which, as far as we understand, are immutable facts. The result of theatre practice is the performance, in its variety of manifestations. Performance, while being the product of rational thought, is still a cultural event, subject to change, indeed, demanding change and transition from performance to performance. Our understanding of meaning in a performance is to a degree subjective and determined by our own ideological location – involving class, gender, race and all the many social determinants that comprise our sense of *Gestus*.

The *études* that comprise the corpus of biomechanics are based on gestures derived from human actions that emphasise either a 'work' task, such as 'shooting a bow', or an action that focuses on what we may perceive as a social gesture, such as 'leap onto the chest', or 'dagger thrust'. The movements involved in executing the *études* involved the actors in emulating the skills of workers in industry. Rhythm, appropriate central body gravity, and stability with no superfluous or unproductive movements were the main focuses of the exercises. The intention was that the body would be trained to execute efficiently the external tasks set; the resulting precision would lead to the quickest realisation of the task objective (maximum productivity). Through this process the theatre should only employ immediately decipherable movements; all else was superfluous. Meyerhold's argument rested, in part, on the premise that previous forms of acting (at least in the nineteenth century) relied on inspiration and emotions (themselves, it may be argued, specifically post-Romantic bourgeois concepts), leading to no regulated control over movement or voice. Equally, in the practices of his former teacher Stanislavsky, acting based on psychology was insubstantial, since psychology is incapable of supplying material answers. Acting based on physiology, Meyerhold argued, is at least assured of clarity.

Many of the *études* are well documented and the reconstruction of them provides an interesting problem-solving exercise for the students. In a context in which there are explicit instructions for a sequence of movements, the student is removed from the more normally accepted practices that involve the concept of individual inspirational creativity, often associated with creative improvisation. It is interesting to note that the written records of the *études* offer a new experience for students of theatre that is akin to the skills required of the music or dance student: the task of translating a notated form into action.

An analogy is often drawn between the play script (text) and the musical score, but it does not really stand close scrutiny. Plays are not direct scores for performance, as is the case with music, or indeed notated dance. A play, apart from the fact that it possesses a simultaneous dual existence as a literary form to be read and as a script intended for performance, is a far more open-ended commodity than either the music or dance score. This is not to say that the music score does not offer room for individual nuance in performance, but more to emphasise the point that there are very few play texts that attempt to dictate how the translation into movement and vocalisation shall be carried out. Even those very few plays that incorporate explicit staging instructions tend to provoke the director and actors to deny those very instructions on a point of professional honour.

It is worth reproducing, in written form, 'shooting the bow' as an example for discussion:

> An imaginary bow is held in the left hand. The student advances with the left shoulder forward. When he spots the target he stops, balanced equally on both feet. The right hand describes an arc in order to reach an arrow in an imaginary belt behind his back. The movement of the hand affects the whole body, causing the balance to shift to the back foot. The hand draws the arrow and loads the bow. The balance is transferred to the front foot. He aims. The bow is drawn with the balance shifting again to back foot. The arrow is fired and the exercise completed with a leap and a cry. (Braun, 1995, p. 174)

Mel Gordon (1974, p. 81) gives a fuller account:

> The actor falls to the floor. He draws his arms and legs together. Rising on his right foot, he slowly draws up an imaginary bow. The actor advances with his left shoulder forward and his right foot back. Spotting an imaginary target, he transfers his weight from his right foot to his left and back again to the right. He draws an imaginary arrow from his belt, or imaginary quiver. Very quickly he bends his upper torso toward the floor. Now, slowly the actor straightens up, holding his extended arms in a rigid position. The left arm is drawn out toward the front and the right arm is thrown back to a slightly lower level. He slowly loads the imaginary bow and draws it back. The actor aims. He fires with a shout. His body immediately contorts like a sprung bow into positions of 'refusal'.

The intention in both descriptions of the exercise is that the student/actor begins to comprehend her/himself in spatial terms, not in the abstract but in the material business of 'performing' a task. The task requires physical self-control and develops elasticity while the extension of the body through the exercise requires a constant realigning of the individual's centre of gravity. The *étude* is also intended to display the complete sequence of intention, realisation and reaction. The reference to refusal at the end of the second description does need some explanation. Edward Braun translates 'refusal' as 'reaction', in the sense that every motion produces energy that must provoke a counter-motion. While, in the direct sense, this refers to a physical action, the meaning should also be seen in terms of social motion and 'refusal'. Meyerhold's purpose in claiming to be scientific was to empower the actor to be able to make rational decisions about the implications of a gesture. Again, Braun quotes Meyerhold:

> The whole biomechanical system, the entire process of our movements is dictated by one basic principle – our capacity for thought, the human brain, the rational apparatus.... That is why we verify every movement on stage against the thought that is provoked by the scene in question.... Not only movements, not only words, but also the brain. (Braun, 1995, p. 176)

Arising from this clear statement is the complex problem of how to display emotions. In 1926, the view of Meyerhold's assistants would seem to suggest that Meyerhold's system pursues the idea of a 'formal display of the emotional' (Braun, 1995, p. 176). Unlike the various historical attempts at veracity on stage, alternative conventions of acting recognise that emotion, like gesture in performance, is a sequence of codified movements that relate to a potential audience's experience of what they read as reality, rather than claiming to be reality. Thus a 'formal display of emotion' is what is intended in the concept of the politics of theatricality.

When, in the context of the project upon which I am basing this chapter, the preliminary discussions had taken place, we were faced with the task of finding a way by which we could reconstruct these exercises. Two questions arose that demanded our attention. First, we had to decide to what extent we were willing to attempt a faithful reconstruction and to what extent should we be prepared to construct a 'reading' of the exercises for our own purposes. The group's decision was to break up into smaller units of four or five people, each group comprising both men and women, in order to work on as many of the *études* as possible. This meant that we were able to tackle 'Dagger thrust', 'Building the pyramid', 'Strike with the feet', 'Shooting the bow', 'The slap in the face', 'Throwing the stone', 'Carrying the sack',

'The circle', 'Dropping the weight', 'The horse and rider' and finally and most problematic 'The leap onto the chest' (a person's chest). The last exercise is problematic because it demands a certain type of strength that, in what we understood to be its original form, could be acquired only by the practice of certain gymnastic and dance skills. If we were to keep to our original 'egalitarian' premise in the physical work, then the exercise would be left out. In the end two students, a woman and a man, made the choice to tackle this *étude*. With a degree of determination they worked out a way by which they could relate the exercise to their needs.

During the course of this phase of our work we became aware that, while the exercises alerted us to the potential for the development of spatial and balance awareness, little attention was given to the *effort* quality of movement. The concept of effort quality in a movement is derived from the work of Rudolph Laban. His work is, in Britain, known popularly through educational gymnastics and what has been termed 'art of movement' in schools. Laban's work was developed through the German expressionist dance movement in the 1920s. However, he was forced to flee Germany with the rise of the Nazi party, arriving in England in the 1930s. In the theatre, two of his pupils have perhaps reached a wider public: Kurt Joos and in particular his ballet *The Green Table*, and Mary Wigman and her expressionist 'grotesque' dance form.

Laban, in his analysis of movement, articulated, as well as spatial awareness, the concept of effort quality. Interestingly, one of his collaborators was the American F. C. Lawrence, whose work on movement analysis in industry was remarkably similar to that of F. W. Taylor. Lawrence and Laban identified the possibility that movement always expressed a quality of effort, as well as direction. Thus the movement required to lift a heavy object possessed, as well as a specific direction or spatial path, a distinguishable quality of effort. The effort, in this case, would be related to a direct, heavy and sustained action, whereas the lifting of a feather would dictate an entirely different quality of effort. Again, an example of a strong/direct/quick movement effort would be the action 'to impale'; or a strong/direct/sustained action would be 'to drag'.

This form of movement analysis enabled us to develop our research into the *études* in a manner not specifically demanded by the written instructions available. The observation regarding the potentiality of effort quality led us into discussions, arising during our practical sessions, related to the possibility of devising an effort quality in relation to the concept of *Gestus* and, to an extent, this also led to a consideration of the role of *reflexology* in Meyerhold's theatrical practice. At the turn of the century a number of schools of 'objective psychology' arose both in Russia and the USA. Schools of 'objective psychology', while differing in their findings, rejected what were seen to be the introspective trends in established psychology in favour of a more visceral understanding of emotion. Mel Gordon (1974) draws attention to William James, an American psychologist (1842–1910) who:

> unable to exorcise his states of severe depression through his own mental faculties, began to investigate the actual visceral [we may now substitute the term materialist for visceral, materialist suggesting an ideological dimension to the perception of the physical/visceral] nature of emotion.... Experimenting on himself, James concluded that emotional consciousness and its transitory states were directly linked to the physical body; in fact, the body's automatic response to stimuli itself was the emotion, preceding the mental perception of the emotion.

In practice this meant that, for the actor to create the emotions, s/he should first observe the physical manifestation of the emotion, then recreate it in order to trigger the sensation of the emotion. The actor did not need to be thinking of that particular emotion for the action to provoke an automatic reflex throughout her/his body signifying the emotion. The acting of emotion thus possesses the potential to become, by a formal display, a means by which effort may be incorporated into a form of *Gestus*. Whether or not there is any scientific credibility in the theory of reflexology, it does offer the potential for the articulating of dialectical theatre as distinct from, but not in conflict with, the practice of Brecht.

To attempt an explanation of this potentiality I suggested to the students that we turn our attention to Meyerhold's idea of the *grotesque*. In *Meyerhold on Theatre* we are offered a definition of the *grotesque* in relation to the arts:

> Grotesque is the title of a genre of low comedy in literature, music and the plastic arts. Grotesque usually implies something hideous and strange, a humorous work which with no apparent logic combines the most dissimilar elements by ignoring their details and relying on its own originality. (Braun, 1969, p. 137)

Meyerhold goes on to argue that his concept of the *grotesque* creates a series of contrasts (we are generally more familiar with Brecht's concept of contradictions) and offers the image of Gothic architecture as an example:

> Like Gothic architecture, in which the soaring bell-tower expresses the fervour of the worshipper whilst its projections decorated with fearsome distorted figures direct one's thoughts back towards hell ... in Gothic architecture a miraculous balance is preserved between affirmation and denial, the celestial and the terrestrial, the beautiful and the ugly, so the grotesque parades ugliness in order to prevent beauty from lapsing into sentimentality.... The grotesque deepens life's outward appearance to the point where it ceases to appear merely natural ... the grotesque synthesises opposites. (Braun, 1969, p. 138)

The reconstruction of the *études*, in the light of fairly free-ranging discussions that attempted to incorporate ideas of effort, grotesque and the concept of disruption through contrast, became more interesting as practical projects. Now the students were at least prepared to consider the idea of a critique as an intrinsic element in their practical movement work. This was a point at which to leave them to their own devices, in order that they might have the freedom to play with their ideas/critique. The outcome was an enhanced sense of collectivity in their work. From the initial stages of small groups working on specific *études*, the students decided to teach each other their new skills, with the adaptations that they had incorporated into each exercise. This process went on for four or five days, during which time the exchange of material skills was also an exchange of ideas focused on the politics of the exercises as they related to the particular students involved. When I was called back into the class I was presented with 'performances' of the *études*, all of which were carried out by the whole group. Without a specific input from me as teacher they had also discovered the *dactyl* and the potential use of vocalisation (both abstract sound and speech) as potential developments in their exploitation of the gestures. The *dactyl* has been described, variously, as a signalling gesture involving the combination of relaxing and tensing muscles through an upward sweeping movement that involves clapping gestures and, in a less obvious way, as a form of parenthesis to specific *études*. However we define the look and purpose of the *dactyl,* the students in this context used it as a preliminary warm-up exercise at the start of each session before moving on to their daily routine of performing all the *études* as a whole group.

Contextual research

Having worked to such an extent on the *études* it was essential that further attention be given to the historical contextualising of what was becoming 'our' theatre practice. The question of history-teaching in the context of the arts can be problematic; as one may argue that practice in the theatre is not ideologically free, equally one has to be clear regarding the treatment of history. A liberal humanist approach to the arts so often decontextualises art as a transcendent cultural event that moves across history, rather than being the result of the collisions of the moments of history. Frequent examples of art perceived as being transcendent of material history may be found commonly in readings of Shakespeare and Brecht. The call to arms that Shakespeare is our contemporary has been well established in theatrical practice for decades. His humane values, so runs the argument, are so profound that they represent the eternal verities of the human condition, unchanging in essence over the centuries. With Brecht the case is somewhat different. The counter to many critics' and historians' feelings of revulsion towards Brecht's Marxism is a strategy of rescuing the poet's artistic soul from the politics which hinder our view of Brecht's humanity. Although very different as examples, in the case of both Shakespeare and Brecht we are confronted by an essentialist ideological appropriation of the 'artist' away from the materiality of history.

Often, when reading accounts of Meyerhold's influence in the work of contemporary practitioners, we find a range of ideological representations, all appropriating Meyerhold to their own purpose, albeit without malice.[3] I am not arguing, in a seemingly contradictory fashion, an essentialist position in which any artist possesses a core of unchanging and irrefutable truths in their work to which we, of later generations, must be true. My debate also stands aside from a crude reading of postmodernist arguments for an endless plurality of meaning, in order to prosecute a debate that focuses on the dialectical relationship that may exist between a clear understanding of the material historical context of the moment of cultural production and the potential readings that may be constructed by our own contemporary narratives. Often what may be most informative, and fascinating, is the range of narratives that lie, potentially, between our cultures and the past. This not a clinging to a belief in absolute historical meta-narratives, although some sense of history continuing is a necessary counter to the essentially reactionary claim that history has ended. Returning to Brecht, as I often do, we find this idea of material historical narrative expressed with elegance:

we need to develop the historical sense (needed also for the appreciation of new plays) into a real sensual delight. When our theatres perform plays of other periods they like to annihilate distance, fill in the gap, gloss over the differences. But what comes then of our comparisons, in distance, in dissimilarity – which is at the same time a delight in what is close and proper to ourselves? (Willett, 1964, p. 276)

Contextualising the work of Meyerhold involved the students in gaining a broad understanding of the ways in which historical context may locate the ideological basis of our contemporary readings of theatrical practice. The students were offered a list of subject areas to be covered. These included:

- an introduction to Marxist/Leninist thought at the time of the revolution of 1917 and subsequent developments in political ideology involving Trotsky and Stalin;
- constructivism in the theatre and in the visual and plastic arts;
- play-writing of the period;
- a short biographical account of Meyerhold's life, particularly in relationship to the privations suffered under Stalin and how those events related to the development of socialist realism and the Writers' Congress of 1934;
- cinefication, including ideas relating to montage.

The students formed working parties comprising four or five people based predominantly on common interest – visual arts, politics and so on. This arrangement formed the basis for choosing the areas of research. We envisaged a specific strategy for this aspect of the work, appropriate to the teaching methodology thus far employed. It was felt that a straightforward gathering and disseminating of material would not address the emergent questions relating to considerations of the role of content and form in this project. A plan was devised whereby the means of dissemination and handling of material were as important as the material itself. The strategy was as follows. Initially each research group would see its task as the production of learning aids for the whole class. This required them to consider the design and manner of presentation of the research as well the information in itself. The second consideration was the means of disseminating the specific material. Some groups found it necessary to duplicate their findings over a period of time, as opposed to handing out the final 'learning pack'. Other groups became engaged with different methods of duplicating information for general consumption. The third stage of the pedagogic method was the structure of the discussion period. All the groups agreed on the principle of a discussion period after we all had time to read and think about the research material, but initially we were in some disagreement as to how the discussion period should be structured. It was agreed, after much healthy dispute (I was often reminded of the tensions intrinsic to party political meetings), that each research group should be given time to develop a critique of the material given to them by the other research groups. By this method everyone, in theory, would arrive at the series of discussion seminars empowered (rather than silenced) by having been involved in the development of a critique. It does seem that this methodology possesses two distinct advantages: the lazy individual is 'encouraged' into activity by responsibility to a small group, and the student who is reticent in large group seminars is encouraged by the knowledge that s/he is a part of a collective view, rather than isolated as an individual.

A number of research groups found that it was necessary to subdivide in order that particular (related) interests could be facilitated. By way of example, the group concerned broadly with political history produced one research line that focused on events between 1900 and 1930; another worked closely on Lenin and the Bolsheviks. Various ways of approaching the exercise were employed, partly as many of the students chose to rebel against what they perceived to be the constraints of 'school type' solid, but uninteresting, accounts of events. Thus the research papers became either witty or contentious in their chosen form. In particular, the project entitled *Your Very Own Guide to Russian Political Affairs 1900–1930: Key Dates for Your Diary,* was inspired to an extent, I suspect, by the comic book form exploited by the Mexican cartoonist Eduardo del Rio (Rius) in his book *Marx for Beginners* (1976).

Textual explorations

The generally accepted principle with the project system at the University of Exeter is that the culmination of the work should be manifest in the form of a project 'showing'. It is worth attempting a brief description of this event. The concept of the project showing, or 'sharing' as it is sometimes entitled, relates to a principle that challenges the convention that a performance is perceived solely as a finished commodity. The intention is to emphasise, in the production of culture, an analysis of the process, rather than its outcome in the 'polished performance'. Therefore the project showing is a space within which the students aim to share, through performance on an informal level, the process by which they have arrived at their performative conclusions. Here it is important to emphasise that there are performative conclusions, from which the audience may make a number readings, *and* that there is an importance in those performative conclusions. Too often the informal workshop, or process-orientated work, may become an excuse for lack of clarity in the ideas to be articulated through performance. We may describe this event as an open cultural moment, where the discussion and questions always remain an intrinsic element in the procedure. This is opposed to the idea of a closed cultural moment, as exemplified all too often by the representation of theatre as a finished art commodity for purchase and passive consumption by the potential audience.

We decided that we needed to articulate aspects of our work to an invited audience, in this instance the rest of the Department of Drama. Emerging from the experience of the research projects was the collective wish to employ a play text from the period. Finally, Mayakovsky's dramatic/theatrical poem seemed to offer the greatest opportunity for the kind of textual appropriation that best suited our current working methodology. The students were in agreement on one principle: that while they wished to articulate their experience of Meyerhold's working practices as they understood them, they also wished to find their own collective voice through an appropriation of what appeared to be a fairly open-ended text. Mayakovsky's text, *Moscow is Burning*, was written in 1930, the year of his suicide, and may be said to belong to a series of plays that mix circus techniques with Russian folk tales, party slogans with poster imagery. The whole sense of the piece is reminiscent of the wild confusion of futurist imagery. Spencer Golub refers to Mayakovsky as the 'Grandiloquent Soviet futurist poet and dramatist, the self-dramatising "loud-mouthed Zarathustra" of his day. His noisy hooliganism and eccentric individualism served an intellectual anarchism which hopefully forecast a new age of freedom' (in Banham, 1995, p. 694). The text seemed open enough and full of so many contradictions in both ideology and style that it was well suited to our need to find a text of the period, but not one which would inhibit us from adapting it to our own purposes.

Mayakovsky's work and attitudes towards the function of art have often been related to the Futurists of Italy, whose celebration of anarchistic disruption at every level of consciousness would seem to fit ill with the purposes and achievements of the emergent Soviet Union. Inevitably the unfortunate juxtaposition of Marxism and Fascism in relation to events in Italy and the Soviet Union raises complications. However, if we accept that futurism (in common with Dada and surrealism) was self-consciously a 'destructive' force that sought to reject the 'beauty' of the past, we may then make an intellectual link with Mayakovsky's rejection of both psychological realism and symbolism. In terms of a materialist analysis of cultural production, we may recognise the potential for any form to be appropriated by an opposing ideology (think of what has been done to the work of Bertolt Brecht by the capitalist democracies). Indeed, we may argue that for art to be considered radical requires a sense that values (ideologies) must be observed to be in a constant state of flux, tempered only by the ways in which history may inform our contemporary appropriations.

Having established Mayakovsky's (and to a lesser degree Meyerhold's) formalistic link with Italian futurism we conducted a search for some of the slogans of futurism that would, at least, aid us in our initial imagery. Some of the numbered agenda that seemed most apposite to *Moscow is Burning* are worth quoting from Marinetti's manifesto for *The Variety Theatre 1913*, with a précis of our thoughts.

> 1. The Variety Theatre, born as we are from electricity, is lucky in having no tradition, no masters, no dogma, and is fed by swift actuality. (Apollonio, 1973, p. 126)

The idea of 'actuality' and 'no tradition' appealed to the students' sense of their own research at this point in the project. This was not a denial of history, but more the attempt to find their own voice in juxtaposition to a given historical context.

> 7. The Variety Theatre offers the healthiest of spectacles in its dynamism of form and colour (simultaneous movement of jugglers, ballerinas, gymnasts, colourful riding masters, spiral cyclones of dancers spinning on the points of their feet). In its swift, overpowering dance rhythms The Variety Theatre forcibly drags the slowest of souls out of their torpor and forces them to run and jump. (Apollonio, 1973, p. 127)

This statement presented some problems between the idea of what may be hoped for and what, realistically, may be achieved. At this point I was perceived as the somewhat tedious brake on their creative energies. However, in the spirit that all disagreements have the potential to be negotiated, we agreed that 'colourful riding masters' were neither desirable, nor possible, but that we did wish to drag 'the slowest souls out of their torpor'. Whether we were capable of achieving this latter aspiration would have to remain in abeyance since, to quote Brecht (who was quoting Engels), 'the inflexible rule that the proof of the pudding is in the eating'. A further quotation that attracted attention was from Marinetti's *Manifesto of Futurism* (1909) (in Apollonio, 1973):

2. Courage, audacity, and revolt will be essential elements of our poetry.

However, the more blatantly misogynist and violent elements in the Futurist manifesto, quite understandably, disturbed the students and gave rise to a further debate regarding the problems in the appropriation of form while disregarding the nature (or at least being selective in choosing information) of particular ideologies. It seemed, at this point, circumspect to suggest that, while bearing in mind these problems, we move back to the chosen text and context. The narrative of *Moscow is Burning* follows in montage form events from 1905 to 1917. There is no attempt to describe in detail the complexity of the historical events. Instead, the narrative relies on a series of images (or we may use the term *tableaux vivants*) representing the downfall of the Czar, the rise and downfall of Kerensky[4] and emergence of the USSR. The media employed are those of the circus, vaudeville, pantomime and agit-prop. The length of the piece runs to only 20 sides of thinly dispersed dialogue and the characters are social types that one would recognise as being at home in a medieval morality play, or in a *Lehrstück*; indeed, *Moscow is Burning* may well be described equally as a secular morality play and as a political pantomime. The characters bear no names other than those which describe their social function: Herald, Clown, Lawyer, Student, General, Worker, Liberal, Kulak (Kerensky is not offered the opportunity to speak!).

On studying the text it was clear that concepts such as 'throughline', or linear narrative, were of no help in discovering a shape for the group's proposed performance. The scenes, or more accurately the episodes, are described in detail. The following (from Mayakovsky, 1974) serve as useful examples:

The arena is brightly lit. Military men, pushing an endless array of pants hanging on clothes racks, spread out in front of the decorated arena barrier. This endless line passes through a palace gate towards the Czar's laundry and disappears. Soon the line of men reappear holding bundles and hiding under a sign reading 'His Majesty's Court Laundress.' A Red-haired Philistine wearing glasses [performed by a clown] appears weaving in and out of the line, fearfully counting the number of pants. He pesters the Major-domo.'

Or towards the end of the text:

Animal trainers, looking like bourgeois [*sic*], appear on the road leading to the palace gate. Each one has a hoop in his hand. Scenery on the stage represents the Czarina's bedroom. There is a bed under a canopy and a statue of Napoleon in the middle of the room. The red-headed Kerensky is forced by the 'Capitalists' to jump through all the hoops to the threshold of the bedroom. Kerensky walks around Napoleon, imitating his posture. Tired, he falls on the Czarina's double bed. The musical Clown enters at the edge of the stage.

It would have been inappropriate to our purpose to attempt to reproduce the whole of the text. The collective decision was to take a number of scenes that dealt, in the main, with the enactment of large-scale riots or demonstrations, with the intention to pursue a performative thesis that dealt with political demonstration: how to choreograph the *Gestus* of a political demonstration became our practical task. The group once more broke down into smaller units, each with the responsibility of creating the working basis of their particular episode in the montage. The next stage was to allow time for each unit to teach the whole group their theatrical realisation. The unifying factor in this stage of the work was the common agreement that we all would attempt to introduce as many aspects of the *études* into the work, with everyone exploiting the performance of the *dactyl* as a form of parenthesis to each 'episode'.

Technical factors such as costume and music were to be dealt with as the need, or the problems, arose. No decision was to be made prior to the problem arising in the work process. In other words, there was a decision (albeit one that was not articulated until after the event) that aesthetic decisions in these areas were to be determined by practical need and not the other way around. The base for the costume gave rise to a particularly interesting consideration. All drama students at Exeter are required, at the start of their three-year course, to buy (for a very modest sum!) working kit. This comprises black karate trousers and a singlet. The very practical reason is to reinforce the attitude of mind required when preparing for work: that is, the students (and staff) change for work. This simple kit was used as the basis for the performance, with whatever emblems were needed to locate the moment in the performance. A number of students did raise interesting questions relating to the function of costume as emblem (rather than symbol), relating the utilitarian aspect of the departmental kit to the idea that making art is a job rooted in material need, rather than transcendental abstract aesthetics. A debatable point, but one worth raising in passing.

The performance that emerged from these elements lasted about 25 minutes, combining passages from the original text with newly devised and written pieces from the group. The montage of the original text developed into the montage of our performance text that included imagery from contemporary politics. To inject, at this point, images from an essay that has informed much of my own work would seem germane to the task of this chapter. The work in question is Walter Benjamin's 'Unpacking My Library' from the collection *Illuminations*. A, more or less, random selection:

> I am unpacking my library. Yes, I am. The books are not yet on the shelves, not yet touched by the mild boredom of order … there is in the life of a collector a dialectical tension between the poles of disorder and order … not only books but also copies of books have their fates.… Other thoughts fill me than the ones I am talking about – not thoughts but images, memories. Memories of the cities in which I found so many things. (Benjamin, 1973, p. 59f.)

Postscript

At the time of this project, the student demonstrations were taking place in China and, particularly, the ruthless action against the demonstrators in Tiananmen Square. The irony of comparisons between the fate the Bolshevik revolution under Stalin and the decline of the people's revolution in China into despotism were not lost on the students. There were two outcomes to the students' response. The first was rooted in the problem of deciding how to conclude our performance/demonstration. The students decided to comment on the events taking place in Tiananmen Square, in particular the image of the man, holding shopping bags, and disrupting the passage of an army tank. The tank was constructed from the bodies of the performers with two students being supported as the tank's swinging gun-barrel. As the

'tank' moved inexorably towards the spectators, one remaining performer emerged from the body of the spectators and enacted the
encounter with the tank in Tiananmen Square. The tableau ended the
demonstration of our project work and was performed in silence.

The second event that grew from our work was an independent
project, instigated by members of the Meyerhold workshop, which took
place over the weekend after the conclusion of the project. Briefly, a
group of our students persuaded a group of sculpture students from
Exeter College of Art to join them in a clandestine project to produce
and erect a sculpture that would stand in the university grounds as a
memorial to the victims of Tiananmen Square. The project attracted a
number of helpers, one of whom was a stone mason who had heard of
the scheme and arrived ready to carve a stone plaque to stand in front
of the sculpture. Inevitably the event created a degree of official
displeasure; but the sculpture still stands and serves as a focus for an
annual remembrance of those 'other' students.

Of course, it is all too easy to perceive this latter event as the
sentimental reactions of university students whose lives will never be
touched by that degree of oppression. However, there is a high
component of reassurance in such acts, particularly when contemporary
students are more and more being required, by the conditions of their
education and material lack of well-being, to espouse a client ethos in
the ways that they perceive the three-year experience of university.

Notes

1. Of course, this is not to suggest that our perceived everyday actions are
    not also, albeit in a less consciously perceived way, ideologically
    determined cultural constructions.
2. Completed 3 February 1926, originally published in *Krasnaya*, No. 6,
    1926. This English translation, by Brian Pearce, appeared in *Labour
    Review* (autumn 1962).
3. We may refer to Ariane Mnouchkine and Eugenio Barba as examples.
4. Alexander F. Kerensky (1881–1970) was, by October 1917, Prime
    Minister and Supreme Commander-in-Chief of the Provisional Govern-
    ment that was overthrown by Lenin and the Bolsheviks.

Works cited

Apollonio, U. (ed.) (1973) *Futurist Manifestos.* Thames and Hudson, London.
Banham, M. (ed.) (1995) *The Cambridge Guide to Theatre.* Cambridge
      University Press, Cambridge.

Benjamin, W. (1973) *Illuminations.* Fontana/Collins, London.

Braun, E. (ed. and trans.) (1969) *Meyerhold on Theatre.* Methuen, London.

Braun, E. (1995) *Meyerhold: A Revolution in Theatre.* Methuen, London.

Gordon, M. (1974) 'Meyerhold's Biomechanics'. *The Drama Review,* vol. 18, pp. 73–88. (Also printed in Zarelli, P. B. (1995) *Acting (Re)Considered.* Routledge, London.)

Mayakovsky, V. (1974) *Moscow is Burning,* trans. E. Bartos, V. Nes Kirkby and H. Wilga. *The Drama Review,* vol. 17, pp. 69–89.

Pearce, B. (1962) Leon Trotsky's 'Culture and Socialism'. *Labour Review* (autumn).

Rio, E. del (1976) *Marx for Beginners.* Writers and Readers Co-op, London.

Willett, J. (ed.) (1964) *Brecht on Theatre.* Methuen, London.

Index